Letters from Prison

"From the first unyielding paragraph
Thompson demonstrates that he has
no ideological axes to grind, no causes
to plead, and no intention of either
condemning or excusing his pen pals.
His goal in *Letters from Prison* is
simply to capture 'the Goyaesque
dimensions of life in federal hell.'
Thompson has a measured, empa-
thetic feel for the material—some of it
grave, some of it goofy, all of it
compelling—and has organized at least
10 years' worth of not-so-belles lettres
in topical chapters . . . fascinating."

—QUILL & QUIRE

Shawn Thompson

LETTERS
FROM PRISON

Felons write about the struggle
for life and sanity behind bars

HarperCollinsPublishersLtd

www.harpercanada.com

HarperCollins books may be purchased for
educational, business, or sales promotional use.
For information please write:
Special Markets Department,
HarperCollins Canada,
55 Avenue Road, Suite 2900,
Toronto, Ontario, Canada M5R 3L2

First edition

Canadian Cataloguing in Publication Data

Main entry under title:

Letters from prison : felons write about
the struggle for life and sanity behind bars

ISBN 0-00-200086-5

1. Prisoners – Canada – Correspondence.
2. Prisoners – United States – Correspondence.
3. Imprisonment – Canada.
4. Imprisonment – United States.
5. Thompson, Shawn, 1951– – Correspondence.
I. Thompson, Shawn, 1951–

HV9443.L48 2002   365'.6'0971   C2001-902526-2

HC 9 8 7 6 5 4 3 2 1

Printed and bound in the United States
Set in LinoLetter

Contents

Eat the worm

No man, I'm not out of the hole yet. I'm back in the hole . . .

Another letter arrives on long, floppy pieces of yellow foolscap. It comes from Leavenworth penitentiary in Kansas, from the dungeon inside the dungeon known as the hole, where the only way out is by mail. By words on paper.

> What does it feel like? I think everyone here is seething with built-in anger. Not many are voicing it out. But you can see it in their faces, their sweaty, solemn and barely controlled expressions . . .

The letter is eight pages long. It describes the latest conditions in D Block, the Dog House, which is a steel-and-concrete wasp's nest for stacking human larvae. It's a big square structure, with one hundred and sixty-five cells. There are bars, not steel doors, so the cons can talk to each other. The heat of a September day drenches the small cells like a tide from a dark, demented sea. The heat makes a man think he has a light fever.

> More guys are shouting for food now. They are about an hour and a half late. Food is usually here by three and served by four. It's five-thirty. One guy is slamming his food slot. Clang. Clang. Clang. I'm not hungry. I'm hot, sweaty, and sleepy. This heat is very draining.

We have never met. After years of letters he calls me friend and wonders why he hasn't heard from me in ages.

> Well, my friend, it's now six-o-five. No food yet. My arm hurts. Even this pen, if you notice, is giving up. So I guess I'll end it. I

1

had to take the pen apart, clean the tip in hot water. Must be the humidity or the bad ink they just love selling in the prisons. Well, my brother from another mother, take care. I'm glad to hear from you. I thought perhaps I had said something wrong.

The letter is part of a conversation flowing back and forth between me, in the university where I work, and José Cruz, or Blaze, in Leavenworth. Why is he in the hole again? I wonder. I ask him in a letter.

I'm an asshole for being in the hole again. Even though I did not do anything but be a member of an organization. The reason all of us are in lockdown is because a knife fight occurred with some of ours and other dudes. Ours was the ones attacked and defending themselves. And this facility has a somewhat legit security concern. Lock everyone from both groups down until it dies down. They don't want it to get bigger. We've all been cool, though. Just hanging in there. One thing's for sure. All it takes is for a needle to drop and see the chain reaction burst. I listen to all these guys in other cells just talk nonsense all day long. For example, dude in cell thirty is yelling over to dude in cell forty, calling him a fat E.T. [extraterrestrial]. Dude in cell forty said back, "Yeah, you remember E.T.'s long finger? I'm gonna shove it up your butt." Now they're joking, talking about each other's wives. It's funny and pathetic.

There are other moments of distraction.

One of the guards tried to break my arm as I was banging, making a nuisance of myself. I yelled that he broke my arm and the nut-job got nervous and injured himself, cut himself around the entire wrist. I was scared to death. Thought I was getting a new charge for injuring him. The disciplinary hearing officer saw through the lie and actually let me go with fourteen day's loss of good time and fourteen days' disciplinary time. Which I admit was a blessing. It could have been worse.

It was no secret why he was in prison. He told me and I also asked the prison system for his official record.

> This is in response to your request for the federal convictions and sentences of José Cruz, Reg. No. 14065-074. Mr. Cruz was sentenced in the U.S. District Court for the Southern District of New York on February 22, 1996, to 180 months for . . . conspiracy to commit murder & threatening to commit a crime of violence.

He was curious about his official record and asked for a copy. I sent it.

> Yah, the info you got isn't much, my record, etc. These people have a file – a confidential file that needs to be carried in a suitcase . . .

I had questions. I wanted to know where the trail went backward in time. What were the experiences that shaped this man?

> As a little kid, I got caught in the park by three or four other little kids, all of us under ten, and they stuffed me in a trunk and tossed me over the edge of a hill into a river. Four black kids. Water started to seep into the trunk. I couldn't get out. It was locked. Then one of them opened it and they fled. I think it was then that I acquired a sense of humour.

I wondered what he was thinking about. How did he survive and not go insane? "This solitude has brought out the best and worst of me," he said. "I'm hanging on to my sanity. My sanity, my word, and my jewels are all I have left." "Jewels" was his term for the treasure of his genitalia. Later, as his mind drifted from topic to topic at night in his cell, he talked about how time slows down when you're wounded. "I've been shot, stabbed, chased and beat by mobs," he said, "and even hunted down by an insane mother who was upset that I took her daughter's cherry – and she was older than me." You have to wonder how one man had the time to do all the things he'd done. Then he said, "I remember, after being shot twice in the chest next to the heart from a guy only a few feet away, laying on the floor bleeding internally, but fading away into a dreamless sleep, wondering, 'Damn! Why does the ambulance always have to take so long?'"

After D Block Blaze was moved deeper into the depths of segregation in Leavenworth.

No, I don't stare at the cracks on the walls – well, at least not too much. Sometimes you may see an aesthetic design from cracks. Come to mention it, there are two stains on my wall across from my bunk. Both look like a man. But the bigger one seems to have an evil grin to its face, longish black hair, slanted almond-shaped eyes, whiskers, and its expression seems like someone with a leeringly gleeful and wicked intent. No, it's not my imagination. Yes, my mind drifts. I asked the psych about it. She said it was natural, especially if you got a lot on your mind. I often fantasize that I'm given powers either by God or a superior alien race. They come to jail and release me and I start changing the world for the better, healing the sick. My wife is a sick woman and she's the basis for the actual fantasy. I heal her. At the same time, I abolish currency and force the rich countries to help the poor ones, or I'll vanish them with a snap of the fingers. I'm laughing, 'cause it's really a silly daydream, but one that I enjoy having over & over again.

Over here, everything is much more quiet than the Dog House. In my cell it's quiet. I could hear the air rushing out of the vent. If I listen carefully, it almost sounds like music, heard barely, from far away. Somewhere else I hear a nutcase talking to himself and the food wagon coming my way. It's grub time. So I'll let you go for now. Peace, bro.

Three months later another letter came:

As for me, still in the hole. No telling when they'll free Willie and his comrade. Our investigation has been over. Six of us (out of thirty) received disciplinary reports. The rest weren't involved (including me). Yet, still, they keep us hemmed up. It's a psychological thing. Oh well, as long as my time [prison time till release] does not stop, they could hang me by my balls. (Hey officer, if you just read that, I didn't mean it.)

To inspire me during the gloom of the winter months at the university, I have an envelope from Blaze pinned to the bunker wall of my office. The outside of the envelope is marked with the words "Have a heavenly day" with a smiling yellow sun on it and the inscription "to the teacher dude." I can almost feel the sun radiate from the envelope. His letters usually start with "What's up, brother?" or "How the hell are ya?" He tells me about the latest stabbing in the penitentiary. I tell him about the latest faculty flogging. I hear about "punks" and "muscling." He hears about intellectual thuggery. He understands my world as little I understand his. But he makes the connection between us by quoting from memory a line from Byron, "The whole world has become a prison unto me."* That makes sense. In my life I struggle with the mental prisons that I make for myself and that others make for me. I suspect that we wouldn't build physical prisons if the human mind didn't have an affinity for incarceration. And so, despite our differences, despite the distance between professor and felon, we write back and forth from our respective forms of imprisonment.

Blaze is one of the men and women writing letters to me from prisons in Canada and the United States. I started writing to prisoners in the days before I donned a professor's gown, when I was a reporter covering prisons in the penitentiary capital of Canada, in Kingston, Ontario. As a reporter I had the freedom to venture inside prisons and talk to prisoners and to the administration. But the relationships were shallow. The writing was superficial. As a journalist with a straitened role to play I couldn't capture the Goyaesque dimensions of life in federal hell.

---

* The actual line is "And the whole earth would henceforth be/ A wider prison unto me," from Byron's "The Prisoner of Chillon."

In my spare time, I started writing letters to prisoners. I built the relationships slowly, the way that prisoners do. I began with men and women I met personally, and then spread to others by recommendations from one prisoner to another. With some prisoners the correspondence started six years before this book was published and will continue after it is printed. One prisoner died during the correspondence. Some prisoners have been transferred and the correspondence severed. Some were overwhelmed by their own problems and the letters ceased. But some kept writing. I'm not sure why. It may have been a rebellion against circumstances, against what others try to make of them, against what they feel is the worst part of themselves. I have no answers, except that prisoners continued to write, from the side of themselves they keep hidden in prison, from a place where information makes them vulnerable.

The letters came from prison after prison, from Kingston Penitentiary and Collins Bay in Ontario, from Kent in British Columbia, from Edmonton Penitentiary, and from prisons in the United States, such as Folsom, San Quentin, Pelican Bay, Marion, Attica, and Soledad. The writers had nicknames like Snuffie, Greasy, Freaky, Big Baby, Miami, Undertaker, Mumbles, Bam Bam, Eight Ball, One Eye, Cadillac, Big Shitty, Do-doo, Snaggle Tooth, Zeus, Bronco, Fox, Upstate, Uptown, Fish, No Brains, Lucky, Speedy, Scissors, Bean Bag, Lump, Cricket, Popcorn, Stone, G Force, One Way, Weasel, Zulu, Kool-Aid, Dolamite, Shorty Big Foot, Rub-a-dub, Hippy, Ladies Man, and Faggot. "I knew an individual named Swamp Thing," said Dangerous Dave. "He had very long hair and would frequently dunk it in water, giving him the appearance of a swamp creature."

One con asked that he be addressed as plain Comrade Brother Yah Yah, although his first name came from royalty. "My beloved mother named me Nebuchadnezzar at birth. I was her first-born child and she chose to name me after a great king of the Bible, king of Babylon, a king of kings. During his reign he rebuilt all the cities of upper Babylonia and constructed vast temples and palaces, including the famous hanging gardens." Nebuchadnezzar was in a prison in Florida. I thank him for the tour he gave me of his new Babylon.

The cons had ingenious names and were locked in prisons in places with lyrical titles such as Road to Justice in West Liberty, Kentucky. They introduced themselves to me:

> I am an inmate doing life on the installment plan. This is my third time in prison. When I go home I'll have eighteen years in state prison. Nothing to be proud of, but it is a way of life. I am an old school convict, and I believe in the old ways of prison life. Please understand that if it is big stories you are looking for, I am not the guy. It will only be wasting my time. If you are wanting the real thing, I know we will get along fine.

> I have been incarcerated in the State of Iowa at the Iowa State Penitentiary since 1981. I am serving a life-without-parole sentence for murder and presently am working on my Ph.D. in clinical psychology.

> I have attention deficit disorder – among "other" psychiatric problems – so I will not just write you a long letter.

> If you may bear with me, I have tremors in the hands. My writing is sometimes difficult, my thoughts are sometimes cloudy. You should know I wrote you a twenty-eight–page letter, between four p.m. and four a.m. yesterday. I was including material such as excerpts from an autobio I am halfway through, chapters of a couple of books I'm trying to write, and all kinds of other mate-rial, all in a package. I got a little manic. I am a captain's clerk in a mental health prison [serving twenty-five years] for first-degree murder.

Many of the letters came from lifers and long-term offenders. They have time to think and observe and write. From my cell in the educa-tional gulag of the university, it was a relief to talk to people such as Richard Abood Lyon in the prison at Lovelady, Texas. He thought "PHD" meant a pre-hearing disposition in a trial. I'd think I'd heard everything, and then a con would describe watching a tornado rip through his prison in the southern United States. Another told me that she was typing letters in her cell with a snake snoozing in her lap. One woman, in prison in Florida, said that every woman has a precise cycle, between twenty-five and thirty-five days, when her sexual passion peaks and she can't resist a man, no matter who he is. "Sex that day," she said, "will be the most sublime experience."

Prisoners keep themselves alive mentally by arguing and telling stories. They debate who is the strongest, who farts the most, who has the most money, who has the most beautiful wife, who is getting sex and who isn't, which guards can be trusted and which can't. I heard how a con escaped by sea using the coffin from a theatre production of *Dracula* as a boat. That happened at the William Head Institution on Vancouver Island. I heard how prisoners in Chino, California, caught gophers on the grounds and made wagers on the gopher fights. I heard how a prisoner got thrown into the hole for having sex with the female officer in charge of him. There was no end to the tales.

I heard the voices, of different pitch and timbre, of various ages, some loud, some soft, some cruel, some desperate, some clever, some heartless, some compassionate, some funny. It felt as though the voices were as close as a whisper coming through a crude, hollow pipe between prison and the university, like water leaking out of the rock from a mountain spring. The letters were glimpses into a secret world where the price of admission was exile from society.

The summer I finished the first draft of this book I flew to Borneo, rented a type of riverboat called a *klotok*, and went upriver to the jungle where there were no roads or electricity or telephones. And yet the depths of the jungle of Borneo were more accessible than prison, and probably easier to comprehend. The reality of prison is elusive. Our images of prisons are manufactured in the delirium of our debates about them. The arguments are familiar. Prisons are country clubs built to coddle offenders at taxpayers' expense; prisons are places of torture run by cruel and sadistic administrations; prisons are society's last defence against criminals who, if let loose, would make Al Capone look like your sainted mother.

But what is life like in prison for those who are not taking a course in philosophy, for those not making headlines as stars of the criminal world? What does it feel like to be incarcerated?

I don't know. As a journalist I visited prisons and talked to prisoners. The administration let me roam through federal prisons for entire eight-hour days, sometimes several days in succession. I saw prisoners after riots when the pressure and frustration of the joint had erupted like wildfire, absorbing everyone, willing and unwilling, into its fury.

I remember walking through a range in Millhaven after a disturbance. I was amazed how angry some cons can get. Ashes, broken metal beds, smashed porcelain sinks, holes broken in concrete walls, metal pipes ripped out, apocalyptic slogans like "blood and guts" scrawled on the walls. There had been a murder inside and a week of rioting. The beast of anger and despair had been let loose to rampage. I stepped into one cell in that empty and ravaged range and found the walls and ceiling painted a deep blue and strewn with stars and moons. Strange. It felt like being somewhere else. It was like stepping into a world hidden deeper inside another world.

I felt the same way looking at the intricate tattoos on prison flesh. It was like gazing down into the convolutions of a whirlpool. How deep does a life go and how many twists and turns does it take? I can't say what it feels like to be in prison doing a serious piece of time. But prisoners know. And if there's one form of brutality at which they excel, it's their sociopathic compulsion to tell the truth. Don't ask a prisoner a question unless you want an answer.

I never worried about asking felons blunt questions like, "Are you a stone-cold killer?" I spoke candidly to prisoners because I knew they respected that. They abhor a conversation that conceals its motive and intention. I remember being in a maximum-security prison in a room out of earshot of the guards when a con the size of a buffalo turned and said, "Aren't you the fucking reporter who wouldn't write my story?" "Yeah, I'm that fucking reporter," I said. He dropped the matter after a brief discussion because I didn't evade it.

And so I would ask a million questions, get a million answers, and scribble at a manuscript that I hoped would someday become a book. I had absolute freedom in asking questions. They had absolute freedom in answering. The prisoners enjoyed the stimulation of writing letters while locked in the security of a cell. They thanked me for allowing them to put their thoughts and feelings onto paper. "Mail call is my only source of companionship," said one prisoner in solitary. "I live for mail call." Another, Mike Schoen in prison in Yuma, Arizona, explained:

> Mail, or "love," as we call it. That little letter that comes means the world to everyone. It could be from a wife, girlfriend, mom, dad, whoever. But that piece of mail is more important than anything in prison. Each day at mail call you know who gets most of the mail because they all stand around the cage and watch the guard sort it out. You might say it is the highlight in everyone's day. But then there are the faces of those who don't get mail. You know who it is, because they just don't care. It is like the outside world has moved on and left them behind. But that is all part of doing time. The longer you are in prison, the less mail you get. People move on with their lives.

My Leavenworth connection relies on letters.

> I've been on my own since I was young and now, in the loneliest hours of my life, the ones who've come to me like family are my correspondents. Whether lonely, depressed, curious, or adventuresome, they've filled that void and we both benefit from it in the heart.

So now you have the professor's epistolary inferno to digest. Be warned. It doesn't always go down smoothly, like the worm in a bottle of tequila that the editor of this book once swallowed. Swallowing the worm is an apt metaphor for a book about felons who endure prison with all its deprivations, despair and rats. The worm is the reality of their experience beckoning from the bottom of the bottle. We need prisons and their depravity to make the misery and degradation of our world outside look good by comparison. The worse the prisons get, the better the conditions of life seem in the larger world.

I remember talking on the phone to Frank Heaney in San Francisco, who had been a guard at Alcatraz from 1948 to 1951 and who now worked for a company that entertains people with boat tours to old, abandoned Alcatraz. I was writing a newspaper story that compared Alcatraz to Kingston Penitentiary, which had been declared a Canadian historic site. Heaney knew the original Birdman of Alcatraz, played in 1962 by Burt Lancaster in a glowingly idealistic film that appalled the former prison guard. "I think people are fascinated by dark histories," Heaney told me. "I see nothing wrong with it. History doesn't have to be nice." Heaney was bothered by depictions that glamorize offenders and turn guards into ogres. And yet, thinking back to Alcatraz, he volunteered that it was an oppressive place that transformed people. "They were good men doing a difficult job. Just being in that atmosphere, it gets to you. The despair and doom got into my bones." Whatever one feels about prison, it is an environment that puts its mark on people. Felons are felons, not angels in a skewed cosmology or heroes from the church of rebellion. But prison is also a condition that society has created distinct from those who commit crime.

This is a book about imprisonment reflected through the minds of those who know it best. It is a book about people, not polemics. It doesn't harangue for the abolition of prison or clamour for the construction of bigger, better criminal asylums. It is a book of letters from prisoners writing themselves out of their isolation, sent to me in my isolation, not unlike you reading this in your isolation. Or, as my Leavenworth contact, prisoner 14065-074, explains in a letter:

> It may not sound like it, since I'm whining all the time about my jail conditions, but in an ironic sort of way, I appreciate all this jail time. It has done something to me, changed me considerably in a positive way. I've grown up & become a man in here. I'm thirty. At least fifteen of those years were spent in prison. Whether this growth will endure once I'm released is hard to say,

considering the high rate of recidivism. I've learned not to say, "I'm not coming back," because, regardless of how much I meant it, I ended up coming back. But I do appreciate the change in me. Even if I never do get to go back into society, that is another reason why I write, because if I physically don't make it out, there will be a part of me that will, my soul in writing, and that's not so bad.

So take from the book what you want. Be a cynic. Be a romantic. But eat the worm.

1 Kiss yer ass goodbye

We will now discuss in a little more detail the Struggle for Existence.
CHARLES DARWIN, *Origin of Species*

My finest Dantesque moment came the Easter weekend I spent locked in federal hell. It started with the guards joking about strip-searching me – several times. Then a guard took me to my cell, telling me along the way stories about rats and cockroaches. I was given a cup and utensils and told to wash them "thoroughly." The guard then closed the steel bars with a click that said the metal might as well be fused in place. In my journal I wrote, "Walls painted white over brick. Bars painted black." Not a very colourful description, but it caught the mood. Charles Dickens wrote more graphically in *Little Dorrit*: "As the captive men were faded and haggard, so the iron was rusty, the stone was slimy, the wood was rotten, the air was faint, the light was dim." In 1842, Dickens had come to Kingston Penitentiary for the same reason I did. We were curious about life inside. I'd spent whole days inside prisons talking to prisoners and guards as a journalist, but I needed to be locked inside a cell in a maximum-security prison to know what it felt like. I made my request to the prison service to be incarcerated and eight months later I was looking out from a cell in Kingston Penitentiary. A prisoner in Florida had written to me before I went that she was "disgusted" by my pretense of being a prisoner. I knew it wasn't real, that I'd be out in a few days, but before long I'd forgotten all that. It's only a few more hours, I kept telling myself. Remember that you're not really a prisoner. Try to get some more sleep.

I wouldn't recommend prison to anyone with a philosophic temperament. I was given a solitary cell in isolation from the regulars. I wasn't beaten or terrorized or raped. The food tasted strange, although that might just have been my paranoia from tales cons had told me about the meals. Sometimes prisoners put urine, spit or soap in the food of people they don't like. One told me that he knew cons did it because he had done it when he worked in the kitchen. Luckily, I wasn't in a women's prison. A female con told me the ladies sometimes put used tampons in the beef stew.

Two or three weeks more in that cell and I would have needed psychoanalysis for the rest of my life. And yet federal prisoners live there for years. They endure harsh conditions, schooling themselves in the culture of prison, perfecting their criminal skills for their return to the street. I have distilled the wisdom of felons into lessons for surviving the dark side of humanity. This is an introduction to hell, with none of the grace of the language of Dante. These dark cantos have been composed in prose by a succession of cons. As you go through this hell you may feel a sense of familiarity. That's not so surprising. Life in the joint is just an extreme version of marriage, work and school. Here's the advice of cons:

- Say "no" to everyone. Take nothing. Hold nothing.
- Don't talk too much or brag.
- Give back anything you borrow immediately.
- Don't barge into the TV room making noise. Cons hate being interrupted from the soap operas. Don't dare change the TV.
- Don't walk around looking into other inmates' cells. Looking into other cells is like saying, "Hey, I wanna rob you, chump." And, if anything is missing, you'll be blamed.

- Don't listen to anything, 'cause once you know about something bad, then you're a part of it.
- Don't skip the line at the chow hall. Don't sit at the wrong table. Every gang, crew and group has its assigned areas.
- Mind yer own damned business.
- Know your cellmate's beliefs and respect them. It can be dangerous to accidentally offend someone's religious or moral beliefs. Also, some religions have the power to cast spells.
- Stay out of debt. Don't gamble, even with friends.
- Stay away from drugs and booze.
- Don't dress well.
- Always search your cell to make sure no one sets you up.
- Don't talk to the police alone or too much.
- Don't pick on someone who is protected by somebody else.
- Have some courtesy when on the phone. Others want to get on too. Cons hate guys who pimp that phone all day long, crying to their girls, and who won't let anybody else get on.
- Never back down. Don't be a billy bad ass – just don't be weak.
- Don't sweat the small stuff. And understand it's all small stuff.
- Don't be a sore loser or a rough ball player.
- Never trust anyone, even yourself.
- Do your own time.

"Do your own time" is a phrase heard often in prison. It means keep yourself separate from everything and everybody. Don't comment, interfere or accept favours. Understand that you are "fresh meat" and need to learn the way of the joint. You have to deal with "Vikings" (slobs, applied to both guards and cons), "booty bandits" (someone looking for ass to fuck), and the "boss," "hook," "grey suit" or "cookie" (all terms for prison officials of various ranks) without "jeffing" (sucking up) to the staff. You have to deal with other cons who want you as a "punk" or a "fuck boy." Anybody can be carrying a "shank" (homemade knife) made out of a toothbrush and a razor blade or a piece of sharpened steel. Probably the more innocent someone looks, the more you have to worry. As Timothy Crockett says from a federal cell in Georgia, "A social blunder or violation of the convict code can mean demise."

Thomas Bodnar is serving a sentence for second-degree murder in the "rock and steel" of Old Folsom near Sacramento, California. Folsom opened in 1880, when it received prisoners from San Quentin, an even older prison that opened in 1852. Folsom was one of the first maximum-security prisons in the United States. Bodnar has served time in Chino, Soledad, Tehachapi and Lancaster. Prison is "kind of cool in a twisted way," he says, and he speaks with the voice of experience:

> Do your time. Don't let your time do you. Get comfy and don't worry about your old lady screwing Sancho, or stuff you can't control. You have enough to deal with. The idea is to have peace of mind. Accept your situation. The alternative is to become a weak, mental wreck and do your time in misery and bitterness.

Other prisoners say:

> Forget the world. Been there, done that, bought the T-shirt, but ain't gonna see it for years, so forget it.

> Most important, don't let time do you. It's only time. What difference does it make if you spend ten years in jail or ten years in a job you hate and a marriage you hate? Who has more stress?

> The only time you see someone looking out the windows is when it rains or the wind is blowing. You can make it hard if you put your mind beyond that fence.

⊗   Don't be a rat.

One rule of doing time is not to "snitch" or "rat" on other cons. It's a rule that older cons say is being eroded by a moral breakdown occurring inside the walls, not unlike the moral breakdown that's occurring on the outside. "Snitching appears to be running rampant," says Shelton Thomas, in the prison at Florence, Arizona, "as younger and younger inmates are coming into the system with a totally different mentality. Once a rat was put to sleep, or near sleep. Now, the most a rat will get is jumped or told to leave the yard." Still, the safest rule is not to take chances, particularly in the tougher joints, where you might meet an old-style con like Paul Wolfe: "I did a fifteen-month SHU (Security Housing Unit) [stint] for breaking a child molester's jaw. I just did six months in the hole in Soledad for battering a rat."

A con in Illinois says that he realized how strong the taboo against ratting is in Western culture when he was in prison in a Communist country. A culture that snitches and has no personal loyalties is on its way to becoming a police state, he says. The same thought troubled George Orwell in his book *Nineteen Eighty-Four*. The difficulty with the no-rat rule is that some guards have the opposite rule, the you-have-to-snitch rule, and they threaten to throw cons in the hole if they don't comply. Cons who understand the no-rat rule prefer hole time. Michael Roger Nelson is serving a sentence for first-degree murder as a result of what he describes as self-defence against five other people. He writes from the prison at Clallam Bay, Washington State, where he has "probably the best view in America's prisons" – the mountains of the Pacific coast. He explains the no-rat concept:

> It's always a good idea to take the fall for something and do hole time rather than snitch on anyone else, even if you're not guilty of anything. When we know about a snitch, that person is first ostracized, then it's only a matter of time before some youngster is sent to earn his stripes by taking that person off the mainline. We call it "cleaning our house." I've seen snitches get beat down here pretty bad. In one incident, half our pod was closed down temporarily due to a quart of blood all over the tables, seats and floor. A couple have been stabbed, and even one piece of shit cop who harassed inmates was beat down severely in another unit. The bottom line is, you can't treat people like shit and get away with it.

Stephen Pang adds from an Ontario prison:

> The same moral imperative applies here as on da street – do
> what you want, so long as it harms no one else. Ratting does
> harm others, to the detriment of the society. On the flip side, a
> "straight john," by testifying [at a trial], protects the great bulk of
> society and therefore properly fulfills his obligation to that
> society. For instance – if you saw me commit a crime & testified, I
> wouldn't consider you a rat, because, as a citizen, you'd only be
> doing your duty. No hard feelings, etc. However, once someone
> takes up the criminal lifestyle, he is bound to die in the electric
> chair before ratting. A criminal who rolls over becomes, in the
> lexicon of the old Soviet Union, a "non-person." Any & all prior
> accomplishments are forgotten. His face is cut out of group
> photos, his name goes into the hall of shame. He is a rat bastard,
> a furback, and nothing that happens to him can be considered
> bad enough.

A con in the prison in Lancaster, California, tells a tale of rats in San
Quentin:

> A Mexican turnkey told a Mexican convict that a white convict
> was a rat and a white turnkey told the white convict that the
> Mexican convict was a rat. Heads up was given by both races and
> both met at the garden area at yard release with five guys left on
> yard (me included) after the gate was locked. The Mexican and
> the white went at it with knives, and one was killed. The guards
> were aware of what was transpiring and were not around. At
> yard I recall the dead white convict was discovered.

⊗ **If you must have friends, choose wisely.**

Dan Rees has been in Old and New Folsom, and in the prisons at San
Diego, Chino and Lancaster. He wrote from a prison in Blythe, Cali-

fornia, on the edge of the Sonora Desert, that "not all inmates in prison are dirt bags." Rees explains his arrival as a new fish at Folsom:

> When I arrived at Old Folsom in the spring of 1987 it felt surreal. At dusk a fog was settling in. The old grey stone walls looked even more treacherous. I was scared as hell – and it showed. My obvious fear led to a few attempts at intimidation by inmates and other guards. Fortunately, two elder lifers in my housing unit took me under their wing and showed me how to conduct myself in ways that I would be left alone yet not viewed as weak. That is a delicate balance to maintain in prison.

Other cons have written about how to pick associates:

> I've schooled a lot of youngsters. The whole thing on that is teach him the way of prison so he will stand tall in here. You take the weak and build them up to be strong so they, in turn, can protect the weak. I don't really like using the word "weak" to explain someone that don't stand tall. I rather call them meek. Because as long as someone has a little heart (balls), they can be schooled.

> I don't believe that you can have friends in the joint, especially in the prisons of today. You can have acquaintances or associates, but not friends. You must remember you usually come to prison by yourself and will go out by yourself. You cannot do someone else's time.

> Avoid contact with prisoners who try to develop a Mr. Macho image. They are almost always cowards with a deep-seated inferiority complex, basically indistinguishable from any other wild animal. Nothing is more dangerous than a coward who fears you are about to attack.

⊗ **Earn the respect of your peers and don't be an idiot.**

From Old Folsom, Thomas Bodnar has some reflections on "dumb shit" and other types of prison guano. Emotions in prison, such as hate, act "like a virus," Bodnar says, and a con has to resist infection without succumbing to weakness. "You will be tested," he says, and explains:

> Do not ever show fear. Do not ever back down from anyone for any reason. It is far worse living in fear and everyone knowing it than to take an ass whopping. Stand up and go down swinging. You will earn respect, even from the guy who beats the crap out of you. People who have been down for a while can spot the scared ones. You cannot fake it.

Other prisoners say:

> A lot of the young guys tend to want to break the rules. But, the guard will talk down to you, as if you were a little kid and you can't be disrespected by an officer, so you open your mouth, and that don't go around here. Then you find yourself in the dog cages for a day and a write-up to go with it. So, just comply with the rules so they don't pull you over and start the whole process of dumb shit. An old con knows this: The less you are known, the more you get away with. I don't sweat the dumb shit. I got nothing but time.

> There are several ways to survive in prison, one of which is to be (not just act like) the baddest motherfucker in the unit, a method which demands frequent proof. Another way is to pretend to be the baddest, and to be very, very friendly with a lot of other pretenders. This method requires less proof. The method I use, and usually prefer, is simply to acknowledge "You're the baddest MF around" and go on about my business. This method works well among the vast majority of primates because they are too

busy trying to scare away others like themselves to mess with someone they don't see as a threat.

You must develop a good convict stride. You need to walk like you grew up on the meanest street in the world and be ready to prove it.

Be the fish or the fish food. It's up to you.

⊗   **Don't look at anybody, but don't let anybody stare at you either.**

Victor Masci, in prison in South Carolina, says, "It doesn't pay to look at any of the older inmates too long. One second is about the max, then it's time to look away or they'll think you're a fag, or, at the very least, they'll ask you what your problem is."
   Others elaborate:

Eye contact in the joint automatically signals aggression, like alpha males or alpha females who command respect by intimidation, and those lower in the order do not dare look at their superiors in the full frontal position. Great apes are especially adept at avoiding confrontations by adopting submissive postures. You look someone in the face casually, and then look away as a matter of courtesy. Maintain eye contact and you might have a problem. But certain assholes use "the stare" as an intimidation factor, assessing the response of a new guy, especially in sexual situations. If someone looks and acts timid, then he might as well tattoo "victim" in red letters across his forehead. I know some men who have intentionally appeared submissive in order to sucker someone in to accomplish something physical.

"Marquetting" is the term used in Michigan prisons for staring at a guy. It is a form of aggression. Marquette is also the name of a town and prison on the upper peninsula. How the term came to mean staring, I don't know. The form I'm speaking of is to meet a

21

man's look. Not to hold it, but to meet it. It's a device I can use like a lie detector or a gut check. If I see you have a habit of looking down or away, I perceive it two ways – you're a liar or you're insecure. It's body language known to cons. Everything you do in here is watched by them or us. An outright marquette is a way of saying, "I've got a problem with you and I'm gonna do something to you, given a chance." Staring is bad, but eye contact is a window to your heart.

Avoid making eye contact with guards when you are carrying contraband or when you are trying to avoid trouble for any reason. Make contact with them when you want to draw heat on yourself so they won't notice someone or something else.

There are many who like to play the staring match. For guards, we have a misbehaviour report called "eye balling." If one stares at a guard too long, he can be written up for this. Consider also, we have female guards, so they get a lot of stares. Often lusty ones.

⊗   **Find a way to sleep, but keep one eye open while you do.**

In prison, sleep and dreams can come to an end. Some prisoners cry out in their sleep, such as Karla Homolka, who appeals in her dreams to her dead sister. One con says that the amount of marijuana he smoked in the joint made dreams unnecessary, another that he only dreams in black and white.

Many inmates snore. I've been told that I snore. A few years ago we had an inmate on our range, lower A, who snored. His snoring was so deep, so loud, that we got complaints from guys on upper A. His cellmate once said that when he snored it felt like an earthquake because the bed and the floor shook. When he snored, he woke everyone up and, as a result, everyone was yelling, banging on the wall, anything to wake him up and shut him up.

Some men talk in their sleep as well. At present I'm sharing a cell with a nineteen-year-old. He mumbles, whimpers and even cries in his sleep. This is not totally unusual, though. Some of the things I've heard have been only the odd word or two, but I have also heard short sentences, threats, screams.

Sleeping in prison is different for every person every night. There are times when I lay down and don't wake up again until breakfast. There are nights when I wake up every hour. Our sleep is controlled by what is in our minds: a bad letter from home, worries about wife or family, an argument with a staff member, or a good happy letter from home, a day when just everything seemed to go right.

I used to be able to sleep soundly until June of '84, when I was gang-raped by seven other inmates. After that, I only felt safe during the day. Now, seventeen years later, I still have problems with sleep.

I sleep with my back to the wall and mostly with my clothes on ready to move if attacked. I manage to sleep five hours a night and have to take medication to sleep. I've not been able to have a good dream since I've been in prison. Most of the time I wake up in a dream screaming with fear. Also, inmates steal off me when I sleep and I sleep lightly so I don't get raped.

Actually, with the one hundred plus temperatures we've had, we don't really sleep. It is more a process of losing consciousness which provides very little of the rest that accompanies true sleep.

I have developed a habit. I go to bed around eleven p.m. but I have six cigarettes by my bed. During the night I wake up two or three times and I have a smoke. I usually have a cold cup of coffee there as well and I have a few sips.

I sleep well. I learned years ago how to sleep. Sleep is a combination of dream and meditation. I can go anywhere in the

23

world and create events, until I am lulled to sleep. I can block out the whole world. I learned this technique in 1980, in juvenile [detention].

It seems that after I had served about twelve years, my dreams all seem to take place in some type of prison environment. I guess with the passage of time, and the small amount of life I had on the streets, my conscious mind can no longer remember things and my subconscious is also inevitably going to lose these sensations too. After about the eighteenth year served, I seem to have no dreams at all, or, at least, no recall.

I am a very light sleeper, so I am always sleep depraved.

Sleep with your head away from the bars to keep your head intact and on your body, once you have been in here long enough to develop enemies, no matter how hard you may try not to. But there is another reason. In most prisons, the door opens across the space by the end of the bunk. If your head is at that end, there is a real chance that your arms may end up sticking out through the bars, in which case, when they decided to open the doors (which may happen at any time), your projecting arms are very likely to be broken. Further, if that happens, they will likely stand around talking about how it could have happened for a half-hour or more before anyone ever concludes that perhaps you should get medical treatment of some kind.

⊗ **Cling to your sanity, for what it's worth.**

David Gaspar, in the prison at Walla Walla, Washington, is trying to survive "all natural," which means without depending on medication or illegal drugs. "People go through emotional and mental changes when they're isolated from others," he writes from the hole. He has served five years of his sentence, "with sixteen more to go" for multiple first-degree robberies.

It's frightening to know that a grown man can be defeated to such an extent that he'll actually smear his own feces on his body just for attention. Right now all the skinheads are yelling "kill the Jews" while banging on anything that will make noise. Why? Just because they're bored. When they're done someone else will get started. It never ends. At times when they scream and cuss, bang on windows, doors and other objects, it reminds me I'm in a place that can hurt me if I allow it.

Others write:

I knew an inmate that set himself on fire by wrapping himself with two rolls of shit paper, pouring a can of lighter fluid on top of the paper and then lighting himself on fire. After which he lived and later filed suit because prison officials did not get him out of the cell and to hospital, and he was a freak. He won the suit for a considerable amount of money. Stayed in prison and was later paroled a rich man. He then committed suicide.

Hard to tell, in here, who is crazy & who isn't. Some people seem just fine, and then they snap when their carrots are cold, or their team loses. Ya never know. It's harder inside, actually, because how do you determine who's crazy, and who's experiencing a situational response? That is, dealing with captivity the only way they can. There, of course, is another point – "insanity" can be temporary, a way of dealing with stress when it overloads you.

How do you keep from getting crazy? Try to recall every bar and restaurant you've ever been in, every movie you've ever seen. That sort of thing. I did it in reception in California. Remembered one hundred and ten Toronto bars.

I stay prepared for the unexpected, because they may come for you at any time. They came and confiscated my mattress about ten days ago, because I was sitting on my bed, reading during the morning inspection. You are supposed to stand. I just told them to keep the mattress. That way I don't have to worry about them coming back to get it. I've been sleeping on the floor with a blanket. I mean, it's rough, but it's fair. This cell is my throne, so I must direct my kingdom from here. This is my twenty-ninth day without a mattress. Yes, the floor is hard and cold with only a blanket, but I have a certain pride about myself and I will carry it to my death. I am very cool and calm.

The clock ticks in my cell and the thought of twelve more years of this is simply devastating to my spirits. I'm always seeking asylums from the rigour of time by inventing mental sanctuaries – places of hopes and dreams where the human soul can escape.

In here, the vast majority exist only for today. Theirs is a miserably shallow world where the only gods they know are television and a few dollars worth of hustled snacks. Do not fall victim to this level of satisfaction or you will imprison yourself forever.

I care about my sanity. It's one of the very few things that is still mine, and being a greedy son of a bitch I intend to keep it. I was placed in a cell with nothing but a pair of boxers on, a set of leg irons on my legs, and a roll of toilet paper. I spent a few months in this cell and I came real close to losing my mind. There were no windows and the air-circulation system ran twenty-four hours a day. The slight hum-whisper of the system was a constant, and over time I began hearing whispered voices. Looking back now, I know it was merely a side effect of the lack of interaction with others, like a minor form of sensory deprivation. But, hell, I was eighteen at the time and had no knowledge of that. At first I thought the whispers were conversations travelling through the air vents from another part of the building and, out of curiosity, I'd jump up to the vent and see if I could make sense of them. But it seemed that the voices would get quiet when I did so. This drove me up the wall. When I lay down to sleep the whispers were more noticeable. I began recognizing voices of friends and loved ones from the free world. Old girlfriends and such, mostly, but there were some strange voices that popped up, strange that they were not people I liked at all. What scared the hell out of me was that after being returned to Texas I still heard these voices for a couple of months, but they slowly faded away.

I knew these were hallucinations, but it was one of the hardest things I've ever done to retain my sanity in this extreme solitary cell. I began making chess and checker pieces out of toilet paper soaked in water or Kool-Aid, shaped and dried and playing against myself, which, surprisingly, isn't quite as boring as it sounds. Once I quit caring about the actual winning and focused on trying different strategies out, it became an interesting intellectual game to see which strategies would work against others. Later, began inventing games – mainly military situation games – that required a lot of mathematics, which wasn't my strong point, but it forced me to focus my mind. I was terrified of losing my sanity. I did everything I could think of to avoid losing my mind. Whether or not I was successful is up to debate. Anyway, I finally pled guilty to all charges, including the murder conviction, in order to get out of that cell and back to Texas before I did go bonkers. Even if reality sucks, it's better than being out of touch with reality.

⊗ **Use the time to plan your funeral.**

Once I am dead, I simply could not care less what they do with the dead meat, although I would not consider it misused if they cooked it and fed it to hungry children. That which is me is no part of the physical body.

I have a cemetery plot across the street from the house I was born in, in Stickney, Illinois, in 1939. I bought the plot in the seventies from an old man who was cold-calling at ten-thirty at night on a work night. The man was about ninety and I honestly felt sorry for him. If I survive my incarceration, I will probably be buried there.

I wish I could have my body chopped up into pieces and fed to homeless animals.

In recent months, I've seen TV programs on mummies. If I can't have that done, I'd hope I could get someone to cleanse and keep my skull and bones in their living room or den. If not, burying a tree on me sounds pretty good.

I would prefer to have my ashes scattered on the water. Why? The oceans, seas and rivers are always moving. Water has life and power. And it evaporates into the clouds, which is probably the only way that I will ever get to heaven.

If I turn forty-five while inside, I don't want out. But maybe I should think about saving myself, get out and start living. I want to be cremated and have my ashes scattered where there are a lot of thermals, so I can ride the winds forever and soar like an eagle – I have a tattoo of an eagle on my back – like my reveries, riding the winds going nowhere.

If planning your funeral doesn't inspire you, consider a simple greeting from a survivor of the joint. It should be chiselled in stone over the entranceway to prison:

Welcome to Mars.

2　Cell diplomacy

A relationship is always better if you don't actually have to live with the other person.

WOODY ALLEN

Envelope and drawing by Michael Ivie in prison in Arizona

I admire someone who can live the life of abandon, unshackled by the presence of others, like a nomad in a wide land. And yet, even though I don't have a cellmate, I sometimes feel as though I'm incarcerated with other people. I ought to love my neighbour, and I don't, and I take a small comfort in the reflection that Jesus, for all his love of humanity, was a wanderer in the desert and along the Sea of Galilee. A sea or a river or an ocean is a great place to seek refuge from the clamminess of humanity. There isn't a parent or child, a teacher or student, a boss or employee, who hasn't felt trapped in a relationship. We're all chained and bound by alliances based on chance and mishap. So how do felons do it, live with strangers whose qualification for sharing the cell is that they committed a crime? What can we learn about the civility of living together from the incarcerated? Ray Medina is locked in the Pelican Bay prison in California, where he never sees the sun –

"I'm so damn pale I look like a damn white boy. No offence." Medina explains existence with a cellmate doing life:

> As far as sharing a cell with a lifer, it depends on the lifer. I usually have problems with strong-minded lifers. They feel as if they don't have shit to lose, so they act like assholes. Some of the older lifers that I had the pleasure of celling with are more calm and respectable. They are fun to live with, cuz they enjoy whatever life they do have and I've always tried to learn as much as I could off them. They taught me how to cook prune (rippie). They've also showed me how to survive amongst all these different types of hard-core dudes.

But others aren't so lucky. The most extreme way to deal with the annoyance of a cellmate is to do what a con did at the Greenville County Detention Center in the United States – stick a pen up his nose and into his brain, and kill him. Relationships sometimes break down. Cellmates have been eliminated or removed. Others have been disciplined and educated. Cons find ingenious ways to oust cellmates or neighbours in the next cells:

> There are many ways to get rid of a cellmate. You can set him up by placing contraband in an area. You can pay to have someone else bust him in the head. You can pay him to leave. You can pay to have someone else ask him to leave, or you could leave yourself.

> Most of the problems I've had were related either to a cellie's unwillingness to share in the cleaning or their unwillingness to go to shower. Whenever there are irreconcilable problems between cellies, there are three main ways of resolving them. You can speak to the supervisor and ask to get a cell change. It's best if both of you go down at the same time. This works about half the time, depending on the supervisor. Secondly, there's what's called "an inmate pack-up" where one person packs up his cellie's belongings and sets them outside of the cell. That's if he's consid-

erate. Many just toss the other's stuff out regardless of where it lands or if anything gets broken. This is usually done while the other person is outside of the cell at chow, showers, in the day room, etc., so that he can do the job without interruption and the other has no chance of stopping him. This method really only works on a weaker prisoner who won't fight back. If a person thinks the cellie won't accept this, it's usually not used – or they'd have a shank waiting just in case. The third method of getting rid of a cellie is to assault him in one manner or another. If a person is really offensive and the other person is the violent type, there's usually a stabbing or the person is "beat down" with a sock or bag full of canned goods. Although a last resort, it's a foolproof method of getting separated from an unwanted cellie.

Most cellmates I hand pick. They've been okay. I did have a cell-mate who used to watch me when I undressed or when I slept, and he would cut his arm to suck blood out of it. That was at Petersburg, Virginia, federal prison. He was a complete nut. He had some sort of skin cancer which bled through the skin. But sometimes he cut himself because he liked the taste of blood. How did I get the cellmate out? Well, the heat was hot in my cell. I opened all the heat vents and actually lit a pipe and smoked the guy out.

I've had my share of problems with neighbours. There was one guy who used to bug me a lot, so sometimes, when I didn't like my food, I'd sling it around into his cell. One day the hamburger patty bounced off his bars. I looked with a mirror and he had cardboard tied from top to bottom on his bars. He'd poured what looked like water on it so I couldn't light it on fire. So I tried to anyway, just to shake him up a little. But, man, as soon as I put a match to it, it went up in flames. The dummy had poured baby oil on the card-board. So it scared the shit out of me. I quickly took a large bowl with toilet water and did the fireman routine. We both did.

31

One neighbour tried to throw a homemade bomb in my cell. But he didn't know how to make it, so it just fizzled on my floor. Woke me up. I was going to rip his head off, so when a guard walked by, I told him he'd better get that guy out of there or he was going to get hurt. That was the fastest I ever saw anybody get moved.

One guy underneath me – the bottom deck – one morning told the guard to get his cellie out of his cell because he was stinking. He'd been dead several days. The dude stabbed him and after, layed him on the bunk and carved words and symbols on him.

You become easily perturbed and frustrated. You find the smallest flaws of your cellmate quite an ordeal. Imagine sitting on a bus next to a man who farts and you can't get away because it's crowded. And he consistently does this without acknowledging his actions or even caring.

I lived with this loser, a junk-alcoholic, but I managed. He'd make hooch and get drunk all the time, and high on cocaine. But get an anal-retentive cellie and, oh, how the time can drag on! Or if you get a cellmate who is just totally impervious to consideration of others and then it's like a bad marriage of dysfunctionals for twenty years.

It's a bad idea to impose your sex life or your drug life on your cellie. Clinton Corbeil is serving a sentence in California of twenty-five years for robbing an armoured truck. At twenty-three years of age he had a dream that he could score two million dollars in a few minutes and retire. The idea came from watching television, he says. His wish came true. He got four hundred thousand dollars and retired to a jail cell. "I am in the hole and have been for seven months now," he writes. He was sharing the cell and had advice on cell manners:

I had a cellie that used narcotics, preferably heroin. We had a verbal agreement that he would show me respect by not shooting the drugs when I was around. I used to sleep in the morning while my cellie had left for the day. I wake up one morning. I do what I do every morning, which is to make a cup of coffee using the extra hot tap water we have here. I don't know that my cellie had stuck a paper of tar heroin on a spoon and left. Of course, I'm sleepwalking and stir my hot coffee using the contaminated spoon. When my cellie returns he is upset that I have ingested his dope. I tested positive for heroin and got charged. I never used drugs in my life, until I came to prison.

Others said:

Cell time is being alone in the cell. A good cellie will give you cell time. Everyone needs to take personal time to write to their families, even to masturbate. I like to get a good first-termer who shows heart or has potential and I school him to the ways of cell living. You have to know that your cellie will be there with you if anything ever happens on the yard. You have to back your cellie up.

I had a cellmate who was having sex with another inmate on the bottom bunk of our two-bunk bed. It was very uncomfortable for me. I am not against lesbians. Everyone is free to select their sex partner. I just don't want to be around girls having sex.

The thing that is the hardest about the hole is, when you have three grown men in a cell you can't "take care of business." Jacking off! So you try and give your cellie what we call cell time. You rotate recreation. So you give everyone a chance to do their thing, out of respect.

⊗   **Do your part to keep the cell and yourself clean.**

How a cell is cleaned and organized is important. Sloppy habits can cause serious domestic flare-ups in a prison cell just like at home. Here are some different views on cell sanitation. As Stephen Pang succinctly puts it, "Be clean. Cons can't stand dudes that smell like ancient funk." Paul Wolfe "just did ten years for killing a guy. I would of got life, but I proved he was going to stab me before I shot him." He has been "to every maximum pen in California," including Pelican Bay, Folsom, Calipatria, Soledad, and so on. In other words, he knows what he's talking about. He starts this section:

> There are respect rules in any cell. You never spit in the sink! You always wipe the toilet seat when you're done using it! You always clean the sink when you're done using it! You always clean up after yourself. When you're done eating, for instance, you immediately clean all bowls and utensils. My cell is my house! My cell is my domain.

> The last one that moved in here had some kind of allergy towards brooms and mops. I'm a fairly clean person. I do my part and I feel the other guy should do his too. It's tough living so close to another man, especially if you have serious time.

> In population I had a cellie, a guy with a serious cleaning disorder. Nothing could be out of order for him. If the labels to bottles ain't pointed and facing right, he'd have a cleaning fit. He washes his hands at least forty times a day, so much that the skin between his fingers was white and peeling, and he's black. Now these are all good guys, gentlemen. But we all have our idiosyncrasies or whatever you call it. Bad habits and oddities. And those are hard to deal with. I must have screamed at Mr. Clean a few times. I'd come to the cell from work and he'd have all our property in the hall, 'cause he'd wanna mop and sweep.

> Years ago, a guy killed his cell partner for using his hairbrush. We tend to be very particular about personal items like that.

> Roaches in my cell? Well, let's see. There's the one-hundred-and-ninety-pounder in the bunk above me. That's about the

biggest one. He keeps, in violation of the rules, stacks and stacks of old newspapers in here, which gives the roaches excellent living quarters and an abundance of food. Yes, the damn things are in here by the thousands. He sleeps all day and sits up all night listening to the radio he smuggled in, and every few minutes either laughs out loud or calls out, "That's bad ass, man!"

Two of the conditions of prison that are difficult for outsiders to appreciate are the noise and the stink. It is so much a part of the penitentiary that cons have learned to measure the passage of time by their noses. Think of prison as a kind of swamp created to manufacture, among other things, enormous quantities of methane gas. Then remember that a prison is not open to the sky, but sealed in concrete, layer upon layer, with a series of airtight steel doors, and that the only wind to blow the fumes away comes from the hundreds of intestines working around the clock to recycle solids and gases. It's like the men's washroom in a large train station when the trains are stranded by a snowstorm for several days. Here's how the ventilated consciousness of a con explains it:

To get the smell, go out into the country and find a farm where they have been using an outhouse for years. In the heat of the summer, lock yourself inside for about a week or two. As your sense of smell adjusts, you will reach the point where you will not be able to distinguish the difference between that and prison. The acclimatization is needed because the outhouse odour is intense while the prison odour is more subtle – but they are the same methane base. Of course, when you take two thousand men and work the hell out of them, then process all of them through eighty shower nuzzles, giving the whole crowd no more than one hour total, in water that is usually bone-chilling cold in the winter and semi-steam in the summer, it doesn't help matters much. When you add to that a diet that is almost exclusively starch, water, pig fat and beans, three times a day, then crowd all two thousand men into a space that, for health purposes, should

35

never under any circumstances house any more than an emergency maximum of five hundred – it's a real gas!

Then the farts, particularly during the early hours of the morning. They range in sound and size. As dawn approached, someone would have to wake up the kitchen helpers and escort them to the gate. Soon you would begin to smell a variety of smells that would tell the inmates what day it was since the institutional menus would start the week off with a menu that could be predicted a year beforehand. Other smells included accumulated fats and grease that were missed by the cleaner, wet mops and, of course, dirty clothes held in different quantities in the one hundred and twenty cells. The pill cart would come trundling through from the prison infirmary allowing a momentary feeling that, maybe, civilization must be nearby.

If you can't live with a cellmate, you may have to live in a cell alone. A cell has its own physical presence in a penitentiary. It's part companion, part extension of your brain, part living diary. In a prison cell in Newton, Iowa, with three grey walls and bars in front, David Hinman talks about doing time by himself in a cell. He was sentenced for second-degree theft as a "habitual criminal" who had spent almost one-third of his life in various prisons. The prisoner, in his late fifties, is married with twin sons who are in their twenties.

I have done time in solitary on and off for over thirty-four years. In the old days, solitary was called the hole and, in Iowa prisons, it was a cell, usually kept dark and cold. You were not allowed to speak to anyone. Food was basically bread and water, for up to twenty-one days or more. I have done as many as thirty-one days on bread and water. If you violated any rules while in the hole you were subject to being beat by guards or hosed down with high-pressure hoses with ice-cold water. Not a nice place. Solitary here, you are kept alone in a cell similar to the one I am in now, twelve feet long by seven feet wide, window in back wall six inches wide by four foot high. You are fed regular meals, can receive mail, send limited mail, and even get books to read.

Rafael Vasquez, in prison in Texas, explains the subtext of a cell:

My cell is five feet by nine feet. I can reach out and touch both walls. The walls are dense cement, painted white. In summer they absorb and retain heat and in winter they radiate cold. The floor is natural, smooth cement, stained by thirty-plus years of spilled food, urine, blood and boot scuffs. Light-blue, vertical iron bars attach to an electrically operated door made of similar vertical tubular bars on a sliding track. This makes up one of the four walls and is the one that deprives us of any privacy. The bunks bolted to the wall are little more than flat iron slabs upon which lies a blue plastic mattress that is lumpy, cracked and about one-quarter-inch thick at its center. I can see outside, all right. About eight feet across from my row of cells is four storeys of ten-by-ten-inch non-tempered glass window panes. The sun shines into our cells and into our bunks with a vengeance. It's one hundred and seventeen degrees plus in our cells in the summer. The intense Texas heat kills the weak and the infirm. To look outside, I see a small grass courtyard and various main-tenance buildings. Beyond the razor wire, there is little of anything taller than a cow.

Solitary confinement is a challenge to sanity, partly because it's not solitary enough. In American prisons being in solitary can mean shar-ing a cell in a noisy range with men yelling and snoring and farting. The punishment of this solitary is that you crave solitude and long for release from the hell of incarceration with people like yourself. And yet, whatever the conditions, prisoners also come to think of a cell in prison as their "house," a haven. Some of the older ones have anxiety attacks if they are forced to leave. Some prisoners feel more comfort-able in prison than they do on the street. They can survive better inside. They have adapted to life in prison, just as people have adapted to living in cities and aren't sure if intelligent life exists outside the urban core. Some of the cons have developed ways to stay in prison longer to avoid the irrationality of life on the streets. The prison system, for its part, works on ways to force the cons out of prison before they are ready, to keep the cycle back to prison alive.

A man in prison recalls himself as an eighteen-year-old starting his round of prison solitary:

> I had no property. Just a toothbrush, toothpaste, my boxer shorts and a Bible. The cell was very small, old, rusty, dirty, dark and quiet. I paced back and forth for a few days, getting to shower once a day and eat to break the cycle of pacing. I read the Bible. I always heard it was a good book! Ha ha. But, no matter what I did, it seemed as though the hours took days to pass and that the days took weeks. The loneliness is humbling. When I was released back to population I remember walking through the main hallway. It seemed as though everything was moving a hundred miles an hour. I couldn't quite get back into the groove for a while. It took a few hours of adjustment to get my bearings back. I had nothing more to lose and therefore could do whatever I wanted with only the fear of fifteen days solitary as punishment. They could do nothing more to me. I had lost all hope. Solitary became my refuge after that. It was a place I could go so I could think and escape the noise and rambunctiousness of prison life. I went to solitary probably fifteen to twenty times for fifteen-day stints after that. I stayed in medium custody for about a year and a half before I was placed in administrative segregation. I live in constant solitary confinement. I have been here now for one year and ten months. In that time I have not touched another human being unless it is when they are placing handcuffs and shackles on me. I get one hour a day in a small cage alone with a pull-up bar as exercise. The cage is about ten feet by twenty feet. Not much bigger than the cell.

A woman writes from a segregation cell in Texas:

> There is a very small crack around the food slot where they put
> my tray in the cell. Little knats [gnats] sometimes get in the cell
> through that. Other than that, there are no critters. The weather
> is always the same in this cell. You don't even know when it
> changes outside. You can't even smell it when it rains. However,
> sometimes you can hear the rain on the roof – that is, if everyone
> is asleep, which is a rare occasion. One other change that some-
> times occurs is the water will turn stagnant and you can taste it,
> so, when this happens, you can almost bet that it is a rainy
> season and water is standing in puddles outside. Other than the
> rain sometimes on the roof, no other sounds come in from the
> free world. No birds chirping or any of that. No mice or rats,
> although it would be quite nice if I could catch the sight of one
> playing now and then.

3   What the guidebooks don't say

In the reformatory we learned to keep our silence and stomp our own snakes.

ROGER CARON, bank robber and author, Go-Boy!

Prisons are like the mountains where I live – big, impenetrable and, for those who know them intimately, all different. I couldn't tell the difference between a cell in Folsom and one in San Quentin, but a felon can. It is the country he knows best. A cell in San Quentin just *feels* different from one in Folsom. The walls, the corridors, the guards, the feverish convict swarm – each takes its own distinct tincture from the history and culture and architecture of a particular joint, from the blood, sweat, beatings and despair of living felons. There may be tours of old Alcatraz, where the "dull moaning" of the foghorn was heard by Sam Spade in 1929. Visitors can cross the water and squint like coal miners into the cell of Robert Stroud, the Birdman of Alcatraz. But that's not a prison anymore. What makes a prison such as Attica, or Archambault in Quebec, different from the others? To learn that, I talked to convicts on the ranges, and sometimes sat in the seclusion of their cells with them. I remember the women who adorned their cells to make them forget where they were. Some laughed, some cried, and then the moment they stepped out of the cell their faces would revert to prison masks. I felt like a civilian touring an army camp. I still didn't know the place as one of the enlisted. I asked my convict correspondents to write me letters that would walk me through their prisons and take me into their cells.

José Cruz was one of my guides in the land of prisons. He'd been to Riker's Island, and to a nasty little joint in New York State called Elmira, known among cons as a coliseum for "young cats making a name" in combat. "Elmira is known as 'gladiator school,'" he said. "Eight out of every ten cons there has razor slashes on his face." Riker's Island was more menacing than Leavenworth, according to Cruz, because the cons are angry and belligerent and haven't settled down to the expediency of doing a stretch of time. The warrior pedigree of someone who has survived the gladiator pit impresses some cons and makes the girls "druel," says Cruz, but it doesn't impress him. He knows that a lot of fancy titles don't mean anything. Here's his account of Riker's Island.

> The air in Riker's was thicker, darker, rancid, fearful, abusive, dangerous, oppressive & hopeless. I mean the feel. I guess that's because the Riker's guys are still fighting their cases, scared, and mad at the world. So there's more violence. In max joints, the guys are more laid back, complacent in wanting to do their time in peace.
>
> I did not get to see much of the island, only the dorm areas and the graveyards. The only prisoners there are guys doing skid beds. The living conditions are like trailer homes, a bunch of square structures put together haphazardly. It was falling apart when I was there, in the winter. It was ice cold. The heat kept on breaking. There was plastic covers on all the windows to keep the heat in. The toilets & showers were flimsy add-ons that was broken down and didn't work. And there was only a few guards there. No one was going to escape.

They brought us on a police boat. Cuffed. The only thing I was thinking about was, "What if it sinks!" We were all chained together and they took us five at a time.

The dormitory was a big, fifty-bed space, real close and real crowded. Every morning a truck would come, pick us up, and take us to the nearby graveyard, and there'd be a truck full of black bags. And we'd dig the holes, dump a bag, cover it up again, and add a cross. No prayer or nothing. Oddly enough, there was never any smells of decomposing bodies, as one would suspect. Just the smell of damp earth, sweat and the sea – or river, or whatever that body of water was surrounding me. I'm not a sea man. I'm a ghetto thug.

As I said, we were all skid bedders. Guys would come and go in less than a month. The guards wouldn't say much, so we entertained each other with our own morbid tales of this potter's field called Hearts Island. The only ones who knew for sure what all that was about was the ones living there. That is, the dead ones living there.

Leavenworth, where Cruz was transferred, is tough and old and famous. Leavenworth is the kind of prison where the guards chew wads of tobacco and have permanently soured faces, according to Cruz.

I guess Leavenworth does have a reputation in prison circles. The inmates of old would boast how this used to be a murder-'em-up joint, one body a week. I think I'd laugh at a con who told me his jail in Riverview is a swinging and funky joint. Meanwhile, they have no walls and turrets and the last murder was about fifty years ago, and that was by accident. So there is a reputation one carries. It makes some cons feel very big.

The hallways in Leavenworth have that sort of gothic feel to it, like a museum, large cavernous hallways. When you walk you can feel the echo. You can always tell the difference between a modern structure and an old structure. The older ones are always very spacious and high ceilinged, often domed. The modern is often cramped and bare and to the point, institutionalized.

Cruz, still in Leavenworth, the Hot House, was moved from a segregation unit in D Block called the Dog House, to a segregation cell with a steel door, similar to the kind he'd known in New York State prisons. Blaze was isolated, in a steely, tough old prison. It was June, with its dreamy, beginning-of-summer promise.

Man-o-man, this hole is the pits. It's called the Dog House for D Cell house. But on the hottest days in the summer and the coldest days of winter, it's at its worst. I mean really, really unbearable. Right now I stay sweaty. I took a shower, but it's like I didn't. This paper keeps on getting wet from sweat, so I got to hold it very delicate-like with another loose sheet under my writing hand. If it's ninety outside, it's like one hundred and twenty up here. I say "up here" because we're also on the last floor, five flights up. As you know from science class, heat rises. The doctors won't make rounds, or rather refuse to see us, unless you're dying. One of my bros is walking around with yellow eyes, his skin is a waxy yellow, and I told him to see the doctor. But the doctor won't see him. What he got could be either of four things that Dr. Blaze knows of: 1. Jaundice. 2. Hippititus. 3. TB or 4. liver infection, and I pray it's not 2 or 3, because we have no circulation here and that shit is airborne and easily contagious. Man-o-man, I hate prison.

A few months later a letter came from Cruz in the hole in Leavenworth in the end-of-summer ripeness of September. It sounded like the same day as the letter in June, as though time had frozen and ceased to move.

It's terribly hot here in the Dog House. The best, most accurate description I could possibly give you is of a gigantic dog kennel. You have cages stacked five floors high, each floor with a range.

You can look down to the first floor if you look over the range banister. A fence is up, so no one gets accidentally thrown overboard. It's like a square of cages within a big square room.There's no ventilation. It's so hot I stay in sweat, dripping all day and night. I have ants all over this cell. I could hear one of my boyz calling to another of the bros on a different range. A third unidentified person keeps on croaking in a nasal voice, "Shaddup!" So the first bro is getting upset asking the third person to identify himself. The response: "Shaddup!" I'm over here smiling to myself. They're nutz. Another guy somewhere else keeps banging his plastic cup on the gate, yelling, "Feed me, C.O. [correctional officer]." It's about five o'clock. Chow should have been served already. I've been writing you since three o'clock. I can see daylight outside the barred windows on the wall opposite my cell and range. I'm on the third range now. Used to be on the fifth. It's slowly getting dark. Probably got three more hours of light time. All I can see past the windows is more brick walls. My back hurts. I have no table, so I sit on my bed, back hunched over this pad as I write you. I could smell the food. Even the garbage food always seems to smell good. I wonder why? This cell is so small. I get off the bed and bump into the wall opposite the bed. This cell is about nine by five. Add a bed, sink and toilet, and you have little room for anything. And, in most cells, they got two men in one cell. The oppressive heat, the sweat, a tiny cell, no air to breathe, only three showers a week, twenty-three hours a day in the cell, and they wanna put another guy in the cell with you? If he's got a gas problem, or, if he's big, I pity them. I'm alone in this cell and it's unbearable.

David Weidert wrote me his reminiscences from Corcoran prison in California, a facility built on an old lakebed south of Fresno. The cells at Corcoran are a few inches larger than at San Quentin and Folsom. He was sent to seaside, fog-shrouded San Quentin at eighteen to serve a life sentence for murder.

San Quentin seemed mid-evil and castle-like. Lots of dark corners and huge buildings and walls. Gun walks with shotgun-toting cops both inside and outside every building. It housed approximately six thousand prisoners. Of all the prisons I've been in, I guess this one would be best described as a war zone. Between January of '82 and January of '84, this prison experienced the single most violent and deadly racial war in the history of the California prison system. It was a thirteen-month lockdown that was a result of a rather long war between various prison gangs. The war simultaneously also took place at Folsom prison. If I remember correctly, the number of dead or critically injured over a two-year period reached up into the seventies or eighties. I was twenty years of age at the time. I watched several people younger than myself die, merely because they happened to have a particular colour of skin.

I spent a year in the hole at San Quentin, back in 1983. It's amazing what the human brain can adapt to, particularly when given no other choice. I was still young then and able to seek some relief through dreams. I tried to sleep as often and as long as I could. I remember I would wake up in my bunk and hear all the noise and smell the stench and realize where I was. This is an insanely unnatural place with people living insanely unnatural lives. During my waking hours I remember playing with the cockroaches, rounding them up, seeing which ones could swim in the sink the longest.

San Quentin was perhaps the one prison that stands out as having the most individualized feel, both physically and mentally. Old Folsom would be a close second. Old Folsom is built with the same five-tiered cellblocks and constructed largely of granite blocks. It has a much smaller yard area surrounded by the housing blocks. Again, the word castle would apply.

New Folsom is by no means similar to Old Folsom, structurally speaking. It is, however, nearly identical to Corcoran or any other of the several new prisons built throughout the eighties and nineties. These new-style prisons are normally built on a barren area of California and are the ultimate in sensory deprivation. Each housing unit is identical to the next. The buildings are all constructed of large tilt-up sections of unpainted grey cement. The interior of the housing units consists of a hundred two-man cells. The interiors of the cells are also unpainted grey cement. Because of the geographics of these new prisons there is little change in the smell of the air or sightings of any animals, with the exception of the occasional stray cat and the scurrying lizards. You find yourself spending months at a time confined to your cell due to the riots that result from the utter stagnation of life.

Another prison with a pedigree is Attica, where Ty Midgette resides. He's a six-foot-one black man with iron abdominals who was sentenced to fifteen years to life for the attempted murder of a police officer in New York City. He had been in the legendary Sing Sing, the historic prison in Auburn, and tried refusing to be transferred to notorious Attica, "the bottom of the barrel," which earned him "ninety days in the box." "Ninety days is really not that bad compared to two or three years in Attica," he said philosophically. From the box he wrote of his resistance to Attica, where "one can get killed, stabbed or beaten by prisoners or guards. So that's why I refuse." When he was eventually transferred to Attica he wrote, "Guess what? I'm in Attica. Ain't that a bitch. What the heck, I'll deal with it. I really don't have a choice, do I?"

Attica is like being in the south during the 1950s and 1960s. Some of the officers are very racist and unprofessional. There's always tension after they have isolated a prisoner and beat his brains out. There's a relationship between officers and homosexuals that is known by this administration. A lot of guys don't even go to the yard 'cause they don't want to be molested or harassed by certain officers. There's a group of officers called the black-glove crew. They are very brutal, they lie in reports, and they set you up.

The difference between Attica and other prisons is that in 1971,

September 9, prisoners took over Attica.* This lasted for five days. State and government troops stormed the prison, killing prisoners and officers who were hostages. This riot started because of the treatment of prisoners by officers. To this day Attica is run with an iron fist because of that riot thirty years ago. I don't blame the administration, but the officers are excessive in their treatment of prisoners, all in the name of keeping control. We are not the prisoners of 1971. They were much more unified and radical than us. Most of these prisoners aren't thinking about overthrowing anything.

I've had somewhat of a rough three weeks. My next-door neighbour, a real lunatic, was banging on the wall at six-thirty a.m., yelling and cursing at God knows who. I politely asked him, "Can you please hold that noise down?" His reply was, "Whoever don't like it can suck my dick." That's a taboo expression that one man doesn't say to another man in prison. Guys have been killed or stabbed for saying these words. I tell him that. "Now you have a problem." We all come out for the mess hall run. I clock the guy upside his head. There's no turning back now. A very one-sided fight ensues. He's yelling, "Somebody get him off me." Actually, I didn't want to hurt him real bad, just rough him up a little. The alarm bell rung. The police came and broke it up. I was given ten days keep-lock, patted on the back by some officers, I guess because everybody knew this guy was trouble. After coming off keep-lock status, I went to the yard that evening. I was stopped and told to put my hands on the wall. I was being frisked by one officer while ten more stood by within three feet. My testicles were squeezed at least three times. Hands searched roughly between my buttocks. This was an attempt to get me to take my hands off the wall. If this happens, that's their excuse to kick your ass, 'cause you're not supposed to take your hands off the wall

* Between September 9 and 13, 1971, forty-three people – thirty-two prisoners and eleven corrections officers – died at the Attica prison in New York State. Thirty-nine of them were killed and more than eighty wounded by gunfire in the fifteen minutes it took the State Police to retake the prison.

until told so. But I endured this humiliation. Even after realizing I didn't possess a weapon, he started verbally abusing me and rubbing my ass in a very suggestive manner. By this time my whole body was rigid and I was consumed with hate and anger. But what could I do to eleven officers with or without nightsticks?

As any con will say, Canada doesn't have prisons of the steely calibre of those in the United States. Prisoners know the differences between prisons, just as travellers know the difference between Kuala Lumpur and Jakarta. Consider the words of Stephen Pang, a graduate of Folsom in the United States, and of Millhaven and Collins Bay in Canada:

> The difference in mentality between here [in a Canadian federal penitentiary] and California is almost unfathomable. When I first went to prison here, in 1988, I felt like I had landed on an alien world. I am a product of an American maximum-security prison, and that still controls many of my thought processes and attitudes. Sheer tension is the best way to describe it. When I emerged from prison in the United States in 1986, people who had known me all my life were afraid of me, commenting later that hate and anger literally radiated from me. The attitude there is basically kill or be killed, no quarter asked or given. Violence is far more commonplace than is ever admitted to. In 1984, we set a record at Folsom with eight hundred stabbings in one year. No mention of this ever on TV, in newspapers, or in any government report. It was a year-long war between various factions, and such are the consequences of war.
>
> To compare joints [in Canada and the United States] would require a few trees. I can boil it down to a fundamental difference: in California, you're surprised when you get out alive; in Canada, you expect to get out alive.
>
> Each prison has its own distinct history and persona, therefore the people you encounter in each prison are likely to be influenced by that persona and reflective of it. At Folsom we considered ourselves the true soldiers, and those at San Quentin to be

pretenders to the throne. Quentin, in turn, was heavily influenced in atmosphere by the presence of Death Row, and by the fact that you can see the lights of the bay area at night, an endless tease for the guys there who were never, ever getting out.

The Canadian versions of Attica, Folsom and Alcatraz are Archambault, Millhaven and Kingston Penitentiary. Bob Moyes, serving a life sentence for bank robbery, compares Archambault in Quebec and Millhaven in Ontario.

After a couple of years in the Haven or Archambault, you would be satisfied if allowed to "retire" and live out your days in the Head [William Head prison on Vancouver Island]. Millhaven and Archambault are identical physically. The joke – the only one – is that Archambault was the French copy of the plans for Millhaven. Everything is opposite in Quebec. Millhaven, turn left. Archambault, to get to the same place, turn right. That's the joke and where the similarities end.

Two of my friends from British Columbia were killed in Archambault, and many were beaten by guards and inmates alike. I, myself, was stabbed and beaten with a pipe primarily because I'm English. It could have been the times or the political climate. It was two years of stress, of fear for life. Sleeping with two bars of soap taped together in a sock wrapped around my hand. Going nowhere in lineups always armed. Every second watching and waiting. Guts in a knot 24-7. Your every sense assaulted by a language you can't understand. Wanting to cry and scream at the same time. But you do it every fucking day, wake up, arm up, door opens, step out on the range, head up, show no fear, no emotion, for certain no weakness. When I was stabbed I went to my cell, sewed my ear and throat up. I stood at my door the next morning and was nodded at by two people. Recognition for not running to the Man. No words. I got in an argument with a guard. I swore in English at him. I got piped and beaten by three inmates for insulting a Frenchman. I hurt, but I stood at my door the next morning. I was still a piece-of-shit Englishman, but I was left alone. I had fought back the best I could. I'm not big or tough, just an animal fighting for survival. Twenty years later it still rattles my nerves. I was twenty-four when I got there. Hijacker, bank robber, survivor of police shoot-out and British Columbia pen riots. Still, I think that place was where I really learned to crawl inside myself. To live inside my mind, totally separate from the physical reality of confinement.

As for Millhaven, walking into that place was such a relief. I slept for days as stress drained out of me. English was in the air and it was like a wave enveloping me. Millhaven is a serious prison with very violent and capable men. A majority are doing life for murder. There are large groups of outlaw bike gang members and white supremists. But, if you are respectful of another's space, you can do your own time. After Archambault, I thought the Haven was great.

In general, a prison cell encapsulates the history of the prison and the occupants, like a living museum, but it takes a con to be able to read it. Anthony Pestello writes from a prison in southern Texas, in what's called administrative segregation, or solitary confinement:

My cell is approximately six feet by nine feet. It has eggshell white walls, a grey bunk and a small desk that protrudes from the wall. One wall has a solid stainless steel toilet-and-sink combination. The door that I face is also solid steel. It has a three-foot-by-three-inch opening that is steel cage. That is my window to the run. All I can see is another white wall outside. The door has a "bean shoot" that is about eighteen by five inches. It takes a crowbar-type device to open it. It opens from the outside only to allow my trays to be slid in. It is also where handcuffs and shackles are placed on me before I am ever let out of the cell. The light is a fluorescent light that is vertical along the wall. It is extremely bright and makes you feel as though you live in a shopping mall or a hospital. The picket (where the officers are located with control panels) can be seen from the door of my cell through the small steel window. In the back of my cell, way above the bunk, is a small window that faces the outside. I have to stack books on my bunk (Machiavelli's compiled works, some Plato like *The Republic, Forbidden Knowledge* by Roger Shattuck – a very good book I would suggest to anyone – *How to Argue and Win Every Time* by Gerry Spence, early Greek philosophy, *The Divine Comedy*) and stand tippy-toed to look out. The window does not open. It is only two-and-one-half feet long and three inches wide, but it allows in sunlight, which is good. If I look outside I see hundreds of yards of chain-link fence topped with razor wire and other types of barbed wire. I guess the razor wire isn't enough! I can also see the guard tower with a lonely guard standing sentry with his twelve-gauge shotgun and AR-15 assault rifle and other prison units in the distance. At night, my first night on this unit, I looked out the window, standing tippy-toed and saw in the distance a lighted horizon. Many lights! I asked if that was the Beeville community. I was told it was two more prison units. Come daybreak I could see guard towers. In the back of my cell in the corners are two rusty steel beams welded and bolted to the corners. They are there because inmates have figured out that you can use different things to scrape the caulking out of the corners of the walls and talk to your neighbours through the small crack. Hey, it gets lonely here and any voice, even through a crack in the wall, is a breath of fresh air! The paint on the walls is chipping, peeling and cold. There are different little writings in places, those that I have been unable to scrub off despite repeated attempts. Some are lines and slashes from a prior inmate's marking of days, some from a workout schedule, some gang graffiti. The ground has the look of an old garage floor. Scraping marks are visible in the corners and under the toilet where a previous occupant apparently sharpened shanks or other homemade weapons. My mattress is light-blue plastic stuffed with cotton, very lumpy, very uncomfortable. The pillow just a smaller version of that.

In a prison in Huntsville, in southeast Texas, it's always hot, and the men are angry.

In the hottest part of summer a few weeks ago, they locked us all in our cells three days and nights and turned off the water. Nothing to drink, no showers, nothing to flush with. And for a lot of those days they turned off the power so we had no fans. Still, we refused to riot. Over the past few months they have reduced the size of our food portions to where what we now get is on a par with the smallest TV dinner you can get. We have never been allowed more than three, or, at the most, four hours of sleep each twenty-four. That's still in effect. They have ripped out all the cable connections to the cells so that radios are all but useless. They have made it so the TV now only gets one channel, which is almost all snow and static. Three weeks ago a man escaped (temporarily) from the Wynne unit a few miles from here by driving a truck through the fence. They used that as an excuse to cancel all our recreation. Since that time, they have allowed us to go to recreation only twice – once each week – and both times they closed the recreation yard early. I have been trying to persuade the other men to refuse to work, instead of rioting. They keep saying, "I will if you will, but I'm not going to be the first."

Though it is officially winter, I cannot legitimately call it so, with the temperatures going into the eighties each day, and drop-ping no lower than the upper sixties each night. The flowers and trees are budding and blooming. The flies, mosquitoes and ants are swarming. The spiders and roaches never even slowed down. Here there's the absolute lack of any hope for any modicum of privacy ever. The damn female guards even come to the cells and stand there giving us small talk while we are trying to shit. (Pardon the term, but I felt a strong word was needed.)

I had to laugh when you said it's hard to get a concrete image of what it looks like from my vantage point. Haven't you seen concrete lately? That's the image – concrete, bricks and steel bars, except when I am at work, where it's concrete, brick and steel walls, and a steel roof. Concrete is the image of my life.

I don't know if the news has yet reached you there of the escape from here last week of a prisoner from Death Row. Seven of them tried, sometime around midnight, in the fog, by cutting a hole through the recreation yard fence, if I have been informed correctly. They were spotted by a guard in a watchtower, who blasted away at them till the place sounded like a Vietnam fire fight. Didn't hit one of them. Apparently though, all the noise did scare six of them into laying down and giving up. The seventh made his own parole. For the life of me I can't understand why six men who are about to be murdered by the state anyway, no matter what they do, didn't keep going when they weren't hit.

The seventh man was found a week later, his body floating below a bridge less than a kilometre from the prison. He had wrapped himself in cardboard to clamber over the razor wire on top of the prison fences. It was the first breakout from Death Row in Texas since a member of the Bonnie and Clyde gang escaped in 1934. The warden was demoted and transferred. The man found in the water had been condemned to die for a robbery in Corpus Christi in which two people were killed.

In the same prison in Texas the cons play a game with snakes.

A couple of years ago the Texas system banned smoking by inmates. Guards are now making sizable fortunes buying cheap tobacco at the store and smuggling it in to sell to the prisoners at prices ranging from $75 to $150 for a half pound. It makes the hard narcotics industry run by the CIA look like chicken feed. Of course, they won't search or punish guards bringing the tobacco in. Instead, they search prisoners and spy on them to punish them for smoking it. They confiscate the tobacco from one prisoner and minutes later sell it to another prisoner.

The cellblocks are arranged in two rows with a corridor called a pipe chase between the backs. As part of the spy operation, the guards began turning off the lights in the pipe chase at night and sneaking down it on their hands and knees, sniffing at the air vents to smell the tobacco smoke.

The other night one of the inmates heard a guard crawling by and jokingly said, "You'll quit doing that shit if you get bit by a snake." Not even two minutes later the guard screamed and ran for the exit, banging into pipes along the way. He had not been bitten, but touched something that felt like a snake in the dark. The riot squad suited up and came down the pipe chase, lights blazing. Sure enough, with their riot sticks they beat to death a small copperhead snake.

Now the men bring in snakes every chance they get and turn them loose in the pipe chase. The guards no longer turn off the lights and crawl behind the cells.

About where the inmates got the snakes – the fields, yards and everywhere else there is a little dirt for them to burrow in or objects for them to hide under, are crawling with them practically year round. We have little or no winter here and, except for five to fifteen days out of the year, they are active on the grounds in the daytime and, during much of the year, they sleep on the surface as well. The field crews encounter them every day they work.

Snakes are fairly easy to catch, if you have the nerve and don't startle them. Just have something or someone moving in front of them to attract their attention while you slowly move a hand in from behind to within about eight inches of their heads and then grab. The thick leather workgloves provide some protection against the smaller ones and are great for increasing confidence. They don't capture the larger snakes, but kill them to use the skins in the craft shop. The inmates do get bitten pretty often, but understand, in here the attitude toward being snake bitten is not the same as it is outside, except for the guards.

After about five years, imprisonment stops being punishment and becomes mere abuse – nothing but an alternative lifestyle that we have adjusted to which no longer has any connection with the crimes committed by those who actually did it. Under those circumstances, the inmates don't look at being bitten by a snake as being anything bad, but instead they see it as two or three days lay-in during which they don't have to suffer through the slave labour.

Women make up a much smaller number of the prisoners in Canada and the United States than men. A woman writes from a prison in Arizona where she is serving a murder sentence:

> When I first got here I was told to forget about the outside because it would make me do "hard time." So I did. I managed to become institutionalized with the rules, regulations and drama. But, for the last six months, I've turned my attention to the "real" world. It's a lonely road because no one here can relate to that. They play the drama. They leave & come right back like a revolving door. The abuse by the officers is so unreal, so the battle is hard every day. It's so dehumanizing. People just don't know.
>
> Almost five months ago we had the first female escape from here. She wanted to go public with the corruption behind these walls, but after two weeks she was caught & shipped out of state. Since then we've been under heavy maximum lockdown. The only way out of our cells is if we work. Not to add that the system has gotten so overcrowded. The yard is made for two hundred and ninety women. We now have six hundred women. One-man cells now hold three women. There are twenty tents holding ten women each. So, within the next three months they are moving the men out of their prisons across the street and shipping them all over the state & moving us to their unit. So it's lots of chaos here.

An earlier letter from the same woman in another prison:

> Where I'm at, the prison fits two hundred women, but we've squeezed five hundred and twenty in now. It's awful. Most are addicts or people who have come in and out four to six times

since I've done these twelve years. It makes me bitter to see it all as my young teenage years were rotted away here.

Each dorm has two sides. The cop's cage is in the middle. It's four individual six-packs with waist-high walls. Each six-pack has twelve women in it. It's a tight squeeze and no room. The bathroom is even open to the cop's cage. It's crazy. Spiders and scorpions constantly come through the doors.

If I'm not in my cube, I feel so unbalanced. There's so much negativity and chaos outside of it. I realized just days ago that I've got to find some kind of balance or all the hard work I've done on myself will have been a sure waste.

I'm doing a little downtime. I got slammed in the dungeon yesterday. I knew I was going, so mentally I was prepared to sit in isolation for two weeks. The room I'm in is room fourteen. Late at night you can feel an uncomfortable presence, like you know it's haunted. I really dislike this room. It feels like death to me. Stagnant.

4   Finding the edge & keeping it

When torrential water tosses boulders, it is because of its momentum.
SUN TZU, *The Art of War*

①

28 April /98

Yo, Reporter Dude!

I had a funny feeling I'd hear from you today and, lo & behold, I did. Wonders never cease, it seems A job interview at a college in BC? Tell me more! Teaching journalism, perhaps? Beautiful countryside, that's for sure, gotta be more riveting than Limestone Land!

I know Claremin — she's as NUTTY as a fruit cake. Met her 6 or 7 years ago. More personalities than a bus full of triplets.

I still haven't heard any word one way or the other on FUCK TO NAC, so I'm keeping The Edge filing grievances for myself & others.

Rosie the Wonder Butt writes me every week like a faithful son should. I saw him on CPAC he look fat as ever! Ha!

Well, I really have no news so let me know when you have questions about The Edge!

Be cool

Pangster

The words came scrawled like a few quick slashes from a knife. They were written by a felon who intrigued me by his skill in surviving the toughest of places. I called him the Pangster.

Yo, teacher dude. It took my July 28 letter three weeks to get there? What is it, pony express? So, there I was, just wondering if you were still alive and – boo-yatt. In comes yer kite! Psych gave me a lukewarm assessment which is, at least, better than the "future Manson" type I got ten years ago. Progress must sometimes be measured incrementally, uno?

Tension is fairly high here in the Land of Plenty. Quite a few beefs over the past couple of weeks, a combination, I believe, of the heat, the overcrowding, and the general malaise. I warned the warden last year that this place was a powder keg, also warned regional & national headquarters, so, when it goes up, just remember, The Powers That Be were given plenty of warning. Part of the problem is we have so many young punks coming in here, young turks who have only done provincial time, and have no concept of how to do time like a man, let alone conduct themselves like adults. I must be getting old, nyet?

The riot came and went like Easter or Labour Day, and the normal chaos reasserted itself in the Collins Bay prison in Kingston.

Da Bay is still in chaos, averaging about a stabbing a week. It'll never change, not for the better, anyway.

Not too much else here. Heroin use is bad here, too, and now the coke is back. But, of course, PTB (Powers That Be) continue to give the junkies work releases, paroles, etc. Makes you wonder, huh?

So, I've started seeing psychology. They've just never seen a real, live criminal up here [in Canada], uno? They also can't accept the fact that some people simply cannot be intimidated into accepting CSC's [Correctional Service of Canada] philosophies, uno? Independent thought completely terrifies these people. Must be a Canadian thing. Now that my UTAS [unescorted temporary absences] are over and the NPB [National Parole Board] shot me down, maybe I can finally get my focus back.

That was the Pangster. Clear in thought, brief in execution, yet intricate. I met Pang inside a federal prison. He was a small man with the deep bass voice of a radio announcer and a body patched with prison tattoos. Even his elbows were covered with webs of inky black tattoos. He had dual citizenship in Canada and the United States, a Canadian mother, an American father. The rap sheet of Stephen R. Pang said he was an American bank robber who had done time in the United States and was now lodged in a Canadian penitentiary. He had been in five United States prisons, including Folsom and Tracy, five county jails in California, four prisons in Canada. He had convictions for multiple armed robbery in 1983 in California, and in 1988 and 1995 in Canada. In the nineteen years between 1983 and 2001, he was in prison fourteen years. "Everyone can recall their first kiss, date, sexual encounter," he told me. "I can recall the first time I fired a weapon, at age five." He found city living idyllic. "To me," he said, "diesel fumes from buses and trucks smell like home, and there's nothing better than dust rising on a city street on a hot August day. The countryside fucks me up because it's too quiet and the air is too fresh." He was trained by the United States military for missions he can't discuss, except to say that jumping from aircraft over Panama ruined his knees. After the military, he turned his training to use in banks. He came to Canada, he says, for practical reasons: "Banks are much simpler to rob up here," and the prison sentences are shorter too.

> If you asked me how many banks I had actually robbed over the course of my lifetime, I couldn't give you an exact figure, although between here and the United States, the number probably tops one hundred. The problem, of course, is that bank robbery, after a time, becomes a job just like any other. You get up, have a shower, shave, coffee, read the sports section, then go off to work. The only difference is, you never know if you're coming home from work that day, or several years later.
>
> Probably my most memorable heist earns that distinction because it should never have worked. I had a target in mind, and a takeout time – 0900. I entered the bank, but it simply felt

completely wrong, so I aborted the mission and went down the street to have a coffee and watch for a few minutes, Sure enough, around 0915, somebody else went in to rob the place. The cops had it staked out, waiting for this particular guy, and they snapped him. Instinct had saved my life.

I decided to call it a day, and started wandering around, window shopping, when I saw a bank I had not previously scouted out. I did a quick check of escape routes, and then saw a uniform cop in there, doing his banking. It was payday for the force. I waited until he had been gone for five minutes, then decided to hit the bank, reasoning that the mere presence of a cop in there a few minutes earlier would have them lulled into a false sense of security. As it turned out, I was right.

I grabbed a bag full of cash and split, but turned the wrong way on my ad hoc escape route. I could hear sirens and realized my clock was running. I improvised a new escape route, and, amazingly, got away. I then utilized three different cabs before finally settling in a different part of the city. I didn't really believe I had gotten much cash, but, when I emptied the bag, I had close to $35,000 in unmarked, used fifties and hundreds. All in all, a great morning.

Going through my head the whole time was that I had fucked up. I was violating every rule I operated by, going on sheer nerve and determination, at a time when I didn't even need the money. It was, however, a tremendous success. I won't say what city it was in, because it's one of many jobs I pulled and got away with.

My best heist? I did a joint in the States, thought I'd only gotten a couple grand. Threw the bag in my hotel room unopened and went drinking. About three a.m. I get back and decide to open the bag, $65,000 inside, all hundreds, not one marked bill. Coolio!

Pang's mind was always whirling brightly, like a fine old Harley on the long, straight road to hell. He had developed a criminal consciousness and a professional persona for himself as a bank robber. He even practised bank robberies in his dreams.

My dreams are vivid, complex and interesting. I never in my life experienced the classic terror dreams of falling or running and getting nowhere. I just don't have those ones. I have a lot of dreams about bank robberies. Once a reservoir dog, always a reservoir dog, I guess. I have a great deal of control in my dreams, something I've trained myself to do. I can change dreams in mid-stream, pre-determine, to some extent, dream content. I would say my robbery dreams are pretty accurate in the way they play out. There is no sensational gunplay or unexpected million-dollar score. Even the thoughts and sensations I have in the dreams are accurate. One could say, then, that these are merely "practice sessions." You have to stay in shape for your career, uno? Is there a deeper layer of dreams? I don't know. I'm not a big believer in Freud. I tend to believe the human mind is a lot simpler in operation, a lot less magical in depth, than we like to believe.

He explained that his mind worked like a logic machine during a heist.

The only constant in terms of thought processes with every job is the clock – from the moment I initiate the score, a clock starts running in the back of my mind. I can count the seconds with a great deal of accuracy. I allow myself forty-five seconds inside from start to finish, which leaves me about two minutes until the first cop car arrives on the scene. Two minutes, if you have properly mapped escape routes in your head, is a very long time. I like to use the subway in Toronto, because, in two minutes I can be two stations away, on an entirely different subway line, all underground, in a mass of people. I always wear a disposable outer coat, which I dump in a trash can, usually something gaudy, so that it sticks in people's minds. I want them to be looking for a guy in a bright orange jacket or some such thing, but not noticing the guy in the blue jean jacket. I never hang around my target zones. That is to say, I don't frequent nightspots in that

area. It's purely a hunting ground, nothing more. This last spree,
52 Division in Toronto was tear-assing around, hitting every bar,
restaurant and street rat looking for me, but I was a ghost,
because I hung around far from their territory. I was in and out of
52 country in a few minutes, and that was that.

Pang's discipline allowed him to control his emotions and responses
with analytic clarity even during moments of stress. Part of that skill
came from his father.

I never, ever panic, no matter what the stimuli. Inside, I may feel
tense, my mind may be racing, but it races in a very organized
fashion. I see things in 3-D when there's a problem. That is, I can
visualize many aspects to a problem as though they had a physical dimension within my mind. The best way to describe it is as if
I had a heads-up-display behind my eyes.

My father taught me to play chess at age four. He constantly
challenged me to play better, because he knew I could. He had an
innate sense of my intelligence threshold, and how much pressure I could withstand, and he gradually increased that pressure.
My four brothers are almost like failures in that sense, as though
they were early experiments that bombed out. They're much
more emotional than I am, more rooted in normal relationship
dynamics. While my mother and sisters would always be shocked
by what I accomplished, my father seemed to expect it, as though
it were a given that I would succeed.

One should not infer, however, from either my demeanour or
my words, that I have no temper. When I was a teenager, I had a
horrific temper. I'd sooner shoot someone than discuss the issue,
once I snapped. I worked very hard to gain control of this facet of
my personality and, in this regard, the [United States] army was
key. The military gave me the discipline I needed to deal with the
morons who make up the population of this planet, and also
refined my father's teachings. Discipline is vital. With it, a man
can work through any problems life throws at him, simply

because it becomes engrained that you have to deal with it! I can drink all night, catch an hour's sleep, get up, shit, shower, shave and face the day, because I have no choice. I have work to do, and that's that. No whining, no excuses.

I still have a temper, although I manage to suppress it rather well. The only person who has ever been able to get through to me when I'm in a total rage is my oldest niece. She's the only person whom I deal with on an equal footing.

I think my father was important to me on many levels. First of all, he was a rock of stability. Absolutely nothing got to him. A nuclear bomb could have wiped out the area, and he would've poured a Scotch, lit a cigarette and asked if the dog was okay. This kind of poise and ability to deal with stress was imprinted on me at an early age.

When I was ten and my parents were fifty-seven, they went completely, totally broke. There was never any whining about that in our household. My father simply took the situation in hand and, three years later, we were better off than ever. I inherited from my father the ability to make chicken salad out of chicken shit.

Pang utilized psychology in planning a heist.

I am, more than most people, alert to political tremors. When the [Toronto] metro PD is involved in their annual funding battle with city hall, I do a lot of jobs. Why? Simple. At that time, police tend to slow their response times, and more cops are "off sick" or "on leave," therefore unsolved crime rises, and they can buttress their annual argument that "crime is out of control" and so they need more money. This is an absolute, a given, in any large city. I strike at holiday times, because people are not as alert to their surroundings, and the cops are stretched thin. There is, of course, an organic "audit trail" for this theory. At Xmas, for example, most people are happy. The Xmas mood is contagious. Consequently, the human body produces more endomorphins and similar compounds, raising the level of happiness in the individual and reducing one's threat-detection abilities.

I allow myself no attachments to anything, animal, vegetable or mineral. Many times I've abandoned relationships and material possessions when I felt a location had become compromised. My old psych assessment from 1990 makes reference to the fact that I applied skills learned in the military to my jobs, which is true. I time police patrols, both overt and undercover. I know when large bank locations change the videotape in their cameras, at which point the entire camera system is down for about fifteen minutes. I know which banks have cameras and which don't, which use Frisco Bay Security, with notoriously poor image quality on the cameras. I know what location ETF [Emergency Task Force] rolls out of each day. The Metro Toronto Police move their ETF command centre around on a regular basis. I know what times of the day the tills are refilled in the various banks. I always pick target locations with at least two escape routes, and I time out each escape route based on worst-case scenarios. I prefer bad weather, rain or snow, for three reasons: (1) in bad weather, potential witnesses on the street are all looking down at the ground and in a hurry, oblivious to their surroundings; (2) in such weather, cops tend to hang out in donut shops, as opposed to properly conducting patrols; and, (3) in bad weather, or when there's a major traffic accident or fire call, the streets are hard to navigate, which slows response time. This is especially true in the downtown core of Toronto, which is one reason I like to do hits around morning or evening rush hours, and lunchtime. Shift change times are good, too, because the cops going off duty are going back to the station early, and the cops coming on have to attend a shift briefing before they can hit the streets, therefore there's only a skeleton crew available on the streets. Police are extraordinarily vulnerable at shift change.

It was almost like reading a novel to see the clarity of his thought in action. I asked him philosophical questions about crime.

Is crime a different morality or philosophy? Both. We need $, we get $. We have a problem with someone, we deal with that person. No "civilized" waffling, no wringing of hands, no guilt. See the problem, solve the problem. We know society is a sham. The same newspaper editor who writes that bank robbers should be locked up for life, goes home & beats his kids. The judge hires male prostitutes. The prosecutor is a cocaine addict. Everyone violates moral conventions. We just do it to a greater degree & more openly.

It seems perfectly natural to me that I should be incarcerated for my crimes. In fact, in less gentle countries, or in less gentle times, I would have been executed, so I'm not doing that bad, in relative terms. I don't view "straight johns" as prey or victims. I do, however, view them as largely being incredibly naïve and phenomenally tunnel-visioned. I find most people incapable of seeing beyond their own little world. The welfare bum can't conceive of normal existence, of actually working for a living, paying taxes, etc., and the middle-class office type plods along, never really believing that his company can be "downsized," or his pension plan found to be inadequate for his retirement. I think most people live in insular little dreamlands, never really aware of how diverse society is, or of how quickly the roof can cave in. Nobody expects an earthquake, nobody expects a flood, nobody expects a car to hit them and paralyze them, but it happens every day, so shouldn't we at least be aware, truly aware, of the possibility of such happenstance occurring to us?

Pang was a felon with wit. Our letters were a kind of strategy game and neither of us could be quite sure how serious the other was. Pang's stories about cats were an example of that. Cats seemed to gravitate toward him and take comfort in him, as though they understood his hunter's instinct. They also brought their problems to him in the joint.

Cats. Cats. Wolfie has gone native. He's more feral than anything now, but he still remembers me, if no one else. Snowball is the great white hunter – five or six years old, all white, catches a bizillion mice a day. Likes to come to my window at four a.m. with a live mouse, wake me up, then play with the mouse in my cage for half an hour or so. He brought home a live duck one night. Don't ask me how. Watching the two cats is a study in barn cat aging. Wolfie, one year old, full of piss and vinegar, is living outside now, fighting and fucking. Snowball, having lasted this long, has learned the value of a safe, warm, dry home. Snowball likes Collective Soul and NFL football, but hates Jeff Healey, and [the TV prison drama] Oz puts him to sleep.

Pang and Wolfie had history. Pang told me about a recent killing in his prison and mentioned that the cat had trouble too.

Wolf was infected – got in a fight, got bitten clean through his paw, so I had to slice the wound open and squeeze the pus out. Can you believe it? The cat trusts me so much that, although he howled and squirmed, he never tried to bite or claw me. I probably saved his life, because he couldn't put any pressure on the paw at all, so the infection would have spread quickly. Good cat.

But sometimes life doesn't go well for cats in the slammer. Pang broke the news to me:

Wolfie, sad to say, went to cat heaven. One battle too many. I'm pretty sure it was Snowball that whacked him, but the Snow-dude isn't saying. Mention Wolfie and he acts suspicious, though. Hmm.

As evidence, Pang sent me a photo of a smirking Snowball lying on Pang's bed by himself. In the photo the cat's eyes had a weird green light offset by the angelic glare of his pure white fur. Who would have thought that Snowball would be the survivor?

Yes, Snowball does have green eyes. He's actually a suspect in several cat killings. The evidence in a couple of cases is pretty strong, but he's denying everything. He's a stand-up cat.

Pang had qualities that could be put to a more idealistic purpose than robbing banks. That's how we started talking about The Edge, after a stray mention of the term in one of his letters. It was another mental game and yet it had a ring of truth to it. The Edge, I gathered, was a kind of finely tuned consciousness that could adapt quickly to the threat of unseen developments. I'd play the disciple and put my questions in a letter. The answers would come as a wickedly shrewd prisoner's version of Sun Tzu's ancient Chinese classic *The Art of War*. The Edge is a set of the traits you develop in yourself to avoid being absorbed into the game of life by what Pang called The Machine. "The Machine," he told me, "is the societal construct which we have created that dictates what is right and wrong, what is acceptable and what isn't, what we should and should not believe." Like *The Art of War*, The Edge had to be pieced together and translated from what I could draw out of Pang by mail. Here is what I was able to distill from the prison letters of the Edge Master:

- When you have The Edge, everything around you that you see on a daily basis seems faded, colourless, washed out. Life is drab, grey, unchanging. You fire up The Edge and take risks, simply to add colour to the world around you. It's as though you are actually perceiving physical reality as a different wavelength, dull, muted, lifeless, until you act.
- Survival in prison and on the streets? Hmm. Only the strong survive, in either environment. Not the physically strong, the mentally strong.
- I think cities force people to raise the level of their game. I believe the pressures and demands are a kind of self-induced Darwinism. The strong survive and breed, the weak fall by the wayside and die. City people are predators. We need the controlled chaos and tension of the urban jungle to keep us sharp.

- Do you have the will to do what's necessary? Can you shrug off the humanity around you? Are you prepared to sacrifice non-essential people around you? The personal cost of survival can be large. You become cold, cynical. At the root, gut level, you trust no one implicitly & very few people to any measurable degree. You cauterize your emotions.
- Flexibility is good. Compromise for the sake of submissive positioning is not. Be rigid in your core beliefs. Be inflexible as a nuke on issues where you hold a strong opinion. As Rage Against the Machine sing: "Why stand on a silent platform? Fight the war. Fuck the norm."
- Be the chameleon. I adapt to any environment, any type of behaviour, any type of conversation.
- Never go around an obstacle if you can go through it.
- If you want to understand The Edge, you have to understand anger.
- The Edge is acting & reacting on a primal feral level, of surrendering to your reptilian brain and allowing your body to release cascade flows of adrenalin & endorphins.
- The Edge is deciding that the consequences of your actions are completely irrelevant.
- How do you get it? I think you've gotta be born with it.

The Edge hit a snag as the prison service tried to "cascade" Pang down to prisons of lower security to prepare him for release. Pang had The Edge in the toughest prisons, where it helped him survive, and it would be his philosophical rudder on the streets of civilized chaos again. But, in between, in prisons of lower security, it was an uncomfortable fit for him. I sensed the Pangster resisting the transformation into something edgeless, less "pangfull." I saw it happen in his letters.

The general feeling, actually, is of chaos. I feel like I'm in some kind of refugee camp. That is to say, in a regular prison the walls & barriers force everyone into narrow, contained areas. You then have crowds and contained, channelled energy, which feeds upon itself. Here, everything is split up & scattered, so every-thing is diffused.

Living in a house here at Bathcatraz [the prison in Bath, Ontario] is very strange. It completely destroys the convict equi-librium, since it is not a prison environment, but it is also not the streets. We deal in absolutes, live in a binary universe, and this throws us.

I'm sometimes more on edge here than I even was in the Bay [the Collins Bay prison], and I can honestly say that, in the four months I've been here, not a single day has gone by when I haven't seriously considered going back [to the higher-security prison]. I'm expending a tremendous amount of self-control daily, just staying focused on why I'm here & what my goals are. After all, I only have three years left until mandatory [release], and I can do three in the Bay on my head. I could not do three here. I can barely conceive of being here a year. This is a fuzzy logic zone.

I really can't see doing a mandatory [sentence length] in this fucked-up place. I think, at its root, it is the lack of anger that galls me here. Everybody is "happy, happy, joy, joy." They seem to have lost track of the fact that c s c [Correctional Service of Canada] is our enemy, not our friend. I can understand first-timers & rapehounds acting that way, but not so-called convicts who should know better.

Then he was moved to a different prison, where he was more comfortable.

This place is great, so much better than Bathcatraz. My cell partner went home today, so I'm all by myself for the first time in eleven and a half months. Thank God! About the only thing they don't allow you here is an automatic weapon, it seems.

The state of penology appears to be in flux. You have to be an incredible fuck-up not to get anything [like parole] here. When I got interviewed for my Correctional Plan, I got the feeling I was taking up space. They want me to put in for day parole, UTAS [unescorted temporary absence passes], everything, right fucking now! Like, get out of jail! Very bizarre.

Life is so much simpler when you know you're in until mandatory, uno?

Another letter came from the game master:

Still no sign of The Edge. This place is just too bizarre to acquire it, although I'm sure it'll resurface if the NPB [National Parole Board] does say "No." If they do, I'll probably take a work release to the apple orchards for a few months and make some extra cash, uno? I've forced myself into a kind of zen calm, but The Edge is still available, just sleeping.

5   Funeral for a prison clown

When you look like your passport photo, it's time to go home.

ERMA BOMBECK

I remember Charles Armstrong as a kind of criminal Woody Allen, along the lines of what Allen's biographer Marion Meade said of the comedian, "He might be crazy but he isn't dysfunctional." Although, on reflection, maybe Chuck was dysfunctional. But he could still think and make you laugh and jolt you out of a comfortable point of view. He and I wrote back and forth at length for four years until, as the publication of this book was near, I asked him for the final summation of his life as an outcast of society, the epitaph of a sharp-toothed pariah. The letter went unanswered. Chuck had died. The slapstick of his life as a prison clown came to an end.

I met Chuck inside Kingston Penitentiary when I was sent to write a newspaper story about his challenge to the income tax system. I found a man with white hair and a mild manner, but who could sting like a scorpion when he put his thoughts onto paper. Chuck was a provocative felon who waged a subversive war of words against the prison system. He forged memos in the name of wardens and put institutions in an uproar. He jousted with the grim folk at his parole board hearings. Chuck said he'd learned over the years that the idea of releasing him was a charade and he didn't want to play the game anymore. "I was scheduled for surgery yesterday," he wrote one time. "Hemorrhoidal, to give me a wider smile for the parole board." He created his own satirical language, like George Orwell in *Nineteen Eighty-four*, with words to describe the prison service as a bungling totalitarian state. In his lexicon, Corrections Canada was "Corruptions Canada" and politicians like the ex-minister of immigration would be "the former minusular of deportation." From the midst of the obscurity and dementia of his life in a cell he sent out satirical letters to politicians and bureaucrats in which he railed against the

![Canada logo] Government of Canada Gouvernement du Canada	**MEMORANDUM**	**NOTE DE SERVICE**

TO
A ⟩

   Charles Armstrong
   FPS 012145A

SECURITY CLASSIFICATION - CLASSIFICATION DE SECURITE

OUR FILE - NOTRE REFERENCE

YOUR FILE - VOTRE REFERENCE

FROM
DE

   A.M. Stevenson
   Warden
   Bath Institution

DATE

24 September, 1998

SUBJECT
OBJET

Inappropriate Publications

I have perused your most recent attempt at "humourous" editorializing (see attached) and find this publication to be totally inappropriate. I reference both the language and the use of staff names, most certainly without their permission. Although I understand that you wrote this in jest, you have exposed staff members to ridicule and I find that the document overall is offensive.

In future, I direct that you cease and desist generating such documents; that you refrain from printing the names of any staff members (other than as required to direct specific correspondence) and that you refrain from dessiminating any publication using offensive language.

A.M. Stevenson

c.c. Offender File
    A/CCM
    Parole Officer

Canada

mistreatment of prisoners. He printed satirical broadsides in his prison newsletter, such as the news that a warden had been charged under the "Cannibalism Act." For a while he was the editor of a newspaper produced inside Kingston Penitentiary that was sent out to subscribers. Chuck claimed that the prison censors would let the word "fuck" pass, but deleted "incompetence" and "intransigence" as foul language. As the editor of a prison newspaper, he said, when the readers yell "kill the editor," they're not fooling.

Chuck was being held in prison as the most reviled type of all felons, the outcast among outcasts, a dangerous sex offender. At the same time his intestine was destroying him from the inside with a vengeance. He had celiac disease, an ailment where the intestine won't digest fats properly. He spoke openly about his mental assessment by the system and told me how he cursed psychiatrists to their faces.

> I've been labeled psychopathic by shrinks in the past and others have said, no, I'm not. But naturally the c s c [Correctional Service of Canada] takes the worse-case scenario because that's the safest for them. I don't for a moment believe I'm psychopathic and, if you don't believe that, I'll get even with you!

But there was a side of Chuck that sometimes got lost in the cynicism and psychosis of his criminal existence. It was as though one part of him was a joke that the other part was playing on him. I'm not sure which was the real Chuck and which the prank Chuck, and I'm not sure I want to know. But Chuck was a natural satirist and a literary man, although he'd never heard of Jonathan Swift. He was what W.B. Carnochan, in an essay on prison literature in *The Oxford History of the Prison*, calls the "picaro." *The Oxford Concise Dictionary of Literary Terms* explains that *picaro* is Spanish for "rogue" and cites *Don Quixote* and *Adventures of Huckleberry Finn* as examples of the picaresque novel. The picaro is never far from jail, says Carnochan.

The funniest prank that Chuck the prison picaro played began with a stack of letterheads belonging to the warden of Kingston Penitentiary. He found the paper in a closet in the prison kitchen. He practised writing the warden's signature, and then fired a salvo of memos.

> I had a lot of fun with that. I was making memos and sending them all over the place and even managed a fair copy of the warden's signature. Talk about creating havoc. The warden was not amused. Anyway, I used them prolifically after I got his signature down pat. It wasn't hard to duplicate because it was just a scribble.
>
> I recall one memo I sent to a prisoner who was waiting for approval for a trailer visit. I had a guard in the kitchen hand it to

him. The memo said the trailer visit was not approved because when his wife was interviewed she appeared to be under the influence of drugs or alcohol, that she swore at the interviewer and threatened to cut off his penis if the visit wasn't approved, etc. This guy was absolutely terrified and he tried to get up to see the warden. He later told me it sounded just like his wife. I had to tell him it was a joke finally and he was ready to kill me at the time.

I made a list of things that were going to be changed in the prison and sent them off to the radio room on the letterhead. The radio room, at that time, broadcast the joint news throughout the prison. The announcer read it off as gospel because he really thought it was from the warden. The news was read over the lockup count at suppertime and the noise was deafening. The whole prison was cheering. I said a swimming pool was being constructed and some famous singer would be doing a show in the gym. I said we were getting a big raise, that the walls between every two cells were going to be torn out to enlarge the cells.

I used the stationery to write to a couple of MPS to complain to them about the budget cuts and to ask how I (the warden) was expected to run a prison and maintain order when my budget was being slashed. I said there could be a major disturbance and I didn't want to be the scapegoat if that happened.

I never knew what came from those letters. I heard through the grapevine that it was suspected that staff was doing it because no one figured a prisoner had access to those letter-heads. In the end, things got too hot and I sent the rest of the unused memos home. They are still in a box in my mother's basement.

Later I talked to the warden of the prison at the time. He told me he never knew who pulled the pranks with his signature.

Chuck was transferred to the Bath medium-security prison with a better view of Lake Ontario and the countryside. It was less oppressive and Chuck was feeling better. The new prison had no history with

Chuck, so he revived the memo-from-the-warden prank. He got up at five in the morning on April Fool's Day and posted a memo on all the bulletin boards in the units. The memo began in the dry and bureaucratic fashion that only a master can mimic, until it got to item nine:

> An Olympic-size outdoor swimming pool, plus a miniature golf course, will be constructed for Unit #3 for inmates and staff in the south field behind lower three unit.

Then, the fake memo announced the warden's retirement and the promotion of a former and unpopular parole officer to warden. It ended . . .

> I trust all of this information will cause many of you to be pleased and enable you to serve your sentences in a more comfortable and leisurely fashion. But remember, it's April 1st, and if you believed any of this, then you're dumber than I thought.

Chuck described the reaction.

> A lot of people fell for it. I heard that some irate staff member took it to the warden and said, "This is Armstrong's work." The warden allegedly read it and laughed.

Then Chuck was summoned to the throne.

> Apparently someone sent it to regional headquarters and someone over there was not amused and faxed it back with orders for him to "counsel" me about using the warden's name on a memo. Then he started laughing and he said he thought it was "pretty good." And he said, "Consider yourself counseled" while still laughing, and he said, "Would you be offended if I told you to fuck off?" I took the hint and left.

I wrote to Chuck suggesting that he send a copy of the funny memo to the parole board just before his next appearance. Maybe they needed a laugh. But Chuck was alternately glum and sarcastic about his fortunes with the parole board, after eighteen years of tango-ing on that dance floor.

> I've got a parole hearing coming up this summer, but there's about as much chance for freedom from them as there was from getting that helicopter from Santa. I thought about calling [the serial killer of children] Clifford Olsen as a character witness, but that might stretch it a bit.

Of course, it didn't help that Chuck couldn't restrain his satire even before a board that could decide his fate. After the fiasco of yet another hearing he'd write to the chairman of the board, replaying the whole disaster to compound the effect like a conductor bringing a symphony to its conclusion. One time he wrote to the chairman:

> At my parole hearing in August the panel discussed at length my use of "sarcasm." One member even brought out a piece of paper on which she said she had written the Webster's Dictionary definition of "sarcasm" the previous evening when going over my case. She quoted it to the effect of "dogs rending and tearing flesh." I would suggest she stick with the Oxford Dictionary, as I do, because all we loyal Canucks know that things American are more violent than things British.

The letter to the chairman of the parole board ended with a friendly tone that was part of Chuck's trademark. No matter how bitter the contention, he tried to end with warmth.

> Don't be a stranger, okay, and stop in and say hello if you're in the vicinity.

Chuck liked to make new friends through letters. He sent a letter to a right-wing politician introducing himself as the Reverend Chuck

Armstrong, director of the Canadian Anti-alcohol Society. He explained that he travelled across the country giving lectures on the evils of alcohol with a man whose life was a wretched example of what booze can do. The man sat on the stage "coughing, spitting, farting and drooling on himself as he sticks his tongue out, makes faces and obscene gestures to the audience." Chuck told the politician that this example of a wasted life had died of cirrhosis of the liver, and that the solicitor general of Canada had recommended the politician take his place. Chuck wrote the same letter to the solicitor general saying that the politician had recommended him as a boozer to join his anti-alcohol crusade. In these letters, Chuck gave the address of the prison, but didn't indicate that it was a prison. He also wrote mocking letters to the commissioner of Corrections Canada, to the head of the Toronto Police Association, and to the attorney general of Ontario. When he had complaints against the local newspaper, he sent the editor some organ donor consent forms for the staff. He tried the same thing with a nurse in the joint and was given a minor prison charge. His typical organ donor consent form read this way:

> I _____, being certifiably "brain dead," as evidenced by my dumb comments, inanimate style and boorish manner, do hereby donate any or all organs to whatever medical institution they may benefit – with the exception of my Hammond Organ, which I leave to my family.

Sometimes he'd create strange companies for the return address on the envelope to embarrass the person who received the letter. He sent a letter to me at work from a fake company that apparently produced condoms to satisfy anyone's penis fantasy. Another time he sent me a letter claiming to be from the out-patient laboratory for people with sexual diseases, saying that my confidential herpes test results were inside. I believe he tried that prank on some politicians too.

Then there were the political tourists who wandered past Chuck's cage. These people are drawn to prison like bugs to a windshield on a warm summer's day.

> We had a visit from the new solicitor general, the commissioner of corrections, the deputy commissioner for Ontario and a large entourage. I ran into them by accident and I know the solicitor general is from Prince Edward Island, so, as he walked past, I said, "You're a long way from Cavendish." He stopped suddenly, looked at me, and came walking back with his hand out for a shake and asked, "Are you from Prince Edward Island?" I said, "Don't you remember me, Larry?" He looked very closely and almost whispered, "No." I said, "We used to chase bikinis together on Cavendish Beach." He reddened and glanced to his right and left to see who was listening and I thought I'd embarrassed him enough, so I said, "I'm only kidding." He looked relieved and laughed.

Another time . . .

> This guy approached me and introduced himself as the deputy commish in charge of personnel and something else I didn't catch. I said, "We've met before." He looked at me closely and said, "I don't think so. Are you sure?" I said, "Yes," then, "I know, we served time together at Warkworth." He looked a bit chagrined for a moment and then smiled and said, "Don't tell anyone." When they were leaving I said, "If any of you get appointed to the National Unparole Board, please keep me in mind." They said they would.

Between letters there were the usual stabbings and riots.

> The bottom floor of the south wing erupted in a mini-riot and it ended with all forty men on that range being shipped to Millhaven [prison]. Damage was extensive from fire and water. It began, apparently, when two or three men got drunk and the staff tried to

take them in custody to lock them up. The other men on the range weren't happy because one guy allegedly fought back and the staff had to manhandle him. Ergo, a riot. They tried to barricade themselves on the range, but they forgot there was a back door, and the ETF [Emergency Tactical Force] came in that way and used tear gas, fire hoses, etc. They brought the large bus over from the Haven [Millhaven] and loaded them on it, a few at a time, and took them away. One guy was badly beaten by the other cons. Some said it was because of his beef [sentence], and others say it was because he wouldn't take part in the rioting. I don't know which is true. But he was hospitalized. It will be some time before anyone can live on that range again because of the damage.

Chuck didn't like riots. He preferred the havoc he could create with his wit.

I learned much about Chuck in his long letters that had nothing to do with his criminal side. He liked to bake cookies for the other felons from recipes he found in the newspaper, and took pleasure in the natural world. He felt a tenderness toward animals. He fed a wounded sand hill crane that landed inside the walls and fed the prison cats. He noticed the small beasts of the field.

Lately I've seen a lot of small frogs hopping around inside the prison. I thought they hibernated for the winter. But then our weather was not really winter-like until last weekend, when it became so cold, so perhaps they didn't realize they were supposed to be asleep somewhere. One was on the pavement today and it looked just like a stone. I studied it for a minute and saw it was a frog and then put it on the grass where it wouldn't get stepped on.

In one letter he described at length an encounter with a deer that was standing on the freedom side of the prison fence. He would stroll across the prison grounds in the early morning looking for the owl he could hear hooting somewhere in the trees.

Last week I came down the hill towards the front of the prison and there was a deer just outside the fence foraging for grass. When it heard me coming it stopped and watched me. I figured it would bolt at any moment, but it didn't. I got right across the fence from it and stopped, and it looked up and there we were at a Mexican standoff. Then the truck that patrols the prison came along, and another deer that had been further along the fence, and that I hadn't seen before, came running along. It ran out in front of the truck and the driver had to brake to avoid hitting it. Then the one I had locked eyes with looked over its shoulder and it took off, again running in front of the truck so that the driver had to brake. There was an apple tree on the other side of the road and the first one put its front legs halfway up the trunk and was eating out of the lower branches. They are quite graceful looking, especially when running. I do enjoy my morning strolls. Each morning there is an owl hooting, but I have yet to see it.

In another letter he recalled being in the Drumheller prison in Alberta, where the lifers were once sent out to collect dinosaur bones. He liked the warden there who came into the cells of prisoners at night and sat and chatted.

I remember sitting in my cell at nights and listening to the coyotes howling in the hills, and I felt some empathy with them because their howls expressed the loneliness I was feeling. All of the normal sounds of wildlife and free world machines take on a special meaning when one is confined.

From time to time I caught brief glimpses of what life was like for Chuck before he was sent to the slammer in his forties. He piloted a whirlybird in the navy, flying the "angel" helicopter that hovered near an aircraft carrier in case any planes hit the water. He also travelled the country to such places as Grand Cache, Alberta, where he hauled propane tanks.

I would never know what was happening to Chuck in the strange saga of his life in prison. Then a letter would come. Once the letter was half a year late.

> Sorry not to have written in such a long time but I've spent much of the past seven months in the hospital. I was a pretty sick puppy for a while and they tell me I just about died on two occasions. As a matter of fact, the hospital called this place to tell them that and to get the name and number of my next of kin to notify them and they ended up giving my room away. See how much I mean to them.

When he returned to prison from the hospital the guards couldn't find his clothes. His cell had been cleaned out faster than the campaign headquarters of a defeated politician. He had to waddle down the range to his prison cell in hospital pajamas. It was the kind of slapstick comedy that happened to him naturally.

> They were a pair of Kingston General Hospital PJs with just a tie string at the waist and an open crotch. I'm afraid I wasn't a fashion statement that day.

Chuck wrote that his mother died and prison officials let him go to the funeral. By that time he was quite ill. He had become a physical parody of himself and there was more of the unintentional slapstick.

> My mother died in April and I was allowed to attend the funeral. I had lost a good deal of weight and the dress pants I wore were too big and I was holding them up with one hand. When I arrived at the funeral home, one of my aunts ran up and said, "Give me a big hug." I did and took my hand away from my trousers and they fell down to my knees. There I was in a room with at least fifty people and all of them staring at my bony legs.
>
> I still look like a concentration camp survivor. I was so weak I couldn't even open a pop can on my own. I still have a long way before I'm back to normal.

At least, the guards were discreet about escorting him to his mother's funeral.

> They did not make me wear any restraints (i.e., handcuffs or leg irons) and they kept well in the background. They even let me take the limo to the cemetery with my children and other family members. I was too ill to flee on them, but even had I not been sick, I don't think it would have been any different, because they trusted me. And I was not about to betray that, because it would have caused them problems if they returned without me. I'll just keep working on my tunnel and hope for the best.

After the letter about the funeral I wrote to Chuck to welcome him back from the dead. I told him that a publisher was interested in the book I'd written from my correspondence with prisoners and that he should stop talking about dying. I imitated his irascible style to say that dying right in the middle of the chapter would be "a damn inconvenience." He wrote back:

> I just opened a container of yogurt and ended up with almost half it on my shirt and pants. I hate those lids where you peel the aluminum foil back, because they inevitably end up spilling on me. Shit!
>   Anyway, that's about the extent of things for now and I'll try to remain alive until your book is completed. But don't take too long, okay. We had a death here on the weekend. A guy with asthma was playing floor hockey when he had a heart attack and died. I knew him to say hello to, but that was about it.

I had some more questions and told him it was time to confront his literary public. "It's time for the bones of your mind to be cleaned and entombed in this book. Pull up your pants and put words to paper. Write your epitaph."

While I was waiting for Chuck to answer, I re-read the letters I'd received from him over the years. I read a letter he'd written following another rejection from the parole board after he'd been in hospital. He said he spent his time lying in bed in his cell staring into space and thinking. His weight had dropped to one hundred and nineteen pounds. His skin was so delicate it would bleed when he scraped it against a surface. His hair had stopped growing and had disappeared from parts of his body. The doctor had put a small camera up his ass and Chuck asked if he could have photos. He was always uninhibited about his body, which had become like a small country that we explored together, letter by letter, learning its geography and culture. I knew the country of Chuck's rivers and mountains and skies, its fields and forests. I knew more about Chuck's anatomy than my own.

His letter continued about another of his lawsuits against "the corruptional service" and about a parole hearing where he said his assistant was told twice they just wanted him to die in prison because that would be the easiest solution. His letters were a living record of the moment, slapstick by slapstick.

> I gave up tunneling, at least for the winter, because the ground is too damned hard. I also tried hang gliding.

Or . . .

> Someone suggested I should donate my body to medical science, not when I die, but right now.

It felt as though the flame of his wit was beginning to flicker and weaken. Still, he was making jokes. He was alive. He recorded the small moments in the life of an outcast. I wrote:

> That's a grim joke about you "trying to remain alive" until the book is finished, but I'll write to the editor of the book to speed up publication. Otherwise, I don't know if this book is good enough to get into heaven. Do you think they have a library in the next life? I'll be disappointed if they don't, because there are a lot of books I haven't read yet. I'd like to have eternity to read,

wouldn't you? To read and read and never get tired or feel the eyelids droop. I hope I don't get hassled about it in the next life. "What, fella? You thought you'd have eternity to read? God, you mortals are naïve."

I'd still like to get a blurb for the back cover of the book from you. From the sound of it, you'd better not wait too long to write it. It doesn't matter that you haven't read the book. Blurbs are a con, anyway. Just imagine the effect you'd like the book to have and write that. Then I'll revise the book to fit your blurb. Will that work for you?

I've been talking to the editor of the book about the idea of either inviting cons to the book launch or having the book launch inside a prison. She likes the idea, although now that I hear you walk around the range in hospital pajamas with the crotch open I'm having second thoughts. You seem to have trouble with clothes. Do you have something nice you could wear, without yogurt on it?

Are you really turning sixty next year? I thought there was a clause somewhere in the Charter of Rights that let people out of prison before that. Is there anything you'd like for your sixtieth birthday?

How's the tunnel coming? I think it's wonderful you have a hobby like that in prison. Some people just sit in the joint and play cards and do drugs. Tunnelling sounds like great recreation. Can you see the light at the end of the tunnel yet? If you can, maybe you're close to escaping. Or maybe you are dead and life has played another joke on you, ripping you off like one of those aluminum lids. What's the prison etiquette for tunnelling? Do you use a spoon, like in the movies, or a fork?

As for the weight, look at it this way, one hundred and nineteen pounds is a big improvement from ninety-nine. What are you eating to put on that much weight? What's happening with your weight? Is this a plan to get thin enough to slip between the bars and out?

Now that you are lying on your cot, what are you thinking

about? Where do your thoughts take you? I'm sure the people reading this book would like to know if you would do things differently in your life. You can talk directly to them, if you like. Tell them what you're thinking and the words from the thin man on the prison cot will fly directly to them. It is a moment in literary history where the walls dissolve, distance contracts, time vanishes. Trust me. It will work.

In the end, it didn't work. Life, the jokester, intervened. I waited months. No reply. Sent a second letter. A third. The last letter came back unopened, without comment. Was he too sick to write? Maybe he was transferred? Phoned the prison. Was told he had died two months earlier. Cremated, then urned in Ontario, though he told me that he wanted to be buried on the East Coast. So what of this man? How do you take a measure of him? He hurt people. He was troubled and had a terrible wit. If anybody had the "savage indignation" of a Jonathan Swift, he did, and people felt the lash of it. And yet, however devious his obscure and unsainted life was, he felt sorrow for his fellow outcasts and loved the simple beasts. Instead of the epitaph he didn't have time to write, here is his expression of his last wish from early in his letters:

My preference on death is to have my ashes scattered over Cape Smokey in Cape Breton and I've made that known to my family. Whether they'll follow through is something else. It's wild country and I'd like some privacy in eternity. There's a nice view of the sea from Smokey, and I just like that place.

Nature looked sternly upon me on account of the murder of the moose.
HENRY DAVID THOREAU, *The Maine Woods*

I lost contact with Huckelbury about the time I moved west to live in the mountains. A con had told me I must write to a man named Huckelbury in a prison in New Hampshire. I did. The letters that came back were like a wild road trip with a man who had survived harsh times. He was talkative and had a brain. He spared no one, not even himself. I imagined the relationship would fill a void in my life. It would stretch out for decades, two men growing old prattling from their havens like boyhood chums. It would also be a kind of literary friendship, like Jack Kerouac and the small-time crook Neal Cassady, since Huckelbury loved reading books and even taught writing to other felons. But then there was my westward migration, a lapse of a year or two, the failed attempts to reconnect. Not long ago I went back to read the original letters again. They were like a travelogue from a previous life.

I have been in prison for twenty-five consecutive years . . .

His first letter began simply, formally, without details, which was classic Huckelbury. I wanted to ask the bluntest of questions, the questions which I was always able to ask as a journalist but that seemed reckless when I wanted a friendship. I wanted to ask Huckelbury why he was in prison. I tried to calculate how much time should elapse before I could ask a person a blunt question like that. The felons that I knew to that point seemed less embarrassed about the details of their crime than I was. With my new correspondent, I started with a harmless question about reading. Had Huckelbury ever read Mark Twain's novel, *The Adventures of Huckleberry Finn*? I was thinking of the road ahead as a writer who would have literary friendships with felons. I loved *Huckleberry Finn* when I read it as a university student expecting to teach English literature someday. I knew that I'd like my Huckelbury simply because I'd heard his voice on the telephone. It was deep and raspy and articulate. It sounded the way experience should sound. I had volunteered to help a group of cons and ex-cons produce a television show for the local community cable channel in Kingston. Huckelbury was a regular contributor by phone from his prison across the border in New Hampshire. His voice had the power of a river. So I asked Huckelbury about Huckleberry Finn.

> I'm afraid I'm not the outlaw Huck Finn was; my crime lacks any sort of philosophical underpinning and was wholly inexcusable.

I liked that. Straightforward, unpretentious. No whining about a man falsely convicted. No pathetic plea to help him get a new trial. No lies I'd have to pretend not to hear. It's so easy to become an accomplice to the fictions of others. Huck didn't want that. A letter came back about prison life, without the rage and bitterness that some prisoners deluge their listeners with.

> For most long-term prisoners, the outside world must cease to exist. Prison time is far easier if the real world is circumscribed. On a personal level, my first five years were the most difficult, when my contacts on the street were still there and I could pretend that everything was normal.

Yes, I thought, and the closer he got to parole, the more vulnerable he would be to the pain of relationships with people outside. The prisoners told me that thinking about the outside world makes it harder to live in prison. The contemplation of parole becomes a goad, a punishment. Parole would open Huckelbury to disappointment, to the wound he had cauterized of the life he had lost. Some survive prison by embracing the oblivion of imprisonment.

> A few men cannot do their time without some sort of affection or companionship, which, of course, leads to homosexual relationships. Some men try their best to sleep their sentences away. The outside world becomes a fiction.

The letter explained life in prison to me, the outsider. The language was controlled, the emotions caught in the bug-filled amber of abstract language. It made me feel excluded. At the same time I didn't want to be in prison myself, and I didn't want to pretend to a fake intimacy. Isn't it strange how we hate to be excluded even from what we don't want? Huck explained how the men in prison create a fantasy world out of their past to protect themselves from the future they can't have, dare not even dream about.

> The lies help to make it through another day.

But it didn't sound real to me, the abstract version of prison I was getting from Huck. I was irritated that he was treating me as I treat my students, the instructor to the instructee. Still, it was early in our letters, and I had to appreciate that he was taking the time to write long responses to someone way up north in Canada. Then this breakthrough:

> From my cell on the third tier I can see over the walls into a valley.

That was good. But he gave only a brief glimpse of his sensations before he reverted to abstract descriptions. I wanted to feel the intensity of his thoughts and his passions, like Kerouac drinking from the bottle of the life of Neal Cassady. Huckelbury's mind was lively, but the ideas lay there in the letters like roadkill. As he said:

> The prisoner sees himself as disconnected, as someone apart, as a traveller in the world but not of it.

I suspected that this abstract detachment of Huckelbury's helped him survive prison.

In the next letter he said he had decided to write in a stream of consciousness. I imagined a Huck with thoughts that came like the sound of his voice, like surf breaking on the ocean shore at Big Sur, full of reckless confidence from some kind of unseen vastness, unvanquished, victorious, pushing forward. He talked about Florida's maximum-security prison system. He had been in the Florida system for eighteen years, before transfer to New Hampshire. In Florida, he did a total of nine years in the hole alone. I was inside. I was there. I crossed space and time.

> After I had been in Florida's prison for about five years, I was transferred to the maximum-security section, a putrid green structure that houses 1,488 men. The day was a stormy one, and I arrived late in the afternoon. I was immediately put in a cell that had two inches of water on the floor. The only furnishings in the cell were a metal bed welded to the wall, a filthy toilet, and a sink clogged with dirt and hair. The mattress on the bunk had been eviscerated, the stuffing gaping from a slit that ran the length of the mattress. I was given no linen and no clothing other than what I was wearing. About two hours later an orderly brought me dinner, what purported to be beans and franks, but what was in reality about six ounces of cold white beans that had congealed so that I could turn the tray on its edge and the mass would not move. I also got two pieces of stale bread. I sat back on my ripped mattress and ate those beans with my fingers and then scraped the residue up with the bread. This was isolation and I had to

take a mental inventory to make sure I was up to the task ahead of me.

You see, isolation, not solitude, breaks men. If I could not find the means to deal with the isolation, then my options were severely limited. I began to call up memories of places, people, events, food, any goddamn thing I could do to occupy my mind and remind myself that, even if I was being treated like an animal, I was still a living breathing human being. Like Descartes, I could think and therefore I still was. The mind is the most potent self-defence weapon a prisoner has at his disposal. It's the old adage, you are what you believe you are, and, if a prisoner begins to believe the myths, the lies that he is fed daily by the attitudes and actions around him, then he surrenders his very soul to the institution that is trying its level best to kill him, perhaps not in the physical sense, but nevertheless in the very real effort to take his identity. And, sadly, the effort is largely successful because of the inability of most prisoners to understand what is being done to them.

In prison, night is the safest time. Movement is restricted and most of the men are locked in their cells. Both predator and prey are secure. I know that while I was in Florida, I never relaxed until I went inside my cell at six-thirty and heard the door lock behind me. Then the tension flowed out of my body. My sleep was sound because I knew no one could get through the steel door until five-forty-five the next morning when the guard unlocked it, and I could always hear that. So, for me personally, night and sleep were both sources of solace and solitude.

Only when the door clicks shut at night can I relax and enjoy the peace and quiet impossible to find during the day. The night has never held any terrors for me, but that isn't the case for everyone in here. Some men literally go to pieces in the darkness. I think that's when memories and fears combine their assault on the most vulnerable. Men miss their loved ones, and the night sounds and relative darkness remind them of their isolation and vulnerability. But, for me the night is a welcome respite from having to deal constantly with the hassle that is daily prison life. I'm finally locked in with my books and letters. Is it tough to think about what I don't have? You bet your ass it is, but, even so, I can indulge my wistfulness and even my melancholy if I want without having to maintain the "face" I must wear when I'm out of my cell.

One huge advantage this prison has over Florida's is the ability to see the night sky. The living areas are like mini-prisons inside the larger whole, walled off and closed by electric gates. But we have a courtyard where we can stay outside until the count at nine-thirty. Before I got here, I had not seen the moon and stars, except through a barred window, for eighteen years. I stayed outside for as long as possible the first few months I was here, just lying on my back on the concrete and looking at everything I had missed. The lights are so damned bright that only the brightest stars are visible, but that was enough.

I wrote back, encouraged by the flow of words from him out of the faraway night.

It's a fine and delicate rainy night as I sit down to answer your two letters. I'm upstairs with the windows cranked open and the crickets have resumed their song in a rolling dark wave after the rain.

His next letter was more personal. Huck was in the prison yard.

No, Shawn, I can't hear crickets or any other wildlife. The steel razor wire and bright lights keep everything living outside my range of hearing. Once in a while, a stray cat will wander in, but that isn't often.

This was the Huck I wanted to hear.

> I have to resist the urge to touch everything. Trees are closer to the perimeter here. I can see into the valley over the walls. The Merrimack River runs through the centre of the valley.

These lyrical moments of Huck were brief compared to the length of his letters, but they were the ones I savoured the most. I was on the road of Huck at last. I wanted to see what he saw, feel what he felt. For the first time, he signed a letter "Huck." I felt like I was being rewarded. I had graduated.

> Thanks for the conversation, Shawn. There's nothing like two minds stretching forth their tentacles to greet each other.

Nothing, Huck?

Well, almost nothing.

Almost it is. I chattered about clouds on the river and great blue herons in the marsh near my home. It didn't feel like idle talk. Herons and clouds mattered to us. I asked about his boyhood and he talked about the time his father gave him a .22 rifle for his twelfth birthday.

> I barely felt the recoil, but I saw a sudden spurt of feathers on the path through the scope. I lowered the rifle slowly, standing still for a long time. Finally, I walked up to it and picked it up. There was no sign of blood, but the tiny body was so limp I knew the bird was dead. I could not believe how light the bird was, how insubstantial it seemed in death.

He ended by saying that was the first and last time he killed an animal. I paused there reading the letter. I knew a line like that could be read cynically in relation to his later conviction for murder. Huck knows that truth of his past and doesn't avoid it. But that doesn't stop him from growing beyond his past. I asked more questions about the relationship of the incarcerated Huck to the fictional Huck.

I am reduced to the status of an observer; the role of participant is foreclosed to me. I can only imagine what lies outside my current world. I know how terribly I miss it. No, I never identified with the fictional Huck, although I could have done much worse. At least Twain's Huck develops his humanity in the face of temptation and trial and learns that Jim, the man he considered less than a man, was in the end the noblest creature of them all. It took a brilliant woman nearly ten years my junior to teach me the same lesson when I was forty-six. I simply don't have the right to claim Huck as my own. I didn't earn it.

I had questions for Huck about his contact with the natural world outside prison. Huck was living in sight of the Merrimack River of Thoreau, a fellow con who picked huckleberries when he was released from his cell. "Thoreau didn't have a clue about prison," said Huck. Thoreau spent a single night in jail for not paying his toll tax, and then changed history with the document "Civil Disobedience," inspired by his brief incarceration. "His reaction to spending the night in jail," said Huck, "is pretty much standard for people in general, but twenty-four hours can't possibly be instructive except in the most superficial sense." He continued:

> With respect to my own contact with nature, I think I want to talk first about my experiences in Florida. The prison sits in a low, swampy area in the north-central part of the state. The land is absolutely barren, the trees having been cleared to prevent any sort of concealment. The nearest foliage is approximately a half-mile distant and limited to oaks and underbrush. Everything is inside: chapel, dining room, medical facilities, cellblock, library. The cells are all single six-by-nines and furnished with a steel rack, combination sink and toilet, and a foot locker. Population cells have one window that lets the prisoner look at an opposing window in another cellblock. Maximum-security cells have none. On the rare occasions that we got yard time, I usually spent it running laps or just lying in the grass. Other than that, there is no

contact with nature's living things at all. No plants, flowers or pets. Zero.

New Hampshire is more progressive. We don't have trees in the prison yard, but we have flowers, and the colours still stun me after six years here. Trees are closer to the perimeter here and I can see over the walls into the valley. The Merrimack River runs through the centre of the valley and, once in a while, in late summer or early spring, the difference in temperature will produce a mist that rises slowly and clings to the route the water takes. I can follow it with my eyes until it disappears among the thicker trees, like an elegant snake slowly sliding into its den. Winter, of course, coats everything in white, but I even enjoy looking at that and feeling the frigid air bite my lungs.

Most of the men in prison in the United States are from the city, many from the inner city. That being the case, they give no more thought to the absence of trees and grass inside the prison than they would to a meal in a five-star restaurant; both are beyond their experience. Prison actually resembles home for many of them, with the concrete structures and basketball courts they grew up with. Thoreau's wonder and contentment as he walked in the woods in Maine and built his cabin in Walden Woods down in Massachusetts would find no responsive chord here.

I wanted to understand what separation from nature does to a human being in prison. That's what Huckelbury is all about. Huck is a sensitive and thoughtful man who needs the natural world in his life and yet has committed a crime that exiles him from that world. Is this what happens to the spirit of the Huckleberry Finns in the great sprawling prisonland of America? The old dream of the American wilderness gets lost in a back alley of the city, where it is thrashed like a dirty wino and thrown into jail for vagrancy?

I found a passage in Thoreau that saw this fall from grace in Thoreau's own experience of the wilderness. It happened in September of 1853. Thoreau was part of a small moose-hunting excursion down the rivers and streams of Maine. He reflected on the motives that bring humanity into the wilderness, which became an examination of the inclination in human beings to murder. As the three men paddled they saw the footprints of a moose that had come at night to drink the water and to eat the lily pads. They heard a sound in the distance like an axe hitting a tree. "By George," said the Indian guide, Joe, "I'll bet that was a moose." He blew moose calls on his birch horn. The men listened. They heard a tree fall like thunder ripping through the air – "a dry, dull rushing sound, with a solid core to it," said Thoreau, "yet as if half smothered under the grasp of the luxuriant and fungus-like forest, like the shutting of a door in some distant entry of the damp and shaggy wilderness."

But when Thoreau saw the moose skinned, his mood changed. "Here, just at the head of the murmuring rapids, Joe now proceeded to skin the moose with a pocket knife, while I looked on; and a tragical business it was – to see that still warm and palpitating body pierced with a knife, to see the warm milk stream from the rent udder, and the ghastly naked red carcass appearing from within its seemly robe, which was made to hide it." What did Huck think about that murder in the wilderness?

I should be disgusted by the death of the moose but I am not. I learned many years ago that survival comes in many forms and some are better at it than others. Prison is a testament to that. We are a group who spend our lives finding ways to survive and we still prevail. Violence is a part of human nature and there is nothing society can do to eradicate it, so I have a hard time understanding why it continually strives to do so. We get locked up demonstrating our aptitude for survival and I think there should be ways to utilize our abilities instead of locking them away in fear. Think of the potential benefit to the country as a whole that an understanding of us and our thought processes could be. So, in my opinion, the moose only got what was coming to it, despite the size and strength that it possessed. The talent to survive is a fickle thing and it is also the reason why and how evolution came to be.

Writing to Huck was a battle against my personal demon of abstraction. I can't just listen to a tree fall in the forest or eat the water lilies like the moose. I found a similar abstract detachment from circumstances in the letters of felons too, Huck included. And then reality would intrude like a big stone shattering a pond with one heave.

> I was convicted and sentenced in 1974 for first-degree murder. I used a handgun to shoot another man to death in a life marked by stupid choices. Last month, the Florida parole board reviewed my case and decided that twenty-five years was not enough. They extended my parole date by fifteen more years. This latest shock means I've had to retain another lawyer to appeal the decision. How are things out there in the wilderness?

So Huck is in prison. I hear from him occasionally, but my attempts to get personal about his inner life are rebuffed. "You've never done time," he says. "You don't know jack shit about it." True, and I have no desire to spend years locked in prison to find out. I tell myself that Huck's reaction is no different from what any human being's would be after long years in similar circumstances. A man survives in prison by making a mental prison to isolate and protect himself. But I know that Huck's mind is still working. I read an early letter from him to enjoy that old raspy river of a voice afresh. Luckily, neither age nor prison can wither the mind of Huck, like the tufts of grass that break through cracks in the cement. I know where he is.

> A victory is getting back to my cell at night, writing a little, and then spending a couple of hours with a good book. I often imagine myself teaching young kids simple ways to understand time dilation in relativity theory or maybe discussing Spinoza with a customer I once tossed out of a bar on a Saturday night.

7   Behind the pink wall

I that was once in the Devils Clutches . . . ingulph'd in Labyrnths of Trouble . . .

DANIEL DEFOE, *Moll Flanders*

A woman I know in prison in Arizona named Kesley Dawn Foreman said she'd miss me the summer of my romance with the jungle of Borneo. I needed a break from the way that university life and writing a book about prison had enshrouded my mind. Borneo, I'd heard, still had some living jungle left. I needed to see. And when I got there, four hours upriver into the jungle, a troop of proboscis monkeys flinging themselves through the air from tree to tree, I couldn't stop wondering how someone like Foreman was faring in prison, a place designed to protect society from reversion to the wild heart of humanity. From Borneo I sent Foreman postcards and letters because I knew she liked wild creatures. It was the language we used to communicate.

I've been corresponding with Foreman for years. She is small, blond, a bit sentimental, a lover of animals, serving twenty years for second-degree murder in a joint in Arizona. She has the typical convict traits, she tells me, and no patience either, after a twisted history as a child runaway and encounters with a series of predators along the way – then murder at eighteen. She started writing letters to me after she'd been in prison more than a decade. Foreman's life reminds me of the story of Moll Flanders, a woman born in Newgate prison in the late 1600s who lived as a criminal and died "a penitent." The story was written by another Newgate prisoner, a journalist with the reputation of "a prevaricating rogue," Daniel Defoe. The old nickname for Newgate prison was "the college," a place of learning, which is still how some see their time in the joint – as an opportunity society has created for them to complete their schooling in criminality. This modern Moll also had a sense of her own history, and described herself unstintingly to me. She sent photos of herself, either coy and seductive, or hardened and fierce. It seemed like two women, two opposing halves taking turns as the dominant self.

> I'm a petite little blond. I'm twenty-nine, but I look nineteen and
> my appearance would fool anyone, but only for a second,
> because I have the true convict traits. I squat on my heels when I
> sit or rest. I eat my meals in five minutes flat. I notice everything
> around me and have no patience.

I told her that the book I was writing was going to include her story, not sure how she'd react, but that didn't deter her. She was open about her life.

> You know I'd be proud to have you write about me. If you go
> through some of our old letters, you have a book I started about
> my life and times. But the basics. Born on an army base in
> Tacoma, Washington. Raised in Montana. B-day 7-9-68. The
> Childhood – groosome. You have all that. Animals, as you know,
> are my love. Someone once told me that if I had as much compas-
> sion for people as I did for animals, then I'd be a good person.

You asked me about what things I remember. Well, I'm great with faces, with names, but can never put the two together. It seems I forget a lot of big events – remember stupid ones. It really is kind of strange to me. I'll write more later. Love, Kess.

I wrote back:

Yes, Kess, I understand your love for animals. So I would prefer that you think of me as an animal, although that's a problem, because I'm not sure what sort of creature I should be. Perhaps a mountain goat, because of the freedom and energy of the beast, and there are mountain sheep outside town where I live. I'm also partial to crickets, the real musicians of our world, and the quirky magpies I see around town, and on campus, self-possessed, as if they had some deeper knowledge. What kind of animal would you like me to be and what kind would you like to be? And how will we communicate then?

She answered:

I like you as a cricket. They are peaceful and full of harmony and I see them as a sender and a sign of good luck. I am a wolf. The wolf is a pathfinder, makes great use of psychic energy, is very spiritual and has an inner divinity. They say that those who find themselves attracted to this animal will likely end up in some sort of teaching role.

In prison Foreman fantasized about her lost soulmate in a mythical kingdom and sent me the love letter she'd written a decade before to the male abstraction of her heart.

My love, there was a time when the winds blew cold over a land lonelier than any of these twentieth-century souls can imagine. The time when me and my warrior stood side by side. Looking to find our destiny, and fate would bring us here once again. . . . I

will not fight the tears as they flow from the river of my torn soul.
For now, the only regret I have is that this life is not yet complete.
Yet I'd give it all to close my eyes and move on to our next world.
That is where we'll be together again.

I was never sure how to deal with the intimacy of these letters. Was
it a real connection or a situation like someone sitting next to a
stranger on a bus, hearing a passionate life story, and then leaving?
It's so easy to confide in strangers who are not part of our lives. I had
the experience of people revealing themselves to me many times as a
journalist. People would tell me what they wouldn't tell their families,
sometimes weeping, sometimes raging. Sometimes it developed into a
friendship; sometimes it passed like a temporary fever. Between
Foreman and me there were long gaps in the letters. Then a letter
would arrive or I'd write one that ignored the passage of time. It was
hard to write because of the intensity of the need I sensed in this
woman, and that would cause a delay of weeks in responding. The
intensity frightened me, yet I wasn't sure whether the intimacy was a
fiction of the letters to soothe the solitude of prison. I'd wonder
whether she had the same question about my letters. I wonder now
why I simply didn't ask her.

Foreman sent me a history she'd composed of her life in a hand-
written, fifty-three–page manuscript with a leftward-sloping script. I
didn't want to read it when I got it and put the manuscript aside. I
wanted to hear from the person she was now in prison, not wade
through a sentimental history of a wasted life. I didn't touch the
manuscript until the time came to finish the book. Then the demands
of research asserted themselves. I read through all the letters again,
last to first, and tackled the story I had been shirking like a pile of
unwashed clothes. The story started with Foreman as an abused child,
beaten, her bones sometimes broken. When she was thirteen, word
came that her father had committed suicide with his army rifle. The
daughter rebelled against an unhappy life at home, snuck out her
bedroom window at nights until one time she came home to find her
mother had packed her suitcase. She felt relief. She was placed in a

state facility for girls. She longed to be a police officer, like her aunt in Texas, in whose home she had sometimes stayed as a child. The young Moll Flanders and a friend set out to hitchhike to the aunt in Dallas. No matter how the story is written, heroines on the road haven't fared well.

> Around Amarillo, Texas, me and my companion ran across two more truckers, who agreed to take us the rest of the way, to only find a gun between our eyes and the cold and sweaty hand upon our young and forbidden flesh. No one could hear our screams upon the desert sands. And still, to this day, I can't seem to recall my thoughts during my struggle to stay alive.

She stayed with her aunt and then took to the road again.

> I caught up with two teenage boys and we travelled the cold, dark nights along the railroad tracks.

After a while, there was just her and one male friend. They hitched a ride with two truckers. A scene from the past repeated itself like a rhetorical flourish.

> I remember me and my best friend Dean were asleep on the bed of the big diesel truck. Just moments before, my friend had given me what looked like a huge Rambo knife, if I should ever run into any problems. Just as we had nodded off, the truck came to a halt. Once again I faced cold hands across my flesh as this man of about forty took me at his will.

She was fourteen, and didn't use the knife to defend herself. The trucker told her he was taking her across the Mexican border to sell her, but she escaped at a gas station. She stayed on the street for a while, then found refuge in the apartment of college students. She drifted again, to places like Utah, and then returned to her mother in Arizona at seventeen. Departed again. Went to Phoenix. Shared an apartment with another teenager. They fell in with a drug dealer, Bobby, and she acquired a crack cocaine habit. The dealer became her protector and gave her money and a gun. His partner was a cop. Life was good.

> For once it seemed I could live without fear. I had a home and people I could turn to if I was ever in trouble. This was a great experience, what I had been in search of for so long, a sense of finally belonging.

Bobby the drug dealer landed in jail, and her life, in the manuscript, became a delirious whirl. Eventually she found herself in a hysterical frenzy in a car with two quarrelling men. Details were hazy. I read the passage several times trying to understand.

> Just then I remember the gun going off, my eyes opening and realizing the gun had pierced the side of the man in front of me. I can remember looking into the eyes of the man before me, his look of shock, my expression of pure fear.

The drug dealer, now out of jail, turned her over to the police after she refused to have sex with him. The conclusion was simple, unelaborate. "I was sentenced to twenty flat years in prison." But all that was history before the correspondence, which had started in the middle of the prison sentence, after prison had changed her. The letters had a life and vitality that the manuscript did not.

> I'm doing a little downtime. I got slammed in the dungeon yesterday [for smoking weed]. I'm going to spend a lot of time studying & I have to do a ten-page term paper on sexual harassment. As far as aging in here, I know that in eleven and a half years I still look like I'm eighteen years old. And I'm a worrier, but, it's weird, because when I'm in isolation I like the silence. Or maybe I just don't want to miss anything. Even if I have a Walkman, I will sit in silence. I enjoy it. On the side of the dungeon I'm on, I

can see a little corner of the yard through a tiny window. Right now the yard's locked down and it's raining. The sky is really grey. It's almost calming to me to know that the rest of the yard is in their areas because of the weather. But I really don't know why. Maybe because I don't like to feel obligated to have to hold a white cloth in the window so my friends know that I realize they are out there for me. It's easier to do my isolation time when I don't have to see anyone. . . . I'm sitting here listening to the rain outside and the slamming of doors down the hall, two noises that are conflicting. But I'm going to relax and just listen.

I had a hard year and kind of lost track with myself. I had some very negative influences in my life. I lost a lot of my direction. The bad part of it is that a little piece of me has crawled in my shell & lost trust in people. I protect myself even when not needed. You know, it's hard to find someone here that can mentally stimulate my mind. Everyone's so caught up in "prison life." I was for thirteen years. But some things happened to me this past year & this is the first time that I have decided that I just don't belong here anymore. And although I'm terrified to fight and bring the truth to light, I know it's time for me to start my life. I'm in the process of filing legal work to the courts. I have excellent grounds to win. As of right now, my release date is January 2007. I could of fought this case all these years, but I was too scared. My murder case involves a police department cover-up, a lot of dirty cops, a judge who's now doing time for the sale & use of narcotics, etc.

She said that she was her father's daughter and explained:

I think the hardest part of my childhood is my father's suicide. Too many questions unanswered. Things I'll never know. I'm my father's child, definitely. My love and compassion for nature comes from his soul, so I hold tightly to it. But it's a side of me a lot of people don't get the chance to see. That's the benefit of our relationship. You get the chance to see what others never take the time to see. That's partly my fault. I love my correspondence with you because there's so much of you in my soul.

A letter in June:

It's always great to hear from you. I've been staying busy with my maintenance job. Summer's here, so it's the busy season with a lot of overtime because of the heat and keeping the coolers up and running. We are getting ready for a big move at the end of July. We are getting too overcrowded, so we are moving to a bigger penitentiary. It's a lot stricter – like it can't get any worse.

About a month ago someone brought me a baby dove that's mother died. He's so adorable. When I got it, it had no feathers & I had to feed it Maltomean & watered-down crackers. Now it's got a hell of a personality. It's got ninety per cent of its feathers and is now starting to eat on its own. It's really spoiled. And loves to be held. Of all the birds I've raised this one has a mind of its own. We are not allowed to keep animals, but some of the staff have let it be because of how much of an animal activist I am & their heart shined through. I have to work hard to get this bird ready to go on his own before we get transferred. It still hates heights because it fell out of its nest. It flaps its wings hard, but can't manage to fly yet. But it's adorable. I'll put it on a towel & crush up crackers & oatmeal and it will play with my fingers like another bird pecking at the food. It gets a hold of a thread on the towel & shakes it like a li'l pit bull until all the food flips every-where. I wish you could see him. It's gonna be hard for me to let him go. But it's urgent I get him to fly, because at any time I could get an asshole who won't let it stay for this last month & they'll kill it. Hey, I heard doves have one mate for life. Do you think I messed that up for this bird – or will it find a mate after all on its own?

Another letter brings her back to Earth:

I just recently put in my habeas to the ninth circuit court to try to get my last five years cut off. I know I deserve it with all the political corruption involved in my case, but they have tried to shove it under the carpet for so many years this is my last chance.

A letter from her from a prison near Tucson:

The most beautiful sound to me is the coyotes early when the morning air has a bit of bite to it. Usually you'll hear a group of pups howling. But the other morning I sat and watched a pup howl and cry so deeply that it made tears come to my eyes. I'd whistle back to him. He'd watch me, then cry out louder, almost as if he couldn't get his point across to any other coyotes.

Sometimes I have such an urge to run over to the perimeter fence just to give them food. But the watchful eyes ain't having it. The pups are my favourite sound.

We had a pet toad in our maintenance office for six months. I got very attached. He had a spot with warm blankets, a pile of dirt and a swamp of water, moss and stones. My toad, he loved his belly rubbed. He would grip his little toes around your finger if you played with his feet. One time he tried to buff up on me and spit some kind of defence poison, but once I held him he calmed down.

Our new boss told me to give him to the coyotes. I snuck Bubba over to one of the counsellors and he took him home and built a pond in the backyard for him. I found out later that he was one of those desert toads that spray out poison, but I guess he didn't find me a threat all those times I handled him.

I've raised baby birds at the max unit before this dorm-style living.

I grew up in Montana, which was deer, elk, buffalo and bear country. Everyone usually gets excited for a moment when they see the coyotes, but I just watch them. The only thing that keeps me from complete happiness is not having a dog. I remember one night I sat outside and, in the darkness, I could see the white eyes of the pups. I cried and watched them. It's those moments when I miss being able to just give playful love.

She was moved to another prison.

I left the coyotes out in Tucson. Here we have pigeons and prairie dogs. The guards don't let us feed them & the inmates hate them because they are dirty. But it's the one regulation I disregard & everyone is used to it. I have one pigeon that has come to my door every day for the past five months & sits and stares at my door. When I get out I feed him. He has a broke leg and no foot. The other birds are pretty hip to it, so they try to take over, but my bird has gotten pretty sneaky to get his share of food. I love him.

She was asking me questions in her letters to prepare her to deal with a world outside she didn't think she could handle. Prison robs people of their confidence to deal with the simple problems of life.

I appreciate your advice & help on questions I have. My fear stems from the money-hungry ones that will try to take advantage. Little things like buying cars, etc. But I will educate myself on everything I possibly can. I won't return, like ninety per cent of these people. I'm terrified because I know what I want out there, but I will need strong friends to guide me, because I grew up in here, so I don't know a lot about life, how to do tax returns, etc.

I am not sure where or which state I'll go to, to settle, because I'm kinda family-less. But once I know I will look into work for a union as a plumbing or electrician's apprentice. That's what I need to get on my feet. From there I hope to meet people & have a career that I can love and settle in. I have faith it will fall into place. I've been working about sixty hours a week at my job [in prison]. I'm working maintenance. Kinda funny because I do all the construction, plumbing and electrical work to keep this place open & running. But I love my job & am good at it.

I'm on my eleventh year with eight more to go. Sometimes I really battle with [the idea of getting out]. I know I could do it if I have a set job. But I know it won't be easy.

Someday she will be released from prison. It may be fifteen years. It may be the full twenty. She would be thirty-eight at the end, twice as old as she was when she went inside, less likely to pass for a teenager. She would be free to wander, to fail, to flourish, or whatever her destiny may be. Nothing is certain. But, if there is any justice in this small shiny blue planet of piss and tears, maybe, just maybe, the song of the coyotes in the hills at night will sound as pure and as sweet and as heartfelt as it did in prison.

[The gorilla] Digit responded enthusiastically toward Simba's flirtatious invitations and showed a revived interest in life.

D I A N F O S S E Y, *Gorillas in the Mist*

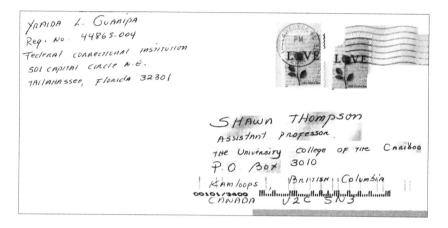

A primatologist told me once that you can see romance in the eyes of an orangutan. It's that old primate gleam that goes back thousands of years and can penetrate the deepest gloom of the jungle. Nothing can deter that gleam, which is why we primates have survived for so long to mate and procreate. In prison, the survival of romance is not easy, but it finds a way. A con let me read a passage from his prison journal about one of those moments of victory: "Sheila can still stir my heart in a way that no other can. Received a letter from her that brought a sweet smell and a smile. I love her and can't deny it with all my will power." I wanted to inquire more deeply into the survival of romance in difficult conditions, so I asked my fellow primates in prison. In Canada there has been a succession of romances between male prisoners and female guards, nurses, librarians and at least one Catholic nun, who married the con after he divorced his wife.

There was an absolutely gorgeous female copper here years ago married to a cop, with kids, who left her husband to move to Toronto with a little Portuguese con from here. He was your typical loud, stupid, uneducated drug addict, which perhaps was the attraction. Maybe the copper wanted to try that, to rebel against her cop hubby. A couple of years later, a copper who was married to an officer here, had an affair with a con, then quit when he got out, and went to Toronto with him.

The thing I find interesting in all these relationships is why? Why would a female cop risk her career over an affair with a con? Why risk her family, her reputation, etc? As for the con, I admit there's a lot of good-looking female staffers here I would gladly fuck, but to enter into a serious relationship with? Uh, uh. I don't see how these guys can forget that these women are the enemy. They lock us in our cells, charge us. How can anyone fall in love with their captor? The whole thing is reminiscent of the Stockholm Syndrome, when you think about it.

Why, indeed, are people attracted to felons? What is the allure of a lapsed human being? How do felons make themselves appealing to the opposite sex? A con who was married in the prison where the nun eloped with the prisoner explains:

The reason why women get involved with inmates is that we are hurt and, for the most part, inmates can be very sensitive, something a lot of women want. Then you add all the individual characteristics each inmate has and, as the saying goes, there's someone for everyone. Prison just isn't strong enough to stop the couple from getting together. The woman may have been hurt somehow in other relationships, physically and emotionally abused, or just had too many would-be relationships fall apart, and somehow met a guy in prison. It's safe because he can't get out and hurt her. She has control. He's sensitive and understanding – or seems to be. He's hurt, lonely and can understand how she feels. Inmates aren't more sensitive than other people. Our suffering has brought the sensitivity to the surface. Our suffering has heightened our ability to feel. And men and women are attracted to people who are suffering.

A realist in the Marion prison in Illinois adds:

Each of us has the need to be bonded with another soul. Most women that get involved with men in prison do so because their most basic mental, emotional and physical needs are not being met. These men and women get attached to each other with the glue of emotional dependency. It has more to do with emotional masturbation than true love, which is not clingy or needy, but desireless. Love is within oneself, yet these people that are lonely, hurt, empty, unfilled, lacking self-esteem, cling to each other and feed one another's egotistical needs and call that sensation love. This type of relationship has the effect of drugs that produce dopamine in high dosages creating the illusion of bliss.

Another says:

I've always messed with older women. They tend to be more settled, relaxed and willing to do the time with you. I have many female correspondents. The young ones are like cats. They come and go in my life. It does appear that when people are lonely, they tend to write to prisoners. A lot of my pen pals are lonely and depressed.

Issues of gender are always a bit tricky when you're only one half of the equation and then only understand half of what you know. Nevertheless, I asked felons, "Will men and women ever understand each other?" "Not a chance in hell," said one. "We're like two different species. Can we think of anything other than sex? Uh, not for long, it seems." Another said, "Men and women are alien to each other, like snakes and eels. Same biological appearance, but different realities inside and out."

I've spent some time with orangutans and anthropologists probing the roots of the affections in primates. Is affection merely biological I wonder. Are primates, like the orangutans I've seen in the wild, capable of feeling? And what about us? Have we evolved beyond our hormones or do we just anthropomorphize ourselves as primates? In prison, sex is revealed as a basic commodity of human beings:

> Females work everywhere and will stand right in front of your shower, which contains no curtain. These female guards will stand there and watch a person masturbate and then write that inmate a disciplinary report. An offender becomes so addicted to masturbating in front of these female guards that he becomes obsessed with it and doesn't even care about getting a disciplinary report any more. Some of the female guards will accept a bag of chips or a soda to let you masturbate in front of her.

From a female prison work camp in California came a letter about how female prisoners open their hearts to lonely old men and get a few bucks in exchange.

> There were men who would get my address in prison and write, "Hey baby, I'm in for armed robbery and looking for a woman." I never answered those. My roommate did once. The man had written a semi-porn letter for his first attempt and the second one was a request for her to get someone to send him money. Luckily, she saw the light. A lot of women do have pen pals. Someone's husband will have a buddy that wants to write to someone. Then there are the women who want to con money. There is a website that has become popular around here. The girls send in photos and look for men to support them. And they find them. They demand money and get it. They go shopping in catalogues and have these men send clothes to people on the outside so they'll have it later. They quite openly call them their tricks. They often have to respond to quite graphic sexual fantasies. The men seem to think they'll connect with these

women once freed, but the woman all seem to profess the end once they get out of here.

I continued to ask felons what love is. Mike Schoen in the Cheyenne Unit in Yuma, Arizona, wrote:

I thought I used to know what love is, but I must have been wrong. I was with my ex for a while. She lasted at least a year. We are on troubled waters right now. She wants to give me problems about my friends. She wants me for her, but she won't even drop me a letter. But the love I felt with her was total peace. I felt comfort with her. I guess that's why I fell in love. Most relationships are really based on sex. And once the sex is old, so is the relationship. Me and my lady had all right sex. It wasn't the best in the world. But, like I said before, when I was with her, I was at peace.

Another foray into the valley of love from a cold cell in Canada:

Prison is a very hard, cold, empty, lonely, sad place. After several years an inmate feels no life within himself. Everything is mechanical, with no feeling. I had placed an ad in the personal columns in the Toronto *Sun*.

Male inmate, 33, seeks female companion for pen pal, friendship, possible marriage. Don't let the usual circumstances stop you from meeting a wonderful guy. Please send photo and phone number to . . .

I received five replies, three of which I rejected. I rejected them based on their letters and what they had to say. One letter came from the Philippines. Another came from a woman who wanted to write but no contact beyond that. The other two I called and became good friends with. Then came the question of visits. One woman said that she lived in a very small town, hated big cities and didn't want to travel. But, we could be good friends. Well, I was looking for a woman to marry right then, not several years down the road. The other woman was more than willing to travel and come to visit. She is a single mother whose son is handicapped with cerebral palsy. With her income and finances being so poor, she could only come every other weekend. We wanted to be married. We put in the paperwork. A few months later we were married in one of the trailers [in the prison yard] by a justice of the peace.

Building and maintaining a relationship in prison is rather hard. We often wrote lengthy letters, talking about everything and anything. All this, plus our trailer visits – which are private and seventy-two hours each – made our first year of marriage a very happy one. But after that it soon became obvious that we had been two very lonely people who had jumped in too fast. Our relationship and then our marriage quickly fell apart. I received the divorce papers the day before our third anniversary.

This relationship, and others like it, were very superficial. We were two lonely, desperate people seeking love, romance and marriage. I believed she married me because she was seeking a man she could trust – she had been deeply hurt before – and a man who would accept her son with a severe handicap. At first, it seemed we were identical people. We had many things in common. We were a perfect match. The three drawbacks were that she is a rather fat woman; when in bed she would just lay there; and I loved her son as if he were my own son, but as she and I argued I felt him pulling away from me, one of the first clues we were splitting apart.

Men and women find their passion in difficult circumstances. I've read the letters and pondered them. When men in prison write to women, they are intense and explicit. But women in the isolation of prison also become intense. One wrote to me from the pastel-hued state of Florida, "I noticed the two times while I was in isolation my sexual instincts were on all the time. My whole body was ready for love, tingling all over my body." It may be that depression triggers sexual fantasies as an escape mechanism. Then again, maybe people just like to pass the time thinking about sex. But the letters of love don't always last.

> I was corresponding with a woman in a California prison. When I first got locked up, the mail came at a regular pace, but, as the years went by, and the woman realized I wasn't getting out anytime soon, the letters stopped coming, slowly but surely.

Another writes:

> A girlfriend is the hardest time. They all say they will be there for you, but that never lasts long. It all starts with the letters, or, as I call it, "love." The letters become shorter, then they come less, then there is no mail. Then you know she is gone. The youngster gets hit the hardest. Puppy love. My advice to the youngsters is to start hating her now. Do I have a woman on the outside? Yes, I do, and why I'll never know.

And still another, in prison in Detroit, says:

> I have nobody. My last sex was April 12, 1996, and that was the woman who testified at my trial from prison for a deal on her case. She pinned an armed robbery on me. I've never married and, frankly, I doubt I ever will. But, I've made a rule. If I do marry, I want to be in my fifties. Then I believe you're both settled and, if you married, it would probably last forever. It's gotta mean something now for us to have sex.

I looked for the idealism of love in the runes of letters. There are romances between prisoners. A woman in prison in California for LSD offences writes:

I don't have a partner on the outside. Rather, I have one on the inside. Franklin was arrested three months after we were married. I went to see him and was allowed an hour visit. Since I was imprisoned, I've had maybe three or four phone calls and none for eight years. We have had correspondence. It isn't easy. About a year ago I started talking about getting out and making plans. He didn't write for a long time and, when he did, he suggested divorce so I wouldn't still be tied to prison and would have a life [while his sentence continued]. I can't imagine not waiting the rest of the time, so now I just don't mention it. I suppose the idea of freedom brings uncertainties. None of us can know what we'll do, but I hope there'll be a happy ending to this all. Yesterday was our eleventh wedding anniversary, so you might say that mentally we're still on our honeymoon. But not really. We will be very different people when we are finally reunited after twenty years. I got a letter Friday saying he was given less than twenty-four hours' notice that he was to be moved. Where, he didn't know. It will be weeks now before we can write. He must get permission, as I have no idea where he will be and cannot initiate the correspondence privileges.

It isn't easy at all [having a relationship in prison]. But what kind of person would I be to abandon the man I love because he will be in prison longer than me? It could have easily been the other way around. I may get out next summer and Franklin will be in [another eight years]. I believe our relationship will be better once I'm out and talk to him on the phone and hopefully be allowed to visit. In any case, if our relationship ends, it will be because of our actions, not the conditions the government would put on us.

I stick with Franklin because he has similar values. He believes in kindness and truly enjoys the beauty in the world. He can appreciate a Monet painting as well as the simple wonder of an orange. I am most fortunate to have him to share this journey with.

The affinity for love in human beings is what Robert Moyes, in prison in British Columbia, calls our "fatal dependency." He recalls the days at the William Head prison by the sea on Vancouver Island. Relationships "blossomed," he said, when teams of university students came inside to play volleyball against the prisoners. "Willie Nelson says, 'Women love outlaws like babies love stray dogs,'" explained Moyes. "Couldn't be truer. I call it our co-dependent heaven! Needy, clingy men and mothering, fix-it, controlling women." One observer in the penitentiary told me: "Let them think they are changing you for the better and tell them how lost you would be without them." Another, a Chicano in prison in Texas, said, "A lot of women like a challenge. In the army I did the major's secretary on his desk! A lot of women get their thrills from the danger of getting caught."

A letter from a con in Illinois brought illumination to the machinery of the affections:

> Dear Mr. Thompson:
> I gave Lee Ann your e-mail address, who lives in Joliet, Illinois. I am more than sure she will be looking forward to hearing from you, or vice versa. You get the picture.
> Kelly, my friend in New York, was nailed with three feet of snow at one time, as the weatherman said. I hope she is all right.
> Kelly, hmm. I love her.
> This is the story with her. Her husband. Jerk !!!!!!! I hate this guy to no end, Mr. Thompson. I have received letters from her. She had been in anguish in those letters. Why? She has what she wants.
> Her husband, he has beat her favourite pet so bad that he killed it with a wooden board. She told me of her husband beating her horses in her stable. She had spoke to me in letters about the need to drink with her horses (rum), to help the stress with what she goes through with him.
> As long as I had written to Kelly, she informed me of other things in her life. Hmm. She had posed naked for a magazine in the seventies. I wish I could get a copy of that issue. I'd give them

blood, my blood. She had trusted me fully. I rosted people for her in the mail, directly. I paid other people money to help me rost people that gave her a bad time. Because of who I am in here, they were ready to punch on the spot, sorta speak. She had to go to court over a guy that took her to court over a real bogus issue, Mr. Thompson.

She used to send me these long letters. Recently, a week ago, I received an e-mail mailed to me from Lee Ann that was sent to me from Kelly, because she is having some type of hard time. She e-mailed that she hurt her back. Hmm. She lifts weights. How could she hurt her back? Because her husband is hitting her? I have no idea. My letters are recently being rejected. Though, I have her love to back it up that it wasn't her that wrote some of the rejections on the letters. I have her MS, I have her love letters, I have her homemade cards.

Now, Mr. Thompson, Kelly is also a cancer survivor. She was in the hospital one time and her husband came to the hospital and asked her for money to pay the electric bill or they were going to shut it off. She was on oxigen at the time.

She sent me a digital imagery picture of her on a letter once. Foxy as can be. Though, that was when she was younger. I bet she is still cute.

Anyway, I had been writing her love letters for a very long time. She even sent me money a few times. She fell in love with me in a very nice way. It was the way of dreams.

Man, I'd go to the end of the world and back for her. I love her, Mr. Thompson. I need her in my life. After all of that pain that she went through, she found the value to still show affection, care and decency. I felt it clear over here in an Illinois prison. But, she was married, and I knew that. She was in prison herself for bigamy. Nasty! But I like it. I like things like that. It is in my jeans to be some type of freak with women I care about. I just get into them too much. Well, I was so into her, I would sometimes mail her four or five letters a day, seven days a week. She just opened up my world. Now I cannot even reach her. But, I am keeping the faith that she is all right. If anything happened to her by the way I know her, I would have some problems. My mom committed suicide and I am not ready for another woman to be hurt in my life. Maybe I guess I should learn to understand when to give her up or not. Women. Hmm.

Another letter came:

> Kelly had cancer, professor. She is like an ex now, but I've been blown off by better. I feel sad over it. I used to love her. But her husband interfered. So, just let Kelly go. Someday I may get to say hi to her. Still, maybe I can give her a bit of a kiss, too. But, Kelly, one never knows what she will do next. She is emotionally unsound. Don't use that against her. She had many hard times in her life. I think about her yet, still. As for Lee Ann "Little Lee," yeah, anyone can trust her. She is so pretty. A Vietnamese knockout!
>
> My difficult romantic situation requires lovemaking. That's all. I burn for it. There is this very cute girl (Queen) here I like named Ms. Somberly (a strawberry Blond). He is so cute! If I had a chance, I'd love to sit and chat with him any day of the week. I miss love. Or my college teacher. She is so nice, like, mannered in voice alone. She is so sexy. You wouldn't believe it! But, I gotta behave myself. That can't stop my dreams. Women are just too beautiful behind my eyes. One day I may find one for me. I'm not bad, professor. Really. Maybe I just need to find a girl my age or younger. I do love that strawberry blond! She is outta this world, professor!

I was trying to understand the difficult passions of women who love men in prison. One of my guides was a woman of mixed Cherokee and Mohawk blood with a deep love for a Cherokee man in prison in Ohio. The man's letters to the woman from the barren landscape of prison were fiery, like a fierce bloom in the desert. The mother spent ten years in prison in Texas for conspiracy in his bank robbery in

118

Kentucky. Such is the extent of maternal love. In a way, it was an emotional triangle of three people – the man in prison, his lover, and the mother. The woman met the prisoner through a letter he sent to her in response to an article she wrote in a Native American newsletter. The letter touched her. She also went into prisons as a volunteer visitor for Native American people.

The prisoner instructed me in his love for this woman. It was difficult, he said, because he couldn't demonstrate his passion. "I mean sexually," he added. The two had the common goal of fighting for the rights of Native prisoners. He wrote to her every day and talked to her frequently on the phone. She visited him four or five times a week. His "warrior spirit" brought them close, he said. I knew he had a warrior spirit because he was convicted of robbing a bank with a gun and gasoline bombs and led police on a chase along narrow mountain roads. Women like a warrior, he said. "I'll say most women like a criminal character of some sort because we face things in life without fear and there is a lot of excitement in a relationship for a man who has been in prison a long time because I can say I'm dependent on her for love and emotional support."

The woman instructed me in the depth of her love for an outcast of society. She longed to be with the prisoner and looked forward to the date of his release. Society had condemned him, she said, but she saw him in a redemptive light. "He has touched my soul to the very core by his words of encouragement, praise, trust, honesty, understanding, love and the beautiful heart that he has within him." She hinted at some kind of dark event in the past which had hurt her deeply, but this man changed that, opened her again emotionally. Her dedication knew no bounds. "If I thought that my life would bring him his freedom, I would give it for this man. This man walks in my soul." I thought what she said was inspiring and looked for clues about the nature of these three people – prisoner, lover and mother – in the photos they sent me. The prisoner's lover was a slender, dark-haired woman, dressed in native buckskin. She looked uncomfortable to have her photo taken. The prisoner had curly, light-brown hair, a strong, hawk-like nose, and fair skin. His smile was warm and beguiling. The prisoner sent me another photo of him hugging the woman inside prison. They looked relaxed and comfortable in each other's arms. The mother was thin and blonde in her photo, with a smile, that, like her son's, was gentle and made you feel relaxed. She looked like she should be playing shuffleboard in Florida.

The son sent me a letter his mother had written to him from a federal prison. It was full of maternal affection, with no jailhouse lingo. The mother was worried about her son's heart. He was having pains in his chest and the doctor found an irregular rhythm. She said her suitcase was packed for the halfway house. "I'm doing okay," she said, "just trying to get things in order before I leave here. I will let you know what my friend finds out from the judge soon about trying to get a judge to move you to Lexington. I have to write your lady friend tomorrow. I love you son. May the creator bless. Love you. Mom."

I asked the mother what her son was like as a child. It puzzles me how we can bring fresh, unmarked protoplasm into the world and, in a matter of years, it ends up in the penitentiary. The mother wrote back from prison:

> William was a well-behaved child. He was very loving and cuddled with me a lot. We watched television a lot together and went to play at the park. His favorite programs on television were *My Favorite Martian*, *Dennis the Menace*, and any movie with aliens, and, of course, astronauts. William told me as a child he wanted to be an astronaut when he grew up. William was also very protective of his brothers and sister. William loves a close family and is especially fond of children. It's wonderful that my son has finally found a beautiful person such as this woman to share his life. She will be a welcome addition to our family and we would love her so much. William is so very much in love with her. It doesn't seem possible that my son has found love in the iron house, but he has and I'm so very proud of them both.

How does the woman know that the feelings of her prison lover are more than jailhouse lust? Is it heart or hormones? Her prisoner had written to her about his sexual love, as men in captivity do, and she was understanding, but shy and uneasy about it. She said, "I have been dealing with Native American male inmates for quite some time now. I know that some will lust over a woman here on the outside." She continued:

> Please know that as much as I love him, he has the chance once he is free to walk from the relationship, if he wishes to do so. Will it hurt me? Yes, it will, deeply, but I feel that I need to also give him that chance. I know that he also loves me as I love him, but this will be the last step that we both will need to take the day his freedom comes. If something should happen and he does leave my life, I will always hold a very special place in my heart for this man whom I have grown to love very much. The tears will come for me I know, but it's also a chance I have to take as well.

Such is love. I was thrilled by the idea of these two people overcoming all obstacles for their love of each other. I could see myself, ten or fifteen years hence, writing the story of how this man and woman found love and happiness in a private sanctuary they created for themselves in the mountains. Maybe they'd have children and I'd visit them one day, climbing the slope to their cabin under the trees. We'd sit down beside the hearth. We'd laugh at the old times and at the distant shadow that the prison had become. But a few days before this book went to the printing press, I received an e-mail from the woman. Apparently it hadn't gone well in the last few months. She told me that she had ended the relationship. The prisoner was tyrannical, she said, trying to control her life from prison. He wanted her to stop seeing her friends and to put an end to her volunteer work with Natives in prison. She said that he wanted to take her to the mountains when he was released and hide her from the world. He took hundreds of dollars from her. Other prisoners – not always the best source of information – had whispered to her bizarre tales of what her lover was plotting. He denied it. She was afraid that the man in prison would hunt her down. She said that what had happened made her feel tainted and embarrassed. She felt trapped, confused, frightened, near hysterical. She wanted to run and hide. Now who's the prisoner, I thought. All because of a humanitarian urge to help people in prison. Some days you wonder if we primates are capable of making any progress in the world. The evidence isn't reassuring. Primates have trouble shaking their bad human traits. But this woman had a good heart. I told her so and said that the mountains aren't bad either. She should try them some time – maybe by herself, though.

9 Magical times in the joint

It's that old devil moon in your eyes

E.Y. HARBURG, "Old Devil Moon"

```
Well I have about 30 more letters to get at here and they have to be
done before I can work on any other project for that is the agreement
that I have made with myself.

You take care and be nice.

I leave you with the words of Chief Seatlle:- "What is man without the
beasts? If all the beasts were gone, men would die from a great
loneliness of spirit. For whatever happens to the beasts, soon
happens to man. For all things are connected."

In Love and Light
Blessed Be


Aspen
```

I've been writing letters to witches in prison since an incident years
ago when I met a coven of them inside Canada's oldest federal penitentiary. I was writing a series of newspaper columns at the time and
learned there was a coven, mostly female, in the local university. I also
found witches in the suburbs. But when I heard there was a coven
inside Kingston Penitentiary the idea stuck in my mind like a bug in
the pitch of a pine tree. I had to go and see. What intrigued me about
the coven in prison was the way that witches bring the creative force
of nature inside the stone walls. They want the natural world in their
lives and know how much they need it, perhaps better than those on
the outside who can have it whenever they want. As one of them wrote
to me, "I learned the importance of nature and its effect on me when it
was taken away from me."

I met the coven, the Stone Circle, inside Kingston Penitentiary for one of the biggest events on the pagan calendar, the Yule celebration. The setting would have been perfect for a staging of Shakespeare's hysterical little murder thriller, *Macbeth*. A witch whom I met that day later described in a letter how it felt to be enclosed in limestone blocks.

> It is a cold, dark, gloomy place. It has the stink of tobacco, the foul smell of body odour at night, and the smell that you find in a basement filled with dust and cobwebs.
>
> In prison, existence is slow, tense and gloomy, and everybody feels everything intensely, and yet these things are small, meaningless and often trivial. You wouldn't believe how many fights I've seen in a meal line and often just because one person accidentally bumped into another. Why is that? Well, our past is dead and gone, our future is non-existent and the present is all we have, causing great pain.

In the midst of that deprivation, that deadened existence, it was a shock for this witch to make a trip to the yard. He could see the stars and feel the wind and the rain. Sensations of the natural world flowed through him with the intensity of a storm.

> It makes nature shine brighter than ever before. The stars are like diamonds in the sky, so bright, so pure. It's impossible to believe that anything could shine that bright. And the rain was always refreshing. I feel like I'm being washed clean when I stand in the rain. I feel the pureness. I feel the cleansing rain wash away all the dirt and tension.

The witches celebrating Yule in Kingston Penitentiary were very different from the witches Shakespeare created for the stage. About twenty people wearing loose black robes, their feet bare, gathered in a circle. There were candles and a small potted spruce tree, brought into the prison "as part of a prayer," the high priest said, "for the world not to be plunged into eternal darkness." The group chanted and sang its version of Christmas carols. One person led with the words, "O

Tannenbaum, O Tannenbaum – I'm sorry we got the last verse wrong." And everybody laughed. Near the end of the ceremony the witches used carnations and cranberries to decorate the little spruce tree. Then they started throwing cranberries at each other like boys having a water fight in the summertime.

I chatted with the witches after the ceremony and they explained that the coven had become their family after they lost touch with the world outside. Sean Johnson, who was carrying a small red pouch of medicinal herbs, said that he lost his twenty-three-year-old wife and year-old son when they were killed by a drunk driver on their way to visit him in prison. "The Wiccan community is my only family," he said, and then headed "back home" to his cell. I kept in contact with the witches from Kingston Penitentiary in the years that followed, as they were transferred to different federal prisons and I was transferred to different newspaper beats. That first coven inside Canada's oldest prison spread the craft through the prison system as witches from there were transferred to other facilities. I watched their progress and heard how they grew herbs in patches of earth behind the walls or scrounged for pumpkins and Indian corn and dried leaves to perform their ceremonies. They said "merry meet" to each other like monks insulated from the wickedness of the outside world. I found new contacts through them, using the network of witchcraft that stretches across prisons in Canada and the United States. I received a newsletter for witches in prison, *The Goddess Inside.* One of the issues talks about a witch I know in Canada getting a letter loaded with "fairy dust" from a female Wiccan in Washington State. The "fairy dust" played havoc with his computer keyboard, he said. He explained in a letter what that is. "Fairy dust is tiny bits of sparkly metal like you see on fashion models on runways. I walked around for a couple of days with this stuff on me and it was rather embarrassing."

As my correspondence spread through the circles of witches in prison, letters came from places like Texas, California and Arizona and I learned about witchcraft. Some of the witches asked me if I had magical abilities or was clairvoyant. I had written a letter to one asking about the effects of pepper spray and, soon after he got the letter, he was pepper-sprayed. I said, no, I'm not clairvoyant, but I am coincidence-prone, which may look like clairvoyance. I investigated the possibility of guaranteeing the success of my book by a spell that the witch sent me through the mail. I abandoned the idea when I was told a secret of magic: A spell that does good in one part of the universe keeps the cosmic balance by doing ill in another part. If the spell made my book do well, another book would have to suffer poor sales. I didn't want that. It would be unfair. I still have the spell, though, if sales slump. I can't divulge it, since another author might use it against me. However, I can say that it involves a candle, a feather purchased at some cost, a night when the moon is waxing but not half full, burning the paper on which the spell is written and then burying the ash, and a series of motions with the feather. I asked the witch if the spell to make people love my book could be adapted to make a woman love a man. He wrote back to chastise me for being naïve.

This particular spell has a dedicated purpose and can only serve that purpose. If you are thinking about a love spell, I strongly advise against such. They almost always produce undesirable results, whether they work or not. By using a love spell one is trying to conquer another and force submission to one's lust. When the energy of a so-called love spell is triggered, it is producing energy to amplify the deep subconscious predatory sexual emotions into a weapon of conquest to overcome the psyche of the intended victim. There is no spell to produce real love. That can only come about through mutual understanding and respect.

I asked another witch to get a second opinion on the issue of love spells.

A love spell is very dangerous. It is dangerous and wrong because it is going against the person's free will, which is also against our Wiccan law. It can also backfire and the one under the spell can become possessive, controlling, stopping at nothing to have the love of another. Very dangerous stuff here. Most people I know wouldn't touch it.

I got the message, and my interest in love spells ended with these letters. Both this book and my love life are accomplishing their ends the hard way.

Most of the spells cast by witches in prison are for healing ailments and wounds, making improvements, and getting parole. One witch says he can cure the aches of the body better than medication. He told me that a con had been prescribed a painkiller by the doctor. It wasn't working. "I did a healing spell for him on a Thursday night at midnight, and, when I saw him Friday afternoon, he said his back was a billion times better. He was walking around, laughing, joking." The witch in Ontario also healed the burn of a friend in Seattle thousands of miles away. I asked how witches get the arcane ingredients they need for spells in a place like prison. The answer is that they grow some of it inside prison and get some of it smuggled inside like the illegal drugs. "The right amount of money will get you anything you want in prison," a witch said, although he didn't sound like a witch at that moment.

Another witch enlightened me about magic and herbs. Jackie Reynolds is in the Estelle High Security prison in Huntsville, Texas, and studies pharmacy through a correspondence course. He is tattooed with elaborate symbols. He dated his letters by the moon under which they were written. We were discussing the witches in Shakespeare's play – which should be written with a capital "W," he said – and he wrote:

> The Witches are conventional stereotypes. The ingredients of their famous "fillet of fenny snake" magical brew, with its grue-some animal and human items, reflect this. One should remem-ber that many such formulae were often codes for ingredients less horrendous to frighten off the inquisitive. "Tongue of dog" and "adder's fork," for example, are simply the herbs hound's tongue (*Cynoglossum officinale L.*) and adder's tongue

(*Ophioglossum vulgatum L.*), which were used against dog and snake bites respectively. Let us take a look at the herbals of Shakespeare's times. In *The Herbal History of Plants* (1633) by John Gerard it says about hound's tongue, "It will tye the tongues of Houndes so that they shall not bark at you, if it be laid under the bottom of your feet." In his days the ointment and decoction were very generally reputed to be a cure for the bites of mad dogs.

He also quoted a fifteenth-century text that says that you can stop the barking of dogs by putting "the tongue of a dog" in your shoe under the big toe along with the hound's tongue herb. I was impressed by the witch's knowledge of herbs and old texts, and I was curious about the hound's tongue remedy, since I was bedevilled by the barking of my neighbour's three hellish dogs at night. What came out of the mouth of my neighbour was like the barking of a mad dog too, but I had no herbs to use against him.

One of the witches I met my first day in Kingston Penitentiary was Doug Lagossy, the coven leader and a stalwart centre of the Wiccan movement in prison. He was serving a life sentence. I remember him telling me that he tried to meditate his way out of prison. "I spend a lot of time in meditation in mountains and meadows," he said. He had taken the name Aspen for his Wiccan pseudonym, which he explained was a tree that grows out of destruction, like himself. From his cell in Kingston Penitentiary on the second floor he had watched the sunset of the winter solstice the day before the Yule celebration. The solstice is the beginning of the period when daylight starts to lengthen as we plunge into winter.

I remember Aspen telling me how he watched a pair of sparrows make a nest on a ledge outside his prison window. It's uncanny that the birds chose that particular window ledge to build the nest. Animals come to him, like the mice and squirrels he turned into pets inside prison. As a boy he used to catch pike in a creek with his hands. "In our faith one of our goals is to find our place in nature," he wrote me later. Letters from Aspen started with the typical Wiccan greeting of "merry meet" and ended with "blessed be."

One of the effects of having Wiccans inside Kingston Penitentiary was a greening of the stony interior, which Aspen described in a letter:

> Our guys there were nuts about plants. Anywhere and anyhow that we could get something planted we would, from shrubs to potted plants to outside plants. I worked in the barbershop there and it was like a greenhouse. I had plants going everywhere and new cuttings always going. Apple trees, orange trees, creeping ivory, you name it and we would get it going. I would talk to the plants and, at times, just sit and watch them.

When he was transferred from Kingston Penitentiary to the Warkworth prison near Campbellford, Ontario, Aspen wrote that it was like "a rebirth – so much open space and green grass and trees. It was like I was given a new breath of life itself." At Warkworth, the witches were also busy growing plants in garden plots, as Aspen wrote in the newsletter:

> Our coven garden is going great guns, more than we can possibly use. We have been giving some of the fresh vegetables to others who do not have gardens. Our carrots sure grew big this year. Mother Earth was not too sure about giving up the carrots, however. I had to dig around a carrot a good four inches, then had a tug of war with it. I did end up with the carrot, but I was on my butt three feet from where I pulled it up, sitting on a beefsteak tomato.

The witches in Warkworth were doing well, Aspen said in his letters:

> The coven is just a wonderful source of inspiration and beauty. I sit and watch the fellows become closer and closer each week.

We are doing introduction to tarot, daily magick workings, runes and the study course material for the coven.

Aspen wrote long letters to me and others for years, which was difficult with his failing health. One of his first letters to me was a brief note after he had had open-heart surgery. He was having heart attacks during the period of our correspondence and wrote, "If and when it is time to go, I believe I am ready." I asked him if he believed that human beings have a soul. In his next letter, he gave the Wiccan alternative to the secular rehabilitation of the soul in prison, a series of lessons and rebirths in the afterworld:

> I am very confident that my spirit will go to the summerland, no doubt to the first isle. In my faith we believe that there are four islands in the summerland. The first is where one goes when it appears that they did not live a full life of belief or service to that which is good. Here you have time to reflect and, when you are born again, you have knowledge of past lives. The second island is where you have done mostly good in your life and you have time to reflect. The third island is one when you have done good and have shown yourself to be of the gods in all you do. Then there is the fourth island. This is the island of great spirits and the one where you remain in the presence of the gods. This is seen by us as the final place where one goes when they have learned all the lessons of mortal man and are now ready to dwell with the gods themselves.

Other letters concerned the battle with prison officials to get Wiccan rites accepted as a religion. His letters often had explanations about what he called his "craft."

> While I was in the main block of Kingston Penitentiary I did not get to see the moon at all, which was rather tough for the simple reason that it is a great focal point for meditations and drawing power in our way. It was not until I was moved to the new c7

building that I was once again able to see the moon in all her glory. For me, my relationship with the Lady in Her different forms is rather private. This much I can share, though: the full moon has gotten much bad press, as well as the craft. For most Wiccans, she is one in four. Each phase has a different personification and each has its own meanings and characteristics. Whenever I am tired, confused or alone, all I have to do is look at the moon and a sense of peace slowly comes to me.

Another witch at the Yule ceremony in Kingston Penitentiary was Doug Strain. I don't remember much about him from that time, but later, through letters, he became my chief mentor and guide through pagan beliefs in prison. Strain's life has the dark and melodramatic outline of a bad screenplay. He was born in British Columbia on Easter Sunday in 1958 as the family was sitting down to a turkey dinner. As a teenager, Strain was rebellious. He enjoyed sex at fourteen years of age. He drank and he smoked marijuana. The excesses inevitably led, he says, to his first prison sentence at seventeen for car theft and break-and-enter. That would not have been too bad if it had stopped there. For a while, his life was mending itself. "I had a beautiful wife, a beautiful and healthy baby son, a job that paid good money cooking in a small restaurant." But he was a drinker. That led to arguments with his wife. She left. He got drunk. Beat a man with a common hammer. Got a mundane sentence of two years less a day. While he was in prison his wife married another man. He got out. In 1981, he killed a woman who was trying to rob him. He was sentenced to fifteen years to life. That was the low point. It was in prison that he met the witches, or Wiccans, and was attracted to the old pagan nature religion. That's the entire story. Nothing to be proud of. There's little real drama in a ruined life. Strain has been in prison since 1981, in places like Kingston Penitentiary, Saskatchewan Penitentiary, Warkworth.

In prison, hope and desire and imagination shrivel and die. That was happening to Strain, without him realizing it.

Prison has a way of sucking the life out of you, if you let it, which I did. We almost all suffer from premature greying, balding, often aging at a faster rate. Many inmates suffer illnesses that older people suffer from – heart problems, pains in the knees and elbows. I'm thirty-nine and have had minor heart attacks. I became complacent to just sit back and do my time. The life was drained from a couple of my friends. All they wanted to do was stay in their cells.

One night he was settled down in his cell to watch television when others on the range asked him to "go out." He said no. They called him a hermit.

I was really shocked by that. I hadn't realized that I had been doing this on a regular basis. Life in prison had become dull, boring, monotonous, and I preferred to spend my time watching TV.

After being in prison for eleven years or so I had given up. I was as cold as the next person. But one day, at a family social in the yard at Kingston Penitentiary, I heard a young boy giggling. I turned and saw an inmate wrestling with his son. That child's laughter was the sweetest sound I've ever heard. Tears came to my eyes as I thought about Allan, my son, who wouldn't have been much older at the time.

Strain fought against the downward pull of prison and became a strong dreamer, a sign of the strength of his inner life. One of his first dreams in prison was a vision of his crime.

Others, like myself, have strange dreams that seem to have no meaning, but I've always believed dreams meant something. Shortly after beginning my prison sentence – I had two years in for second-degree murder – I had recurring dreams of the face of my victim looking right at me and saying, "Hi. I'm here. I'm never going away." All I ever saw was her face, looking down at me, surrounded by blackness. She had black hair, dark eyes and a voice that was crystal clear. The dream started shortly after I started my sentence and didn't last very long. I had the same dream several times but, for reasons I don't understand, it stopped. Several years later I dreamed of her again, only this time I was looking at her from a distance. She was standing on a street corner, looking as if she was lost, not knowing which way to go.

I was not being haunted or simply having nightmares. It was my subconscious telling me I had to face what happened and deal with it so I wouldn't go insane with guilt. It was also telling me that something had happened that would be with me all my life.

Strain recorded his meanderings through the dream world. He studied what he had written as clues to his path through the dark wood of life. One February, he had a dream about the ocean.

I was on a beach and a massive tidal wave came up, but never hit me. The wave came two times. The water was very dark blue with grey in it. There was a row of white buildings that protected me from the wave.

He interpreted the dream to mean that he had unusually strong emotions, both dangerous and yet offering redemption. Later, in March of that year, he had another dream. The dream was intense, involving water again, and a female figure. It felt like a breakthrough. At that time he had just been moved to the Bath prison, near Kingston and within sight of Lake Ontario, after his ten-year stint in Kingston Penitentiary, located on the shore of the same lake. The dream has a female figure, since men will dream of women who support them and guide them, particularly at a time of need in their lives.

It was a beautiful sunny day. I was in a field of green grass. I heard a woman calling my name. I followed the sound of her voice and it led me into a forest of tall trees. Inside was a path that went in a circle with a large pond and waterfall in the centre. I felt strangely at peace. A woman rose from the centre of the pond and smiled at me. She was beautiful. I was filled with a sense of peace and love. The woman was slightly shorter than me, perhaps five feet five. She had a very thin shapely body, slim waist, round hips, nice size breasts. Her hair was long and blond. She had round blue eyes that sparkled and thin red lips. This is how I see the Goddess Aphrodite.

There is a line in *Macbeth* where the moon withdraws, a line that has unusual power for Strain.

Midnight is the witching hour and that is when the moon is at her peak. She does not normally set until dawn. So Shakespeare was saying that the moon was pulling away from Macbeth, unwilling to shine a light on what is about to happen. When we do wrong or go against nature, we notice nature pull away from us, as the moon did in *Macbeth*.

Macbeth was greedy, unrealistically idealistic, and lonely, very lonely. He wanted too much and had delusions of grandeur. He showed bravery and courage, willing to do the nasty deed, but only after he was reassured he'd get away with it.

I see similar characteristics in myself and also differences. At times I'm greedy and idealistic, however, I don't believe I'm unrealistically greedy or idealistic.

When the bond between man and nature is broken, humanity is on the wane, says the convict. He believes that the moon, particularly when full, affects the human body. Surgeons need more blood to perform an operation at the time of a full moon, he says; workers in psychiatric hospitals and cops on the beat feel that people are more emotional when there is a full moon. Prison officials have said similar things to me about the unrest in prison on the night of a full moon. The moon can cause strong emotions, most noticeably love, my witch said.

In his own life, from the time he was a child, the moon for him had been a comfort, a companion, a healer. His father ran into financial trouble, and the marriage, with six children, fell apart. The boy was devastated. He grew angry, resentful, confused. Yet he had flashes of pleasure when he immersed himself in the natural world. His mother told him she thought he was part fish because he spent so much time in the water. Alone in a troubled world, he would commune with the moon as though it were a spirit of purity and goodness.

My parents divorced when I was only eight. I have never cried so hard as the day I watched my father pack his suitcase and leave our family. I lived with my mother and sister. I really had no one I felt I could confide in. So, at night, when the moon was full and I could see her face, I would tell her all my problems, worries, and cried sometimes. I poured my heart and soul out to her. I felt there was always someone listening, absorbing what I said, wiping my tears and making me feel stronger. Once in a while I would ask for something, make a wish, and like magic I would get it.

The full moon was true beauty. When I was young I asked the full moon to make the school bully stop picking on me, help me do good on a test, help me find a girlfriend, all the little things a child would ask for, help me see my father again.

I felt then and feel even more strongly now as if there is a real person in the full moon. I can see the moon and stars every night that it isn't cloudy. I know where the full moon is, even when it is clouded over. I feel a great presence, a loving woman and mother and goddess who wants to wrap her arms around me.

Today, being a Wiccan, I know the Full Moon is the Goddess and I was actually talking to her. Perhaps that's why, all my life, I've felt as if someone was always with me, always looking after me, always guiding me. I have seen the moon at night in prison shine so bright there was a glow around her. She just lights up the whole sky.

I can even hear the cuckoo in the distance.

DIETRICH BONHOEFFER, German pastor
imprisoned and executed by the Nazis, from a letter

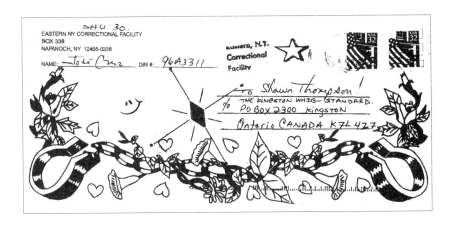

The wind blows fiercely against Kingston Penitentiary. It comes off the flat expanse of Lake Ontario, where nothing restrains it until it grows strong and willful. On the islands nearby, the people have seen tornadoes and waterspouts. They have seen trees uprooted. A good gale can lift the chickens out of the barnyard, and maybe a frail old cow or two, and blow them across the water like tumbleweed across dry land. I remember the storms when I lived in the area. The winter wind would come booming off the lake, a flowing, rushing roar of wind, like a river flooding, pouring through space. Crystals of ice would fall from the grey limestone sky and snow would cloak the city of Kingston with a shaggy gown. At those times, in bad weather, it feels good to be outside in a prison yard. It's a moment of exultation in a power that doesn't submit to human pettiness. It's freedom from the claustrophobia of being human. I heard this from cons in Canada and the United States who fight against being institutionalized. I asked them if they felt the wind and the rain.

Depending on how hard the wind is blowing and the direction, you can hear it howling and sense the fury of the storm as it beats against the windows. If it's happening at night, I close my eyes and imagine being swept up to be carried to a strange and mysterious land. I wonder how many other inmates are listening, what they are thinking, do they wish as I do sometimes that the wind would blow the walls down.

I call the section of the prison along the west wall the wind tunnel. This section of the prison grounds always had a breeze. Depending on the season and the type of day it is, will usually dictate how forceful the wind is. Every day it never failed to cheer me up. With the wind blowing in my face it would bring back memories of when I was free.

In my youth I skied and raced bikes and boats. I love speed. I never wore a helmet because with it you can never get the full effect of the wind in your face, at times bringing tears to your eyes and sucking the breath right out of you the force is so strong.

One of my most vivid memories was when I was about twelve years old and my dad stopped at a go-cart track. No one was on the track but two older boys who were drunk. I remember climbing in the go-cart, the smells of gasoline, grease and the leather seat where many people had sat. My heartbeat quickened and I could almost feel the blood surging through my body. When the man started it up, it was like the roar of a Formula One racecar to my ears, the excitement and exhilaration.

I was off. There was the rush of the wind, tears forming in the corners of my eyes, the roar of the go-cart's engine, the blurring of the fence posts as I sped by. Since then I have been hooked on speed.

When I think of memories like this of my youth and allow myself to be swept off by it, it takes me out of here. I am happy and free again, until reality comes crashing in. Still, when I feel the wind on my face I associate it with being free. As I used to walk along the west wall and the wind would blow by me, I'd envision it blowing the ugliness of the prison off me.

Depending on where I feel it, the mood I'm in and the force of it, will dictate what memory will come to mind. When it is blowing gently and I hear a low mournful sound, it reminds me of a friend who took his life here. I think he's riding the wave of the wind and he has come to check on me to see if I'm all right and to say hi – at least, that's what I'd like to believe. I think of the other men who have died in here and wonder if that mournful sound is their spirits. They are still imprisoned here and crying for their release, which will only happen when the walls come down.

The wind is unique. The wind is how I send messages to my sons. I see a white light and as the breeze brushes past me I send the messages, trusting the wind to communicate them, feeling the warmth, feeling my presence around my sons.

When I feel the wind I realize that it has been here since the beginning of time. I sit on the grass in the prison yard with the warm wind on my face. The sun beats down. When I close my eyes I pass through the wire fence into the open space.

I walked on the beach of the North Sea as a small child and I could hear the fishermen selling the salted cod I loved so much. I can still smell the salt air and the aroma from the smoke house thirty-five years later.

When I feel the wind it touches inside me. It can transcend time and I can feel myself beside anybody from my past and talk to them.

Wind is the spirit of movement. I have lived through several tornadoes and have come to see the wind as a powerful god. I have seen its anger. I have seen its peace.

Rafael Vasquez, in prison in Texas, has seen the power of the wind:

One spring day I sat in the day room as I watched a rainstorm turn for the worse. A funnel cloud began to develop right over the building I was housed in. Keeping in mind that one wall of this particular prison is primarily glass, we were easily afforded a four-storey view of the havoc in the making. Emboldened, killers grouped up at the windows to whistle, clap and cheer the funnel cloud on as it would develop, then dissipate, develop, then dissipate. Finally, it made up its mind. The thick black tail of the thing reached down to grope us and, with that, came a shattering of glass and upheaval of debris. It was at this point that our fearless killers and murderers turned into girl scouts. The first breaking window was this group's cue to stop cheering and start squealing in fear, as they literally hurdled benches like so many deer over a fence along a country road in their attempt to escape the locked day room. These guys were pissing down their legs and rattling the door, trying to be let out. It did not dawn on them that their cells would afford less protection from flying glass and debris. Likely, it was their security blankets they sought. Oh, it was a riot. Utter chaos. What did I do? Being ex-military, I am trained for natural disasters. Accordingly, I remained seated on the bench where I had been and calmly kissed my ass goodbye. The end result was that the twister barely skirted our building as it touched down in the employee parking lot where, much to our enjoyment, it trashed several officer-owned private vehicles. From the parking lot the twister headed on to our chicken farm where it levelled the place, tossing up one-hundred-and-ten-mile-per-hour chicken salad. We didn't see a single piece of cooked chicken or a fried egg for months. Feathers, however, were plentiful.

I asked questions about the last vestiges of the natural world that break into prison. The Pelican Bay prison is located in northwest California near the ocean. From the prison yard, when the wind is blowing through the trees around the facility, the cons can smell the bold, rank fustiness of the sea. Here's the perspective from the yard:

Sometimes, like on Wednesdays, when I go out to yard, I go right out after breakfast and it's damn cold, but it's the best time to smell the strangest aroma of the sea, and it's the only time of the day that we can see birds fly over the top of the yard roof. As for the sun, which is what we all strive for, it's very fucking rare for me. Only on Fridays at three p.m. do I get a piece of the yard. The sun shines on my corner for my whole yard time, one and a half hours. I usually just go out and sit in the corner and read or lay out as if I'm on the beach. One time I got sexually aroused. Ha ha. But, seriously, it brought back some damn good memories. On the other six days of the week, if I want to feel sun on my body, I have to jump up and reach the part that shines on the upper wall. I drew a solar calendar on the wall so it tells the time the sun is shining on the wall. I did it so that in the year 2065, the people that find this prison all smashed up full of rust and broken concrete and plants and weeds growing in our cells with li'l animals running in the halls and tiers, they will find my solar calendar and cut it out of the wall and put it in some *National Geographic* movie or museum!

The William Head prison on Vancouver Island is surrounded on three sides by the sea. It is unusual among prisons for the way nature breaks into the facility. In a prison like San Quentin, the walls obliterate the sound of the waves. Robert Moyes reflects on the sea's influence at William Head, on the power of nature and on his own tendencies.

Anywhere in Canada, bar none, William Head is the physically most picturesque of all. I grew up on the west coast of Vancouver Island, so for me it is like home. I know the view, the smell, the climate. You can hear the sea lions mating there below, echoing across the water. How many people have ever stood on a rock fishing and had a killer whale (big ball-huge dorsal) break the surface thirty feet away, blow and submerge, leaving hardly a ripple? All you can do is sit down, feel your heart pound with the excitement and beauty of it all. Billions of free people on the Earth and I get to experience such wonders in a federal prison. Doesn't seem fair, does it?

I grew up just miles up the coast from the Head. I fished in small boats all around the prison property thirty yards offshore as a kid for years. The beaches you see from the Head are beaches I played on, dug clams on, even partied on. I grew up smelling the richness of low tide, kelp and sand drying in the sun, the salty air sometimes light and breezy, sometimes heavy with the moisture of a coming storm. The sea feeds you, gives you a good life, regular rhythm and tides, easily defined seasonal behaviours. It's a real and healthy way to live. But sometimes its power is beyond the control of humans. All living creatures are at its mercy. It can freeze you, drown you or smash you to pulp on its rocks. Flesh and bone or reinforced steel hull, it doesn't differentiate. It simply takes. Watching logs tossed against the rocks, feeling the wind and rain, tasting salt, the thunder of large waves. Losing myself in it, watching and listening, wondering what it would be like to be out there, could you live up to it. The measure of a man is what he challenges. As a kid I didn't want to be a fireman or a forest ranger. I wanted to be a pirate.

The Head was originally a quarantine station from the early 1900s till after World War Two.* The small, well-tended grave-yard holds headstones with Slavic and Oriental names, but no inmates. I was in the Head for almost four years. Most days I swam for twenty to thirty minutes after breakfast, fished for salmon six months a year, four to sixteen hours a day. Shrimped and crabbed in a bay below the tee-off hole of the par three, nine-hole golf course. Dove for abaloney and octopus. I ran a kind of seafood supply business. The staff tolerated it because they could get fresh salmon for a buck a pound. With the other inmates I traded for cash, tobacco or pot. Eighty acres of woods

---

* William Head was originally a quarantine station from 1881 to 1958. It was renovated by the prison service and took its first prisoners in 1959.

and ocean, definitely my type of place! It was hard to find me not smiling or up to some mischief. Fall days at the Head were spent smoking joints, playing chess and backgammon in front of a wood-burning stove in the greenhouse. Some of us had pet cats which ran wild on the property. Tons of wild blackberries grow there. Pick the berries, add sugar and yeast, bury in a large compost heap of cut grass to keep it warm, dig up in the fall and enjoy a glass of three-month-old brew.

From the old four-storey-high honeycomb of cells in Kingston Penitentiary the prisoners looked out the peepholes of windows. Years ago, the windows on the top floor stretched upward like those in a cathedral. The men saw snow hanging in the dusty windows like a curtain shredded by the wind. "The only time the windows get cleaned," says a prisoner, "is when they get broken, and even those repairs are not high on the list of priorities."

From a cell here, a prisoner sees the bars of his cell, painted black, then the railing of the catwalk, "a dirty green colour," and then, obliquely across from his cell, a window with a torn screen – "I presume to keep the insects out." There is a fragment of the kitchen roof. At night, the moon or the stars are usually obliterated. Prison is not a place for astronomers. The lights outside obscure everything but the brightest stars, and the moon rarely crosses a prisoner's small, square wafer of southern window.

I can only recall seeing the moon once in the past year or so. It has to be in the periphery of my cell and the window across from my cell or I can't see it. And since it moves across the sky, I have only a few minutes to see it before it disappears.

When it snows, the view only changes in colour, to a virgin white, but the snow gets dirty quickly from whatever dust seems to be constantly in the air, and it usually melts quickly because of the building's heat.

Another prisoner here says:

I prefer winter a lot more. You look forward to seeing the snow on the ground. You look forward to walking through the snow, how it blows on your face. The cold enlivens the body. It gets everything circulating. I despise summer because you get burnt. The snow gets me wondering what it's like out there, what the trees look like with all the snow on them.

One year it snowed early in Kingston. The wind blew the snow from the lake towards the prison in big, wet flakes. I remember a con who was released from the penitentiary at that time and bought himself a bicycle for the joy of riding it through small banks of snow in town. He told me that one of the deep resentments of his life was not having the money to own a bicycle as a child, and so he started stealing.

Others wrote of nature glimpsed through prison slits.

Snowstorm? The building whistles. The wind blows through the windows that don't quite shut and it's got an eerie feeling, that constant blowing whistle and you look outside and you're watching the snow horizontal. It has a chilling effect on the inside as well as the outside because you remember where you are. Any associations? I tried to look on the positive side and I was thinking that at least we're lucky and we don't have to go outside and struggle to work. I was wondering how everyone else on the outside felt. For myself, I was grateful that I was inside. Associations? No.

Sun, rain, clouds? When you do have sun, it's beautiful. It's very nice to enjoy the sun and to get out whenever we possibly can, when we have yard and to be in the sun, because you always feel that you're in the shade here, because the building is so huge and the walls are imposing when you are outside, and to feel the sun on your face. We have a little area in between the wing where I live now, which is just a little piece of grass, and there are several tables, and when I used to get away from work and I would have a particularly stressful day, I would lie on top of a picnic table and just look at the clouds, sort of carry myself away and pretend that I was free, feel the sun on my face and have that feeling of travelling somewhere in my mind. In fact, there was another girl and me. I used to do it, visualizing with her. I used to say okay, where do you want to go today? The sun's on our faces. We're going to get in the car and we're going to go here on the boat. We had all these trips that we made. It was kinda fun.

I think it depends on your perception of things and how you assess things. You feel as though you're not in the nature world, but you have to take steps to try and live it. People took pictures of the fall colours for us and brought them in. We were living in those pictures, because you do feel like you're in this stone tower and so things are going on outside that you have no control over, that nobody really cares about you anyway, the public at large rather than your own personal family and friends. So you don't have any sympathetic ear. You do feel as though you are cut off. When you have things like fires you feel that nobody would care if you live or die. Feeling that you're part of the whole while you're in here is probably worse for others. I try to maintain a very positive outlook.

When seasons change. There's one tree in the yard and everything seems so different there. It's like a fixed area. It's not part of the outside. It's just the yard. You don't feel as though it's happening there. The yard is the same as the inside, really. It's really a space where they let you walk around. There's no smell of fall. We're able to see the stars. On some occasions we have night yard and you can go outside early, around seven o'clock. You can look at the sky and the stars. And from the ranges you can see the sky and the stars, because you look out right over the lake. In fact, it's like Alcatraz as you look out over the lake and because there's a little island out there and it's usually ice and snow. It kind of looks bleak. But, yeah, you can see the stars.

I think the lake is beautiful. When I moved down to the wing I desperately missed the view. I think that was the one thing. The ranges are, in all senses of the body, unpleasant, but the one thing that I used to do first thing in the morning is just look out the window and look across at the lake and it was very soothing. I think water is very soothing for most people. You feel at least you have a bit of a reach. Sometimes you can see sailboats on the water and you can see the yacht harbour, a little bit of it. It's very pleasant.

One day when I was inside the Collins Bay prison I heard the sound of a small bird chirping inside the layers of concrete and steel. The others heard it too. It seemed like a miracle that a bird could penetrate a tough prison like that and get so far inside. But it wasn't a miracle. It was an illusion. A prison official told me it was only the squeak of a metal fan in the pipes churning air through the prison. The mechanical bird music made me think how the sensations of nature affect us. In prison, the sound of water running through the pipes can trigger a reverie about a creek. A glimpse of birds or clouds through a window can revive old memories. Prison is a place of stone walls and sensory deprivation, yet nature leaks through to those with the strength to feel it. Contact with nature is a need that the mind struggles to restore in prison. I wondered what it does to people to deracinate them from society and nature and put them in places like a penitentiary. In what sense does taking people out of the world make them more human and natural?

A few prisons are more open to nature, like William Head prison on Vancouver Island and the Kent prison in British Columbia with a view of the mountains from the inner courtyard. I kept asking prisoners across Canada and the United States questions about their sensations of nature in prison. Here are some of their replies:

> Hi, from the deep south, I am now at a minimum-security work camp. The day I got here it rained for a while and, once I put my stuff away, I took a walk on the grounds with a guy I knew from Turbeville. I got to stroll through a stand of pine trees and smell that fresh pine smell. First time in over five years since I smelled that wonderful scent. Here we get to go out all day until eight

p.m. They got cows grazing in a field right next to our compound. I've even seen some deer in the back, as well as some hawks. They've got some beehives here, too. I watched a couple of humming birds the other day. First time I've ever seen a live one, and then two. They also have cockroaches two inches long. I've seen several of those little lizards that change colour – chameleons?

When I arrived on this unit [in solitary in a Texas prison] my first few weeks I spent about three hours a day looking out the window across the field watching the grass being blown by the wind. It seemed as though a giant hand would sweep down and smooth it out as the wind blew. I saw birds playing on the razor wire and wondered how they could dance so quickly about it without being harmed by it. I could hear no chirp from the birds, due to the thick concrete walls and thick glass, and I wondered what they sounded like. I couldn't remember the last time I had heard a bird. I watched the buzzards high above. The clouds like cotton balls drifted through the blue Texas sky. I wished I could be as free as the clouds! The nights were beautiful. One night just before bed I saw the biggest full moon I have ever saw. I watched it until it was out of view.

I watched two birds building a nest in the razor wire that was spiralling on the outside perimeter fence. These two little birds were working their butts off building this nest. This black bird was sitting back watching the two smaller birds. Then I observed that every time the two little birds brought some long straw and placed it in their nest, and then fly off to get some more, the black bird would fly over and take what they had just brought to a nest that he himself was building. I thought to myself, "What a thief." Do you think he learned that from the prisoners?

We have mocking birds [in our prison]. One has taken up residence in a tree right outside my unit. He sings quite loudly and I

taught my co-workers that they could whistle and get him to
respond. We have lots of frogs in the spring and this mockingbird
even has one call that sounds like frogs. I like to hear the killdeer's
call or the mocking bird sing as I walk in the fog, or watch the
buzzards soar or the herons search for food in the ditch lines.

As a child I enjoyed nature. I remember when my parents would
go out drunk (just about every night), I would run to the woods
and, on this hill was a big pine tree, and I used to climb it and I
would go all the way to the top and just look at the beautiful sight.
We lived in New York State, in a valley of two hundred people.
The only thing in that town was a welding shop. Everything was
miles away. I was at peace when I was in this tree. I would hold
on real tight and close my eyes and feel the wind blow against my
face. As a child I swore up and down the trees talked to me.

I remember when I first found the woods it was total freedom. I
could do what I wanted, when I wanted, and did not have to
answer to anyone, or tell anyone. It was a secret that nobody
else knew.

I came from a very abusive past, both mental and physical. I
think that is why I became so close to animals and trusted them
so much. It was rather simple. You hurt them and they hurt you;
you loved them and cared for them and they loved and cared for
you. I thought that was the way things were supposed to be.

I am fifty-seven years old, but clearly remember events from
when I was four or younger. My family was among the poorest of
the white underclass.

I recall a trip with my father into the forest with my two brothers, one older and one younger. Late in the year in rainy,
intensely cold weather I remember walking through the forest
alone, barely clothed, with bare feet, wishing there was some way
to get warm. It was wintertime and extremely cold, in Texas. I
was about three years old and returning from my grandmother's
to the cabin where we lived. I chanced upon a hollow tree trunk

that had recently been struck by lightning. The entire inner surface of the cavity was alive with glowing coals. Delighted, I crawled inside, smearing myself with soot and ash and stayed, surrounded by live coals, until I was warm enough to go the rest of the way home. By morning there was nothing left of the stump but ash. I never gave a thought to how dangerous my act might have been, nor did I have the slightest burn.

We lived in the woods part of the time and on a farm part of the time, before moving into the city when I was four. I wandered about a great deal. I can't say I was aware I was looking for anything, though in hindsight I know I was. I was looking for something or someone to be with me, something I could be part of. Basically, I was looking for love.

As a child living in the woods and farm, I was almost never hungry. Food abounded in the wild everywhere and somehow, instinctively, I always knew what was good to eat and what was not.

We lived in a logging camp in the woods. It was a very small operation. There was only one log cabin and it was small. The men slept in the cabin. We slept in hammocks in the woods. The children thought it perfectly normal and natural. We bathed in the same rivers and streams that we drank from. Our only income was the little pay that dad got from chopping trees from sunup till sundown.

Sometimes I get to enjoy the wonderful healing aroma of a rain in prison. Sometimes I see the beauty of the monarch butterflies as they pass through, migrating either north or south. I am no longer living on the punishment wing and now I go out to the recreation yard every evening to look at the moon and the stars. Halley's comet comes only once in a person's lifetime. I wasn't allowed to see it.

Most of my childhood memories of the forests and rivers were of something alive. It helped me to feel more alive myself. You can reach out and touch a tree and feel its life flowing through you.

The same happens with water, though not nearly as strong as with wood. Water is much wilder than wood. There is a difference between rivers and forests. The ones within the city become tainted with negative emotions. The best way to describe it is as a symphony of Chopin's performed by Wagner – strange and different. The city just doesn't feel right. I mostly block out the emotions I get when entering a city because I don't normally like having the urge to start breaking things. Cities are an attempt by humanity to force communal living on an extreme basis. Mankind has done the same with prisons. A prison is designed to be a place to force men to live in extremely close proximity with other men. Only this time it is not for protection, but to foster a more violent individual, which will give others a reason to play at the great game hunter. A prison is, in truth, nothing more than a smaller city. A modern city feels unnatural and corrupt in its base nature, somehow a perversion of what might have been or could be.

11   Get thyself inked

On his palm was a rose, freshly cut, with drops of crystal water
among the soft pink petals. I put my hand out to touch it, but it was only
an Illustration.

RAY BRADBURY, "The Illustrated Man"

"A prisoner in Kingston Penitentiary" by prison artist Steven W. Zehr

Prisoners write to me out of the deep need to be the authors of their
lives. For a moment or two, writing in their cells at night, they can
control the way they are read, without being edited and corrected by
others. The need to be tattooed is a similar kind of authorship, called
"getting inked." I remember sitting with a bank robber in the Collins
Bay prison, hearing the pride in his voice as he talked about the

tattoos on his body. "I'm a walking billboard," he said. "In prison, it's just like an art form. I'm an individual and I like to express myself through art." We were sitting with a thin, nervous con who had a scorpion tattoo biting his jugular vein and teardrop tattoos at the corner of one eye. The bank robber said that he was inked with "the tool of my trade," a gun. He had lots of "tats" on a body he'd shaped with prison barbells. His head was shaved to bring out the form of his skull, like some kind of fleshy, bald gourd. He had a tattoo of an eagle with the slogan "in cash we trust," which he explained by saying, "The reason I'm here is robbing banks because I love money." He had a tattoo pinup of a ripe and curvy fantasy woman that went with him everywhere. He had a skull, "my dead head," with prison bars for eyes, and explained, "This is the angry part of me."

With tattoos, the body of this man had become a piece of paper on which the images of his life were written. It was partly self-defence, as most writing is, fighting for the clarity of one's own thoughts against the onslaught of others. The tattoos were a way of preserving his sense of himself in a place where his identity can be assaulted or obliterated. Nobody can take away a man's tattoos, he told me. A man can be in segregation, stripped of the few clothes and possessions that reflect his identity, but his tattoos reassure him that he is who he wants to be. Some cons ink themselves in segregation just to fight the system. One of the main joys of tattooing in prison is rebelling by performing an act that's illegal in the joint. "It's a victory over one's captors," says Thomas Bodnar from Folsom.

Stephen Pang, the Pangster, has tattoos on his arms and web tattoos on his elbows. It was hard not to look at his elbows when I talked to him inside the Collins Bay prison. He told me about his tattoos in a letter:

> Spiderweb tattoos are a symbol of doing time – things which lie untouched in dark rooms, collect dust & cobwebs, n'est-ce pas? My tattoos don't tell a story, really. They present a visual image of my world at the time – violence, death, patriotism, finality. I find, here in Canuckleland, most guys got tattoos for the wrong

reasons, with no thought given to what is a permanent insignia. They get inked just to get inked. I was in the pen a year before I started getting my arms done, and at every step I consulted with my artist about whether what I was considering was right for me. Most guys in here have at least one design they deeply regret getting. I don't. I got them in Tracy, California, 1985. (This is a high medium-low max joint, "gladiator school." Now it's a reception centre.) I have two dragons battling around a vortex, a skull with a knife through it, a guillotine, two guns, a rebel flag, two swastikas, a scimitar, a cobra wrapping around a skull, a grim reaper, Harley wings with lightning bolts where Harley-Davidson would be, and others.

Tattoos can be put anywhere on the body, across backs and bellies and thighs, across foreheads and bald heads, even on the inside of the lip. Some tattoos are symbols that represent certain prisons or gangs, and are taken seriously as badges of honour. A beefy ex-con told me a story of threatening to beat a man who pretended to have been in a prison by having the prison tattoo. The pretender was told to have the tattoo changed or suffer for it. Gang member Paul Wolfe explains the brotherhood of ink from a prison in California:

> I've got tattoos from my neck to my waist and both arms are sleeved. When I got my ink put on, it was mandatory you earned certain tattoos. Lightning bolts had to be earned, war birds had to be earned, White Pride had to be earned, and a teardrop had to be earned by killing someone – and that was only if you wanted a teardrop on your face.

Says Thomas Bodnar:

> Almost always a tattoo in prison has more meaning than on the outside, even the crappy ones that are worn with pride. Some are gangs, for example, a clover, the Aryan Brotherhood. Most gang tats are street or neighbourhood names, Eighteenth Street being

a gargantuan Mexican group. But the gangs now are so numerous it would take an encyclopedia to list them. People used to put FSP to symbolize Folsom, but nowadays that kind of thing is nonexistent. Most gang tats are supposed to be earned, usually a stabbing or an assault on someone. But a tattoo does not have to be a gang tat to have meaning. Most just are expressions of an individual's personality or life. I have a goathead (Baphomet) on my back symbolizing my evil past, peace sign over my heart for my peaceful future, many snakes and skulls that are just good art done in less-than-ideal circumstances. I love them more than anything and will never regret anything about them.

Craig Scott, in Pelican Bay State Prison in California, did tattoos in the joint and then "tried to make a living off it" when he was out for a while. He recalls a con who had his armpit tattooed to look like a woman's crotch. Another tattooed letters on his forehead himself using a mirror. He got the letters backwards. He didn't believe it when the other cons told him the letters were reversed, because every time he looked in the mirror the letters looked fine. "I have seen a lot of bad work," says Scott, "and I don't think it is the work so much as the body it goes on that is ugly."

The ink and the tattoo guns are made from materials scrounged inside prison. The ink is sometimes concocted from melting foam cups and mixing the liquid with black ash and shampoo or toothpaste. Some "scrape the dew off the bottom of a painted shelf to get the colour black or use newspaper since the paper has ink on it." "Bad ink," says Thomas Bodnar, "is usually homemade with water or ammonia in it. It would itch for life or blister or spread like spilled coffee over time, or fade. I have seen people get beat up for selling bad ink, saying that it's good." Needles are made from sharpened paper clips or a piece of guitar string sharpened by sandpaper or rubbed against the cement floor. The motor is taken from a battery-operated razor, a tape recorder, or a fan. The whole machine is held together by electrical tape and dental floss.

I've seen some felons with so many tattoos it reminded me of Ray

Bradbury's story "The Illustrated Man." A convict I met in the kitchen in Kingston Penitentiary was writing a symbolic novel of his life through emblems he had winding around his body. That was a novel lost to me because I could never get the man to write letters back. I regretted that, like discovering a book I wanted to read is out of print. But I found others with stories about the elaborate tattoos on their bodies. Mark Fisher, in prison in Detroit, plans to have an old Norse saga inked on his back:

> I have a pattern put up for my own back piece. I'm just waiting for the right artist and opportunity to begin work. It will be a Viking ship with a wooden dragon head for ramming, coming out at an angle with a Viking standing on the bow, leaning on a double-edged axe looking into the distance. Several other Vikings are seated and rowing. You can see the intricate work of the ship and the brawn of the men, and, under it, across my lower back in Old English will be the word "onward." I just need the right artist.

Cons discuss the style of tattoo artists the way the women in my wife's book club discuss the novels of their favourite writers. The cons make their own best and worst lists.

> Best tattoo I've seen? An intricate map of Ireland.

> Best tattoo I seen was of a helicopter flying out of a prison yard with convicts hanging off and guards shooting. The caption said, "I did it my way." The tattoo was on a man who escaped from prison by way of a helicopter.

> Worst tattoo I heard of, the devil pissing on Jesus, almost like a painting on a wall as I hear. The owner is a respected person and had been ruined by mishap. He needs to go home.

I think that the worst tattoo that I have ever seen was a crown of thorns across the forehead of an inmate. Good tattoo, bad judgement.

The worst would be mine. They are all homemade, but basically my last name and a crooked horse that I could never get finished. I was out in an open yard and found a guy who thought he knew how to tattoo. Well, when we started, we got busted and thrown in the hole. Never finished it. So it's crooked.

A fellow with the last name Gonzalez was having his name tattooed across the back of his shoulders. The tattoo artist miscalculated the size of the name and letters and thus ran out of space. Thus, the final letters "lez" ran down under the right armpit in decreasing sizes. I'm sure the recipient didn't think it was funny since he has to live with it for life. A Mexican national wanted the name of his home region of Mexico, Michoacan, tattooed across the base of his back. Instead, the tattoo artist spelled "Michigan," as in the U.S. state.

The worst prison tattoos are "fuck the police" across a man's forehead and two men engaged in a sex act on a man's back. He thought he was getting a Harley-Davidson logo.

I knew a guy that looked like a homemade newspaper. He had every name of every person he spent time with on him, even pets. It all looked artistic, though in a morbid sort of way.

The worst tattoo I saw was actually an intentionally bad tattoo. There was this "roach" who was really bad about thinking everybody owed him something. He actually expected someone to do him a tattoo for free. So, this tattooist finally got pissed and told the roach that he'd do him a back pattern, which should have warned the dumb ass, but didn't. Well, he got a back pattern all right – of a tremendous dick & balls! The balls spread across his shoulders, and it was some detailed work, but, for some reason, the ol' roach wasn't too happy about the tattoo.

The best tattoo I've ever seen, in or out of prison, was done with a single razor blade broken out of a safety razor, wrapped with tape, and scraping the person's arm and shoulder with the razor blade, occasionally wiping the blood away with a rag. After about an hour, he washed the wound with soapy water and then with alcohol pads swiped from the infirmary. Then he rubbed the ink into the wound – wounds actually, they covered his shoulder and upper arm – and, after dabbing away the excess ink, wrapped a bandage around the wound/tattoo, and, after about a week, when all of the scabbing had flaked away, there was the most awesomely detailed tattoo I've ever seen. It was a Native American collage with a white buffalo, an eagle, and a portrait of Sitting Bull, all blended together along with some designs and smoke. If I hadn't seen him do it with my own eyes, I'd never have believed it. I saw every step through because I was "holding jiggers" (watching the run for guards making their rounds, with a mirror stuck out of the bars) for my cellie, who was the one getting the tattoo done.

But, whatever the tattoo you want, however stupid the design, never get a tattoo of someone you love. It's more permanent than marriage.

I will refuse to put a girlfriend or wife's name on anyone. Bad karma. It seems to be a curse. I've seen it many times. A guy is all in love with some girl, comes to prison, gets her name tattooed to show her that he really loves her. Six months later, she's gone. Then the guy comes back to get it covered up.

And finally the epic Lorna tattoo, a body written in dedication to the name of the beloved:

I ran into what can only be described as an obsessive compulsive tattoo nut. At some time in his life he became infatuated with a person named Lorna and had a very obviously handmade tattoo of this name on his left forearm. Then, as if to make a crossword puzzle out of this word, he wrote Lorna across the original effort sideways at every letter. Then, obviously not satisfied with his efforts, he continued this process until every square inch of this man's body that he could reach was covered with this woman's name in a giant crossword puzzle. The man's face, tongue, eyelids, ears were covered. The palms of his hands and even his penis and testicles were covered. I cannot begin to imagine the agony that this man endured to be able to cover himself this way.

Seen a shooting star tonight and I thought of you.

BOB DYLAN, "Shooting Star"

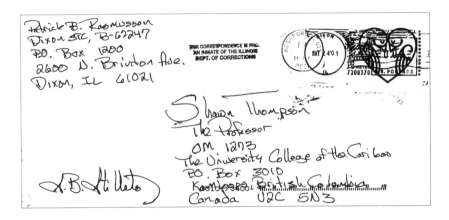

One day I got a letter introducing me to a prisoner in Illinois called Patrick B. Rasmusson. The name was sometimes written as Rasmussen, or Raz, as I call him for short, and he was answering a small item I'd put in a prisoner's newsletter in New Mexico. Rasmusson was prolific. Corresponding with him was like watching yourself lose a marathon from a distance. During one day alone this man produced three letters and mailed them in three separate envelopes.

Dear Mr. Shawn Thompson, (Sir):
I am a beginning wanna be Author. But, I want Authorship something bad. It burns feverishly in my soul to write. It is all I have been allowed to do in prison. . . . I choose to be as neat and as personal as possible to you in these correspondents. However, these are my three handicaps: #1 My typewriter is aging fast. #2 One of the problems with the typewriter is it only has a sixty-thousand-word spellchecker. # 3 I am bipolar. That has a

dramatic effect on my relations with correspondents on the outside. . . . Mania has addictive qualities. You will see that. It will be evident in my writing. Other correspondances could not keep up with my letter writing. The result, I had been blown off.

Raz is one of the lucky ones. He has been diagnosed and put into a prison mental hospital, unlike the thousands of mentally ill people in Canada and the United States – sociopaths and such, people with addictions to drugs and alcohol – who are declared sane enough to be sentenced and dumped into the joint. I witnessed the parade of cases through the court system when I was a court reporter. One time I saw a woman leap out of the prisoner's box shrieking. She was wrestled to the ground by four officers, strapped onto a stretcher, and hustled off in an ambulance. The woman had been in and out of mental institutions and once chased her daughter with an axe, naked. But the prosecution said she was just pretending to be insane and the judge agreed, rejecting her insanity defence. I read another story in the newspaper recently that reminded me of these cases. A Crown attorney in Halifax asked the court to declare "a narcissistic psychopath" a dangerous offender so that he could be jailed indefinitely. What kind of an argument is it to say that a man should be locked up in prison because he's a psychopath? But that's typical of the rationality of the times. I asked prisoners about the sanity of other prisoners and one wrote back from Texas:

> The prison system is being used as a thoroughly inappropriate and unsuitable substitute for a psychiatric institution. The literally genuine psychos in here outnumber the relatively stable prisoners – and guards – by a hefty margin. Sometimes you can't tell the difference between the psychos and the "normals" without long, close observation. My current cell partner is borderline bipolar and I wonder each day if I'm going to make it through the next twenty-four hours without him going ballistic.

The explanations I got from Rasmussen were garbled, but he mentioned a "bipolar, schizo-effective disorder with an anti-social personality disorder." In this chapter I'm throwing away the shackles and giving Raz his wish to be a writer.

> Now, I have tobacco, and found some rice papers to roll a ciga-rette, hold on. I am going to roll a square . . . Remember what I just typed about addictive qualities in bipolar patients? Bipolars usually have other addictive qualities, ei: smoking, drinking too much beer, smoking pot, doing other drugs, writing too many letters, enjoying sex more than the average person.
>
> I just came back from the med line. It is a journey of (approx.) 1 football field. . . . At the med line, always, always, there are mental health inmates that look up to the sky at night, eight-thirty p.m. At this time of the year, Winter yet, there are plenty of stars to look at. They are all fascinated by the sky. Some even choose to point out exactly what planet they are from. . . . They either stare up into the sky with the DAH look, like they are drifting, or they drape their eyebrows over their eyes starring with a complex look.
>
> I had chose three inmates for you tonight. One, I had asked, "So, what do you think of Mother Nature?" He is a paranoid skizo. His answer was decent. "I wish I can be free." I asked, "Why?" Him, "So I can take a walk in the park." I asked, "Do you like the park, RED?" His nickname, due to red hair. He said, "Yes you cannot be alone." I asked why can't you be alone to him. He said, "There is only one alone I want."

As a writer I felt a grudging admiration for Rasmusson. He was a torrent of words. I felt like Cervantes meeting a real live Don Quixote in the street and being overwhelmed by the mental energy of the man.

> A guy I work with, him and I always look up at the stars at night. He is Viet Cong, South I guess. He said he is from Dang Nang. Well, he likes to mimic me. He sees the respect I get from the people that ascertain the same respect from others. So what does he do all the time at eight-thirty p.m. med line? He looks into the

blackness on a clear night to witness the pinholes that shine through from the other parts of the universe. It is amazing actually. He just looks. It is hard for him to talk English, so he just looks and occasionally he even smiles. He appreciates the wealth in the sky, But, would he appreciate the same wealth of the sky if he was free? Why does it seem to appear to be more fascinating to him now than I would guess it may have been before he was locked up? Because the sky is that beautiful. Sometimes people do not recognize the night sky until they are cuffed in chains the rest of their natural lives.

I caught a field mouse in here, big little critter if you ask me, for a mouse that is. Though, it was pissing off the female secretary. I caught the mouse by an artillery of devices. The little bugger was too smart. Almost human like. I was appointed the job to catch the mouse. Okay, fine. I thought that one ordinary mousetrap would be sufficient. Ha! It was a very fast mouse. The only way I was able to catch the mouse was to enstall not only one mousetrap with peanut butter, but also assisting the mousetrap with sticky pads all around the trap. This little guy was taking the bait every time scott free, and making the human look like one big fool, particularly me. "Think, Patrick," I told myself, so, since I was in the National Guard, one thing I was taught, "If you want to make sure you get the enemy quick, good and fast, give him no room to breathe. All righty, so I did. I fixed the trap up, by bending the food arm back, so I could adjust the touchyness of the trap itself. Put on the peanut butter, and then grabbed all of the sticky pads, and laid a minefield a horse could not get by on. I was so happy the next morning, that I had caught a mouse that no one else could catch. I shown it to everyone. The mouse was still alive. It was not originally caught by the trap of peanut butter. It was caught by the sticky pads, then by the trap. . . . But, it only caught the toes on a front paw. The mouse shown signs of struggle.

The boss said, "Okay, you caught the mouse. Now take it out back and kill it. . . ." I should of just let it go. I should of thought ahead. I told the boss that I cannot kill this thing. Mr. Thompson, the mouse was scared. I could see it in his eyes. It was shaking, and trying to free itself for the perdictiment it made its own nest in. All field mice should know it is unauthorized to enter a building when it lives in prison. The penalty is death. "No, boss. I am not going to kill this mouse." "Patrick, you killed your Grandmother. Why in the hell do you have a problem with killing a mouse." (Now you know, don't you?) There was conversation about this once later. "Oh, he could not kill a mouse but, he can go out and kill a human being." Something like that anyway. Mr. Thompson, I snapped from a medication overdose in a private Chicago hospital, when I checked myself in for my mother's pistol suicide. . . . (Man, am I tired. I have to get this out to you as quick as possible.) so, since I could not kill a measley little mouse, the Boss said. Hey you, an officer, follow Rasmusson in back and kill this thing so it don't migrate back indoors. The secretary will throw a fit if it comes back in.

The mouse, it had ears, it knew it was walking to its own electric chair, which amounted to a work boot. The march to the manhole cover in the back of the building was on. The mouse sure was cute-looking. Frankly it had no idea what it was in for. He was strapped into the brown paper bag to ensure the manhole cover wouldn't be messy from mouse guts flying everywhere, and for a bit of human dignity. Why step on a mouse while it is looking at you, right? The boot came plunging down. A faint noise was heard. That was it. The sound of bones breking, but little bones. Then I was to throw the mouse away, in the garbage can. I did. Then I was instructed to clean the mousetrap for the next mouse. I did. Then, I returned the trap to the kitchen, where the trap belongs.

I don't know. You tell me. What do you think I felt like? That it was not that big of a deal, that it was only a mouse? No-sir-eee. It was a big deal. I didn't keep my trap shut. It could have been eating some corn kernels in the farmer's field today, from last year's harvest. I compare that to what I barely remember on the next morning of my case. The body just laying there. Listless. No breath. I am sorry Mr. Thompson. I am sorry for what I had done, in both cases. In my murder case, I just wasn't thinking (in a way) like with the little mouse. But, in my case, as too some of the case with the mouse, someone else pulled the trigger by the use of my hands. I have a strangelation murder I do not remember as much as I remember this mouse case. I had a nervous break-down. As one writer to another, brother, I am being totally honest. In nine years of being locked up, there does not go one day that I do not think about my case. Maybe, if my attempt of suicide worked, Grandma would still be here as well as that mouse.

Who am I? This letter is being mailed out right now, so I can get the other letters in the box at the same time.

It was exhausting to read a Rasmusson letter, he was so intensely alive. And yet I wondered whether someone was playing games with me. Was Rasmusson a real mental case or a character that a prisoner had concocted to fool a writer like me? The story of the homicide and the murder of the mouse sounded almost too clever. But then there aren't many sane people who could sustain the illusion of such a perfect blend of insanity and creativity. Raz had sent me photocopies of court and police records, which added an eerie sense of reality to his existence. The prison records on the Internet initially refused to divulge the existence of the man. The problem was that the prison service uses a date of birth for him that he says is wrong, in addition to a wrong spelling for his name. Sometimes it's hard to know who has the simple facts right. In the end I found a photo and description of a six-foot-one brown-haired man serving a life sentence of twenty-five years. Rasmusson told me he was serving the sentence for the first-degree murder he committed at twenty-eight years of age. "I killed my dad's mom," he said. "That was a direct result of an unexpected suicide of my mother's blundering a year before." I asked Raz how rational people see a bipolar personality.

I see people afraid of me, or intimidated, or unworthy to my output. I max all day long. It is all from getting my thoughts out of my mind to rest the thought itself. Seriously. Even though I may not be as educated as others, I find most people (rude), unorderly, lazy, and filled (with what I call) the cool pride. People have this need to be tame and mellow, and show relaxation to associate, or mingle. Don't get me wrong. I can too, but most cannot handle my intensities of my dramatic moods that are very very real. I'm a better actor than most of your Hollywood super-stars. Yet, it's no act. My feelings change due to what emotion is presented in front of me. My emotions have truce to everyone. I'm light inside but no invert at all! So others appear weak inside and out, no matter how brilliant, or how big. I am an emotional competitor. I'm off of meds still. My psych saw a light no other doctor had. I owe her a clear thought.

Another letter arrived with talk about his family:

Man, I can't wait to get outside and see exactly what computers can really do. A website? Easier mailing access. And ensured mail in a way, I guess. Sounds a lot more interesting than trying to catch the voltage from a lightning bolt. That is an idea that my dad wants me to work with. He said, "Son, if you can capture the voltage from a lightning bolt and store it with the high amps, your family will never work again in generations to come." That means two things. With all that money, why would any of your later generations want to go to school? There are your two things. A bunch of rich dummies. Sorta like me when dad regretted kicking me out of the house. His newest wife at that time made that decision. It wasn't his choice. Dad is a nerd. Any good-looking girl would have him tied around her finger. Oh, the family victum? That was my dad's mother. He was on my side, but not his wife. You know she has a wart on her nose? I asked her why she don't cut it off to look more appealing. What does she do? She gets upset at me and then has my dad limit the calls I can make to the shop to once a month, and tells him not to send me any more money.

When I was arrested for murder I was literally threw into a lockdown cell. . . . I was in that strip cell from January '92 to August of '93. A year and a half I remained naked in a cell with no clothes and at a cold temperature to refrain from thoughts of suicide. Because I was in the mental hospital for an attempt to take my life before the murder, they had to be sure that I wasn't going to do anything funny. And they sure didn't take any chances either.

In the cell I was completely stressed out. I entered the cell at one hundred and ninety-eight pounds. I left the cell at two hundred and ninety-three pounds. They claimed they had to feed me to make me balanced. And it was quiet in those gloomy hallways of too much silence. I didn't like the silence then as much as I complain about the noise levels here at times. The silence. Poe should have written exclusively on silence. You would sing to yourself. You would begin to hold conversations with yourself. Some of the nurses would see you talk to yourself and truly believe you were crazy. But, I was only trying to break the monotony of silence. My conversations included people of Presidency, War Soliders, Made Up Friends, or K-Mart store clerks, and the conversation that I would hold to myself would be just asking questions to how they were doing. Or if they were all right, and if I could help in any way possible. It does happen to everyone. Even those who are well adjusted in the head. They try to see what it is like to talk to their selves and actually become good at it, and choose [never] to talk to anyone else again, because they sure can swear at their own self or hit their self, or make their self feel bad.

I grew up living behind Statesville pen. I know what the different personalities of prisons hold. I knew the guy that came into the county jail when I was there on this case, who killed the last prison guard there. . . . He was a good friend. I will never let his secrets out. He died while in the county jail at the age of approx. forty-eight. He could not trust anyone but me. He began to bleed from the butt. He stank bad. As his friend, I chose not to leave his side because of his health problems. I stayed with him to the end. He felt that the prison was getting back at him, that they have him poison of some type because he didn't know why he was experiencing these types of medical problems. Then, one morning, the guard said, "Patrick, he was your friend, go clean his cell out. He is dead."

Dear Mr. Thompson, (Sir), (or may I use the name Professor?) You know the movie "The Blues Brothers" opened and ended with the same picture of a prison that is practically in my back-yard? Joliet Corrections C.C., or also known as Joliet, or as the people that live in the town call it, "Collins Street Prison" because it is on Collins Street. Is that too compelling for one day? . . . The prison Joliet was odd to grow up next to. And, I want to talk about the feeling I had looking at it as a teen then being in it as an adult on the inside.

I had walked by the Collins Street Prison many times as a boy. It is on the other side of the river that parts Statesville Prison and Collins Street Prison. . . . It is smack dab in the middle of a town, Joliet. There are working people all around the prison, there is a street that is no more than fifteen feet from the main wall, and kids, grandmas, grandpas, dads, mothers, sisters and brothers all over the place that hang around it treat it like a regular glorified monument that has been there more as a symbol of time rather than something of incarceration. People do not talk about prison inmates when they walk by the prison, they talk about, "Man, look at the size of that wall," or "That is a bad looking stone there." The wall is made of carved stone from some poor bunch of whoever's. . . . A gigantic wall pissing people off. . . . Professor, I knew humans that worked in Joliet Prison, my own dad did TV repair for inmates in Joliet Prison. I never heard of any account that mentioned anything about the humans that live in there. And there are a lot of them.

His use of "sir" and "professor" was making me feel like a character in a novel he was writing. Rasmusson talked at length of the effect of newspaper headlines on the town.

I wrote to that newspaper in Joliet. After they found a letter from me that they liked, they decided to print it and use the word "crazy" behind it. I am far from crazy, Sir. I am only bipolar. They would not even allow my condolence properly in the headlines of the paper. I apologized to the whole town of Joliet. They printed it on the front page. Then, during their process, they also decided to include their remarks about how they thought I was generally full of it.

Dear Professor, (Sir):
Good morning Professor. I hope it's not too cold up there for you [in Canada], or is that why you're going to Borneo? I think of your life. I wonder about your students and who they are; what they are; their dreams and thoughts; and if there is any relation to mine. Once I become your friend, Professor, you can't shake me loose too easy at all. I try hard to attach myself to people with quality and emotional spirit. When I see that adjacent, I become a vicious Stiletto, if ever needed, and I'm not kidding! I come from the heart of despair. I'm not going back there as I was abandoned. My pristene family left mom all alone because they didn't care to associate with a bipolar person. They done the same to me, also, and only on account of the M/H reasons. If you looking at me, you may wonder why they did this to me. I'm thirty-four, six-foot-one, one hundred and seventy pounds, blue eyes, blond hair (dishwater) no tattoos (just a party dot), no major scars. When I look at me in the mirror, I see a handsome person, but inside (honestly) I feel like a boy yet. Not scarred. No. It's just my innocent value I see that is always taken advantage of. I am

sullen in a crowd. Others make so many insinuations; all but the
State Employees. None, (or really most) inmates trust me, only
because I am an Administrative Clerk who is polite and respects
who I am told to do. When I have to, for my own reasons, I can
put the fear of Hell in any man alive when they are not worth the
words they speak. I do so regularily. I do it, also for reasons other
than, say "I don't care for you dude. Ya better leave me alone." I
do that to try and wake people up, individually. And it works. For
example, I'm trying my damedest to teach this wrongly steared,
eighteen yr old gang banger how to write. He looks up to me and
listens, because I teach him words out of the dictionary. His own
race (Spainish) abandons him, as his gang, like he is this little
victim. So my attempts to lift his lonely world is to make how he
thought was his friends look like fools, (which they are). I taught
him one word at first, "Concinnity." I made him study the one
word inside and out, Then, I told him to use it in front of his
friends. He did. His friends want to know what the word means. I
told him to tell them, "What? Ya stupid, or what? You finish any
homework in school?" He did that. They got mad at him as I was
listening in my cell. They provoked him. Then I stepped out, and
put the fear of Hell into the whole group. Now, he has friends.
Then, I kept sliding him new words, like these: "alight, barren,
disrupt, dynasty, foretaste, germinate & humdrum." I gave that
list to him tonight, with diction and sentence form. I told him he
has got two weeks to know these words inside and out, then I am
going to test him, (again), to see if he learned them. His problem
started with his foxy-looking girlfriend, blowing him off, because
he is a high-school dropout, (like me), bullied and teased in a
letter; still writes to him, and he gets depressed. But, he won't let
her go, because she is this flower to him. She knows that, and so
his letters are now starting to twist his college girlfriend's heart
just a wee bit. I gave him a fresh slate. And he is using it. And he
uses those other few words in speech. Yeah, he defines them
wrong in structure when I listen, but I pull him to the side and
correct that. His pals now want to know, why a kid with no

dictionary, knows these $50,000 words. It's so funny, Professor. He blew their heads totally! So awesome what one word can do. Now he also wants to learn how to write poetry.

I enjoy the part of Raz that makes sense, like the part of me that I hope makes sense to others. Some days I feel that the only way I can make sense of the people around me is to imagine that the planet is one big insane asylum and that all the people in it are inmates. I'll let the bipolar writer have the liberty of the last word.

@ approx. 1 a.m. to 1:30ish
Dear Professor:
My cellie is fast asleep. I valenced the bunk bed with my soft blue blankets, so the bright light don't wake him. My writing is silent, but that damn light is more piercing than any stereo at this time of night. . . .

I have my small library out. I stopped on a chapter I was in the process of rewriting. The chapter of a Receptive News Anchor Woman. People, the general society here, tell me I need a sexual scene in this book.

I'm still bipolar (in a way) as I see things so much different. I have to leave my wreckless (occasional) attitude behind, if my intent is authorship, which it indeed is. An author still must be somewhat wreckless in spirit. Wouldn't you think? If you get a letter you do not comprehend, don't freak out professor. Sometimes I am that hard to understand as I am told. But, I mean well, and that is what really counts. . . .

The lightning is streaking across the sky. I'd like to dim the lights. Maybe I'll turn on my nightlight, a snowy picture screen on the TV. Let's see if that will set the mood. It worked! The thunder is heavier. I hope it continues. The rain is moderate, but it was much heavier earlier. Such a shame that I can still see the razor wire with the beauty of a perfect mellow storm. The mood is set. I'm going to write about bipolars and sex now. I feel comfortable with it anyway, anywhere.

13   The optimist in prison

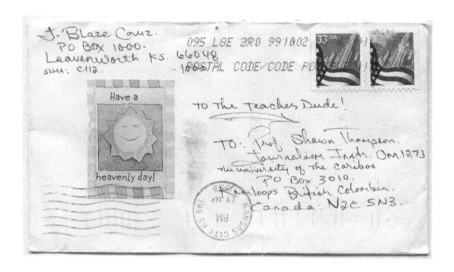

Angels . . . become images of our freedom: from the past, from authority, from the necessity of dying.

HAROLD BLOOM, *Omens of Millennium*

Everybody should have an optimist of one's own like my man in Leavenworth, José Cruz. He always has a good word to say, no matter how bad his life gets. He has a long list of people he writes letters to outside prison who depend on him to buoy their spirits up. He writes to his family, to women, to friends, to an elderly lady in Lewisburg, Pennsylvania – and to me across the border in Canada. One time I got a condolence card from him, even though there had been no deaths in my family. The card had drooping purple flowers on the front and was about loss and grief. "I could not find no Christmas cards," he wrote from prison, "so I figured I'd send you this one and let you know I sympathize with you if you ever lost anything." He ended it with "happy holiday, 'cause to me, every day is a day to celebrate." Not exactly, but sometimes, perhaps, even in Leavenworth. In the midst of being transferred from one prison to another, he sent me a Father's Day card. Nice touch, although it made me feel older to know that the son I never had was locked in prison.

How much can you learn about a person from letters? Not much, I suppose, and yet this man seemed to listen to what I said and to respond thoughtfully. He was able to detach himself for a moment and reflect on himself and his situation. He seemed to learn and to make discoveries, no matter what the circumstances. I've read plenty of letters from prisoners where I had doubts about their sincerity, particularly when they asked for money or wanted me to write to an official to get them out of prison. But this man never did that. He seemed genuinely interested in what was happening to other people.

> Pray you are well. You caught me the night before leaving for court en route to Riker's Island. Hope you're feeling better. Drink lots of water and juices . . . I write a lot of letters, study the scriptures, work out, and read. I have this routine that leaves me exhausted by eleven. You'll be surprised how busy a person could be. The entire cell is your universe and your mind is this highway, a web of highways in the universe.
>
> I'll continue answering your letter in my next scribe. Gotta go. You are in my prayers.

I knew little of this man beyond his existence in prison. I learned he had the nickname of Blaze, which sounded like a fallen angel consigned to the flames of the inferno. He was born on April 10, 1968, in the Bronx, "when I came into this world and started dying." I opened one letter to find he'd sent me a photo of his wife, his mother and his son. Sometimes he sent me photos of himself and a friend inside Leavenworth, such as the Native American leader Leonard Peltier or the Canadian bank robber Patrick "Paddy" Mitchell. He seemed able to make friends anywhere. He would mail me a card and sign it, incorporating me into his extended family, "with much love and respect, your baby bro, Blaze." He called me his guardian angel, but I don't think from anything I did so much as the need to feel that his image of himself was protected somewhere outside the mundane realm of prison. "Don't make me look like a goof," he said, thinking of this book. The word "goof" is the foulest term in the prison lexicon. I wasn't sure whether he meant don't make him look silly or don't make him look soft, either of which could be fatal in prison.

Blaze, as I said, is an optimist, a real one, tested by circumstances and not just the product of a lazy and sheltered life. He wrote once when he received fourteen days in the hole for causing a ruckus from his cell. A guard who injured himself trying to stop him blamed Blaze for the injury. Fourteen days wasn't much, the sanguine con said. "I admit it was a blessing. It could have been worse." But then the guards who thought he was getting off lightly took his shoes in retaliation. He was forced to walk through the range in big slippers. "But it could be worse," he said cheerily. "They could take my slippers, too." It seems that the optimist can find progress in a setback. Or, as Blaze summed up the wisdom of slippered feet, "We all contribute to mankind's growth in subtle ways."

I wanted to share the good fortune of having my own personal optimist and so gave Blaze the address of a friend, Dr. Rosa Garriga, a Spanish woman I met in the Far East. It must have startled even her durable Catalan blood, for she wrote, "I have to say that I was shocked when I read that you gave my address to someone in prison. But then I thought that could be interesting." Yes, sometimes it takes time to understand the blessedness of our fortune. Here are some short letters to read. They are from the period when the lives of Blaze and me were in transition and flux. Blaze was being moved from prison to prison and I was leaving a newspaper for a job teaching journalism. I was also struggling to write this book. Luckily I had encouragement from prison.

Hey Shawn:
What's doing, bro? I pray that you are, as we say, chillin. I'm doing okay. But not exactly in a federal prison yet. I'm not transit and presently I'm at Passaic county jail, Gestapo capital of the

world. Not only do these guards wear all black, they also walk around with snarling, barking guard dogs. The visits are held through a glass partition by a phone. And this is beat-down city.

As soon as I got here I felt the tension. They began screaming at us, hollering over the barking dogs. Eventually I got tired of the disrespect. They must have thought I was a new prisoner fresh off the street and easily intimidated. They were shocked when I screamed at all of them and their dogs, telling them to go fuck themselves and I don't care what they do. Naturally they cuffed me up, took everyone else away from sight, and roughed me up while cuffed. That actually felt good. It healed my sinuses. I had no more problems after that. But this place really sucks. They even got cameras in the cells. They could watch you as you shit.

I was in a sixty-man dormitory for a week, dirtier than a garbage dump and noisier than the girls' club at gossip hour. So I started laying down the law, getting it cleaned up and whatnot. Then someone dropped a slip on me, saying I was starting trouble. So they moved me to an isolation unit. Now I'm in a two-man cell with a big black guy as my cellie. He admits to being a snitch and has a mental problem. Next door in a cell with a wild Mexican is a guy who beat up and robbed a nun. And, in the other cell, two murderers. One of them is nuts and begging for anything. "Give me something to eat. Give me a match. Let me get some lotion." And on and on. That was the first guy I had to put the brakes on. These beggars are the worst. The nun beater said he did not do it. The murderer says his friend did it. This shit is crazy.

Having a cellie is the pits. Can't shit or fart in peace. There are so many things people of the free world take for granted. I can't read or write here because the TV immediately outside our bars is loud. I'm already trying to get out of this joint. One way is to write up complaints with threats of lawsuits. My complaint is already seven pages long, front and back. And, believe me, they are all legit complaints. This place is abusive, oppressive and violative.

About your cell experience [being voluntarily incarcerated in

Kingston Penitentiary], you should have focused some anger at the staff. Really. Curse them out, rave, spit and, if that went well, without getting an ass whipping, you could have also flung some shit on em! I'm laughing. But really, we all usually release anger on the guards. In a way, I feel bad for the fools at times. They get treated like shit quite often.

Thanks for writing. It was nice to hear from you. Kamloops? Sounds like a cereal. I hope you get the college job. No need for you to feel you must start writing your book with a vengeance. I think you're coming along just fine. If you push yourself too hard, you'll burn out. Relax.

Well, my friend, you take care. I'll reach out to you soon again. Yours, Blaze.

Another letter came as Blaze kept me informed of his pilgrimage through the prison system:

What's up buddy?

I pray this finds you well. I'm doing okay. I just got over an ordeal. I got myself thrown in the hole, a real hole. You get nothing but a blanket. Not even toothpaste or a book to read. So you could imagine the stress. Actually it wasn't that bad. (If you know how to become one with the universe.)

As you see, got transferred back to N.Y. I guess the dudes in Passaic, N.J., did not enjoy my cool disposition or frankness.

I can receive books here, so I'm going to start having everything I sent home returned. Hey, guess what? I'm in a large dormitory with about eight different units situated in an octagonal form with the sleeping quarters at each end and the dayroom in the center of the octagon. Can you picture that? Anyways, as I write you, there's a guy somewhere doing his Muslim prayers. It's quite musical. "Allah akbar allah-ah akbar." He's doing it with a nice deep baritone voice and it's echoing off the walls quite melodiously. I get the funny feeling as if I'm in a Turkish jail. Did you ever see the movie *Midnight Express* about a dude

who gets caught transporting drugs out of Turkey and this begins
a terrible ordeal. It's no joke. If you get the chance, rent it out of a
video store. (Excuse the paper and my sloppy writing. I'm not
trying to be neat today.)

By the way, bub, happy Daddy's day. When I was thrown in the
hole I could not write anyone, so I got backed up. I'm lucky they
kicked me out. I didn't do half the time I owed them in the hole.
But I got a new charge, aggravated assault. Jesus, I got to chill out.

I'm glad you heard the crickets [from the cell in Kingston
Penitentiary]. So I gather you had a window close by, huh? Did
you get to see out of your window while in the cell while you were
doing your newspaper article? What did you feel as you looked
out the window? When I look out windows I get a longing feeling
to be free, to be travelling. As I alluded to in the earlier missive, I
didn't actually see the cons playing ball from my vantage point in
solitary. I could only hear them playing, yelling in joy and
triumph when, I guess, they were scoring or getting in a good
play. The day was twilighting. Just getting dark, or dusk. It was a
bit foggy out. It was warm. And, yes, the crickets were out in full
force along with the humming and flitting of other insects. As I
looked out the window, I became annoyed at their cheering,
upset that these men could be so happy at being in prison. I actually felt as if I was on a controlled substance, so dreamlike it was.
But I wasn't and have not been in such a state for almost ten
years. The closest I can get to describe it is the feeling one gets
very early in the morning stepping out of the house and no one is
out. It's nice and warm. The air smells good. The fog is out and
it's just beginning to get light out. You're still drowsy from
dreaming, but alert and refreshed. And there is something on
your mind in a thoughtful kind of way. Gosh, I don't know if I'm
coming through to you. The feeling was induced by the solitari-
ness of my mind and the frustration of hearing human beings
actually enjoying their captivity. You don't even see lions in a
cage at the zoo so ecstatic. We are the smartest creatures on the
Earth and the dumbest and, at times, the most pathetic. And

strangely enough, we're happy only when it's like that. Go figure.

Well, I'm glad to be out of that Hitler jail for real. It was nasty. I'm at an okay place. I promise to try and be a good kid. I can't afford no more trouble.

I love you pal. Good luck in your job search. I think Kamloops is best. Like I said, you look like a gentleman and a scholar, so a college job is most fitting.

King love.

Another letter:

Dear Shawn:

What's up buddy? Well, I'm now in Kansas, writing you from the general population at Leavenworth pen. It's not bad being in GP. There's more to do. But, to be totally honest with you, I like the hole more. Less bullshit and it gives you more time to study, write and exercise. Now they want me to do programs. So I won't have any time for self. I don't know how long I'll last. But I'll give it an honest try.

Well, did you get my paper tissue letter? I hope so. What would you like to know about GP? Do you know anyone in this joint? I read a psychology book called *Lifestyle and Criminal Behaviour* (or something like that.) The guy who wrote it was a psych here named Walters. I wanted to meet him and tell him what I think of his theories. It was kind of accurate – kind of. But he no longer works here. My tough luck!

Did you write me at Jersey? That place sure was the pits. Hey, enclosed is a letter to one of the people you wrote an article about. I reread the article [about a mother whose five-year-old son died of brain tumours] and felt like writing a li'l something of encouragement. Who knows, she might need it. Stuff like that is hard to get over and often can sink a person.

As for me, I'm well. Just figured I'd let you know I'm alright. Alive. Did you get the new job at the college? Did you get the Dad day card? Are you still going to move to Fruitloops? Oops! Sorry.

I think you called it Kamloops. Same thing, I guess. I got a lot of
letters to write, so I'll get back to you. Until then, I'm ghost.
(That's a slang way of saying, "c-ya later.") You take care and
good luck.

Yours, Blaze

I'd sent Blaze a newspaper article I'd written about a mother who
lost her young son, her only child. The boy died at home on Good
Friday with his mother holding his small hand. I had taped the interview and play it sometimes to a journalism class as an exercise in writing an obituary. I watch the eyes of the men and women in the class
grow watery as they listen to the mother. It seems that the power of
words can still affect an open and unjaded heart. The way that Blaze
had expressed himself in letters made me think that the article would
interest him more than what I'd written about crime and prison. It did.
And he surprised me too. He wrote a letter to the woman, which he
asked me to pass along. Here's that letter from a felon:

A while ago an article on your beautiful son was sent to me.
Yes, all the way to the good ol' U.S.A. New York. I read it
entirely and could not suppress a tear from sliding down my
cheek. The story was touching. I was going through my papers
today and saw the article, which I had put away and forgotten
about. I read it again. To my surprise the article touched my
heart just as strongly as it did the first time and I felt obligated
to write and let you know that you have a beautiful son. He was
and still is an angel who carried a deeper message to us all, a
message that eludes us because we are not yet ready to grasp it.
I know with certainty that he is well, very well.

I hope you find comfort in knowing that there is a place where
all souls go, a beautiful place that cannot be explained by those of
us of flesh and bone, but a real place none the less, a glorious
place.

I pray that you've been able to endure and even continue living
your life. I understand that it's not easy. It never is. I'm not sure

if you will ever get this letter. If you get this letter, be advised that there are many who care.

Take care and God bless.

José B. Cruz #14065-074

Leavenworth, Kansas

14   Blessed are the cockroaches

I always liked animals more than humans. I like their independence.

DR. ROSA M. GARRIGA, orangutan vet, Kalimantan

I lay on an iron cot in an old, brick-lined cell thinking about rats. The cell was in Kingston Penitentiary, the oldest federal prison in Canada, with the oldest rat population. Cons always have a story about the wildlife in this joint. "Many times," a con told me, "going to work in the morning, we would see a dead rat on the ground or the floor of the shop building. Usually the rat had its neck ripped open. Some would say it had been attacked by a bat, but I do not know for sure." Another said that cons sometimes chop up pieces of rat and use them to spice the food of people they don't like. Folsom is another joint that gets a high rating on the rat scale. A con told me, "The rats in Folsom would scare the crap out of any cat. I've seen some as large as house cats. They must eat well. Maybe they eat cats." A felon who had travelled from prison to prison in Canada and the United States said, "San

Quentin – rats, bats, everything! Wharf rats, no less. In Canada, I've heard Kingston Penitentiary is the worst."

The old port city of Kingston, on the edge of the natural sewer where Lake Ontario joins the St. Lawrence River, has a thriving underground population of rats who landed by ship years ago. The rats are in the sewers. From time to time they erupt through lawns like groundhogs. When I lived in Kingston I wrote a newspaper story about a rat exterminator who killed thousands of rodents in the city during his career. Rats are a reminder of the limitations of civilization. No matter how hard cities have tried, they've been unable to expunge the rodent. There are fifteen hundred different types around the world, comprising forty per cent of the mammal species, according to rat expert David Alderton. They have endured and prospered in the worst conditions we could create for them – which are also the worst conditions we could create for ourselves. The nasty truth is that the only way to get rid of the rat is to get rid of us. As one con said to me, "The reason we are afraid of rats is because they remind us of ourselves."

So I lay in the cell for my voluntary weekend in federal hell and wondered if the rats would come while I slept. A prison cell makes you vulnerable and a prey to fear. I might die in a fire. I might go mad from hunger. Rats might nibble at my toes. I was thinking about the sound rat feet would make as I fell into the fitful half-sleep dream world of penitentiary steel and stone. Would I be able to hear them? Feel them? I swear that a rat can sense when a person falls asleep. It must be the smell of sleep that attracts them. And yet in the lonely hours of prison some cons welcome the footfall of the rodent. They make pets of rats and mice. They treat them like their children. For others, mice are a distraction. The cons put necklaces on them and tattoo them and give them Mohawk haircuts. They use their skins for crafts.

> Kingston Penitentiary was rat infested. In other words, when you took a shit or a piss, you flushed the toilet first and take a fast shit, 'cause a rat could come up and bite ya in the balls. They would get their pillow when they went to bed and put it on the toilet with some books on top.

A mouse was in the garbage pail in my cell one time. I guess he climbed in and couldn't get out, jumping around. I thought it was a rat. I'm scared of rats, 'cause my mother said they jump at your throat. Holy fuck, I didn't know what the fuck. I kicked the pail over and I'm holdin' my throat and it's a little mouse. I've heard of guys that would get cheese from the kitchen and put it out for a rat. They'd call that their mouse. To amuse themselves.

In Oakalla Prison in Burnaby, British Columbia, there was a drag queen named Donna. Actually, she was cute and she had small breasts and a tight butt. In a dress with makeup, you couldn't tell the difference.

One day Donna was sitting on the toilet and suddenly let out a very loud scream. Everyone thought she was being raped. Four guards went running into her cell. Donna was lying in her bed with her pants down around her knees and a large grey rat was running around her cell. The rat had come up out of the sewer pipe and had bit Donna in the ass. She had to have four stitches.

All of us were scared to sit on the toilets for about two weeks. I myself ended up becoming constipated because I refused to sit on the toilet. I suffered craps, but I figured it was better than getting bitten on the ass by a dirty rat.

In my cell in Kingston Penitentiary rats weren't the only wildlife I had time to think about. Through the window across from my bars I watched the cat that lived inside the prison. In their letters the prisoners wrote stories about this cat, which now seemed like a celebrity to me. It lived under the chapel in the prison and I heard when it had a litter and how it was fed. Then a guard took me for a chilly hour by myself in the small segregation pen in the yard. I positioned myself in the tiny section of the pen where the sunlight penetrated and watched a small bird perch on the razor wire. It ignored the existence of prison walls.

The prisoners filled their letters with stories about snakes and toads, groundhogs and seagulls, and a profusion of insects. I wondered about the psychology of people whose passion for animals exceeds their sensitivity to people. Is it pathology or a deeper human-itarianism? I also noticed that prisoners could write longer and more coherent narratives about the wildlife they saw in prison than other things in their lives. They turned the animals into a prison version of soap operas and old Norse sagas.

When I was in a cell I had a few books to read, as the other prisoners did. But my love of literature faltered in what I thought would be an ideal reading situation. I was hungry to watch something living with a story to tell, to have the material to make a story myself. Prisoners like Ray Medina, "a southern Mexican" in Pelican Bay State Prison in California, find the materials to make their own wildlife stories:

> The exercise yard is nothing but concrete. In the drain I once found a little green tree frog. I was so fucking happy. I brang it in with me in my mouth. Tasted sour. But he became my homie. I called him Ranna ("frog" in Spanish). I built him a little pad out of milk cartons, some melted-down soap and oatmeal for glue. When they would hit my cell I would slide him over to my neigh-bour's cell or I would tie him to a string and let him crawl in my TV. Of course, getting him out took like two hours. But, like I said, he was my homie. When I would go to yard, I caught as many spiders as I could catch and often there was none, so I would feed him rice. In the mornings I would fill up my sink with lukewarm water and let him float and drink till after I'm done with my studies or workout.
>
> I guess I would say that I felt like a bully the first days I had the frog. Kinda like the Cyclops in that movie with that big one-eyed dude, had all them men trapped inside his cave and to get out they had to move this big ass rock. Well, after about a week or so, I think he started feeling comfortable with me. When I would take him out of his house, instead of jumping away he would jump towards me and on top of me. I guess he knew I wasn't gonna hurt him, or her. I even tried to check to see what sex it was. But one can't tell by his genitals, 'cuz they don't have any?

Anyway, we were at one with each other. I think he knew that when my cell door opened he was gonna get fed when I came back from yard. I usta make some long sticks out of newspaper and soap, so I could lure the spiders and insects out of the holes for him to eat. I even had to pay this black inmate for a moth that he caught in his cell. He charged me one cookie and six sheets of writing paper. I paid it, 'cuz I had meat to feed my frog in four days. And guess fucking what? The damn tree frog didn't eat the fuckin' moth. I researched and found that moths have some poison or some shit on their bodies that frogs don't like. Well, it was cool, 'cuz my neighbour brought me a big juicy worm he found.

One day I woke up and didn't find him in his house. I searched the cell and found him behind the sink, next to the door, trying to plan his getaway. I snatched his ass up and discovered that he had somehow squeezed through a very, very small hole. I thought about our relationship and his freedom, so I took him outside with me and let him go. I figure it's no use both of us being locked up. And, if he escapes, at least he'll take a piece of me to the outside world.

From another con, a woman in a prison in Texas:

I asked one of the guys that worked in the fields to see if he could get me a snake. He did. I named the snake Bing and he got quite used to me. He would crawl around in my bunk. I had him about a year, then he started getting too big and I let him go and wished him well.

The biggest thing I noticed about Bing was that he was real smart. I liked watching him and his creativity. That is, he decided that he was not going anywhere soon, so he started making arrangements in his house. He would move the stick to where he wanted it, the grass, and even move his water bowl and the rocks. I had two rocks so that he would sorta feel in the wild. I had one of the rocks at one end and the other at the other end of his box.

Bing moved one of the rocks right beside the other rock. Then I noticed he would crawl between the rocks. It wasn't until a few days later that I discovered what he was doing. He was actually making something to help him shed his skin.

I had to keep him hidden. Some officers did not mind it, but others would cause you trouble. So you learn who to hide him from and who not to. You will always find an officer who loves to cause trouble for the prisoners. It almost seems as though they got picked on all their life and now that they have a little authority behind a locked door they abuse that.

Bing was just great. He was the right size for crawling around in my cell. I would type and my table is right beside my bed and Bing would crawl off the bed and into my lap where he stayed most of the time when I was typing. Sometimes he would even punch a key or two on my typewriter. I suppose he wanted to write some too.

Some prisons tolerate relationships with animals and even have pet therapy programs. The Regional Treatment Centre inside the walls of Kingston Penitentiary had a fish tank. I was told a story about a prisoner there who was upset when a fish died and insisted on taking it to bed with him like a tiny teddy bear. At the maximum-security Saskatchewan Penitentiary in Prince Albert, men have been allowed for years to have aquariums in their cells. "I had one myself and kept goldfish," says a prisoner who was in the Saskatchewan prison in the 1960s. In those days, televisions and radios weren't allowed in the cells. "Having goldfish has a calming effect. I could lie in bed at night and watch them swimming around the tank." Some of the inmates bred fish and sold them. At the former Prison for Women in Kingston dogs were allowed to come inside to visit prisoners. One time a horse was even brought inside. The practice ended after staff complained about the dog belonging to Karla Homolka. The argument was that dogs carry fleas and they get nasty at times. A former prisoner of the now-closed facility wrote of the wildlife and the effect it had:

The girl next to me, she's doing twenty-five years and she's been in and out of prisons all her life. She feeds the squirrels, every day no matter what, from her window. It's amazing to see how gentle they [the inmates] are. There was a girl that was also very institutionalized. She left for out west in the summer and there was a pigeon with a broken wing. This girl would rip your heart out soon as look at you, but she was gentle with this bird with the broken wing. She went out every day and cared for it and fed it.

Wildlife can't be kept out of prison. Creatures find holes and cracks in the walls, and they squeeze and fly and tunnel through to get inside. And so people in captivity can always find an animal. In a penitentiary such as the Chuckawalla Valley State Prison in the California desert there are small rattlesnakes, kangaroo rats and the Chuckawalla lizard. There are the brown recluse spiders, the vinegaroons (whose venom makes you feel like you've tasted vinegar) and other scorpions. The cons catch the scorpions to wager on in fighting matches. In a prison in southern Texas near the Gulf of Mexico, prisoners catch turtles and turn their toilet bowls into temporary aquariums, throwing crickets and June bugs in to watch the turtles eat them. When the doors are left open on hot nights at the Sussex II prison in Virginia, skunks and possums wander into the buildings. A con there says that occasionally someone will throw something at a skunk and stink up the whole cell block. Years ago, Kingston Penitentiary was full of animals. It had a stable for the horses that were used as mounts by the guards. There were hogs and chickens. And there were rats. And where there are rats, there are cats. The cats were said to be down in the sewers with the rats. The cats kept the rats under control, but they were as wild as the rodents. Doug Strain says sparrows flew around inside Kingston Penitentiary. "They flew in and out the range windows and up and down the ranges."

Bats were once plentiful in Kingston, but they disappeared following the reconstruction of the dome after the 1971 riot. Fred Hyatt in Pennsylvania says he kept a pet bat in prison. The bat flew through his open window and used the cell for sleeping during the day. Hyatt fed him insects and fruit. Thomas Bodnar in Folsom kept bats in the maximum-security Tehachapi prison:

> I have been in five different prisons and there have been plenty of wildlife, especially in Old Folsom – bats, owls, cats, frogs, snakes, lizards and birds – all here living among us. Most animals in prison wind up being pets. Only the occasional rat gets mistreated. But the rest are treasured. Old Folsom has a giant vaulted ceiling. The most unusual animal I have seen is a huge barn owl, a white one that nested in the rafters. I have seen him catch a rat.
>
> I have had many pets in my life but none that I will love and remember more than a bat. Birds take a while to domesticate, but a bat, trapped in a cell, has absolutely no fear or apprehension. My cellie, who worked on the yard crew, somehow got hold of a bat for me and brought it in. At one point the bat crawled up me and sounded his echolocation into my ear.

Insects are also a form of entertainment in prison. When my son was small he used ants as an experiment in miniature behaviour. He would interrupt their supply line or circumscribe their universe with an upside-down jar. Then he would come and tell me the story. In the hole, insects supply a miniature life-and-death struggle. They may be the sole connection to a world outside that doesn't think like prison. Mark Fisher, in prison in Detroit, says, "Anything in a cell is welcome – ants, mice, spiders, roaches. Fuck, even a rat. The hole is so isolated it's a time passer just to watch those ants crawl."

A prisoner told me a story about a man in the next cell who made a pet out of a cockroach. The cockroach is blessed among creatures because its sturdy little carapace can survive anything unscathed, from nuclear radiation to a federal penitentiary. The man in the next cell "was convicted of armed robbery and had a large wood roach he trained to come to him and eat from his hand. That love story went flat on one of the rare occasions when a crew came around to spray for roaches and the man with the sprayer stepped on it." In this case the man writing to me was making a story by watching another con making a story with insects.

In a series of letters from a prisoner in Texas I watched a saga unfold that joined human beings and insects in a single drama:

> We have a "pet" black widow spider now. Of course, we are kept separated from her by the window glass, otherwise someone would have killed her by now, even though she never leaves her web and hasn't harmed anyone. Another man and myself have, for the past two months, enjoyed watching her build her maze of webwork, swell with eggs, cocoon them in webbing, and guard the cocoon. The newborn should be emerging anytime now.

Next letter:

> Our black widow spider generated a second cocoon full of eggs about a week and a half ago, then yesterday she opened up the first one, and now there are about two hundred little ones in the web. This morning when I woke up, one of the babies had already built a web in my cell about six inches from my foot. Regretfully, I killed it. That was just too close for peaceful co-existence.

Next letter:

> Our black widow spider seems to have recovered, both from her injuries and from the depression she seemed to suffer for about two weeks after destruction of her web, theft of her cocoon egg, and killing and removal of her babies from her recently hatched brood. The coward who did all that to her never admitted it, I suspect because he was worried about how many of us got mad about it. Anyway, she appears ready now to lay another clutch, but has been delaying. I don't know if she's delaying because of the cool weather or from fear of another attack.

Next letter:

> Nobody was bitten by any of the black widow spiders I
> mentioned. The lady recovered and, in spite of the lateness of the
> season, laid another batch of eggs, and, a month later, she laid
> yet another. Still, the assholes who destroyed the first two
> batches – there were two men involved – came along just before
> time for the third batch to hatch and destroyed all of them again.
> This time they managed to kill the widow too. I would only give
> them a ten per cent chance of living through the next summer.
> They figured they could do whatever they want because the man
> who was caring for her is over sixty and they figure because they
> are big and black, they don't have to worry about him. They
> completely ignore the fact that he is serving two life sentences
> for murder for hire. Besides, he's not the only one who wants a
> piece of that action.

The risks of spider watching are explained from another prison in
Texas:

> Sometimes I keep spiders in a jar. Like a real dumb ass, I had a
> brown recluse spider that I noticed one morning had taken up
> residence in the upper corner of my cell, right above the head of
> my bed. I decided to leave him where he was. My thinking was
> that as long as he stayed out of my bunk, I'd stay out of his corner
> of the ceiling. The arrangement worked just fine until one
> morning I woke up, swung my legs over the side of the bunk, and
> suddenly was dive-bombed by my ungrateful visitor, who
> promptly bit me on the side of the neck. This will wake a person
> up faster than guzzling a gallon of expresso! Well, my neck began
> swelling up, and I was a wee bit concerned, as you can imagine.
> Being locked in an administrative segregation cell all day makes
> it hard to get medical attention at the best of times and, even
> then, unless you're half dead, the best you'll get is a sick-call slip
> to fill out and in a few days will be called out to see the nurse. I

figured that if I was going to get anything done about this spider bite, I'd better do it myself. So I got a razor blade, used it to lance the bite, then began packing a mixture of salt and powdered bleach into the cut. It hurt like hell, but after doing this about ten times nothing was coming out of the wound but blood and it healed up just fine.

Some people need wildlife in their lives and go to unusual lengths to satisfy the urge. In prison that need has a rougher, troubling edge, captured in the ambivalence of a comment I heard about a con who'd befriended a cat in prison. The con said, "They can do anything to me, but they'd better not fuck with my cat." I heard a similar comment about an offender who made pets of squirrels in Kingston Penitentiary. "He was a rotten bastard, but he liked squirrels," said a man in prison with him. The squirrel man could be harsh with his fellow creatures, and yet he cared for small animals, like Robert Stroud, the Birdman of Alcatraz, a psychopathic murderer romanticized by the film with Burt Lancaster.

Keeping a pet in prison is partly a game of wits against the system, but it also makes the prisoners vulnerable to others. Some guards will destroy the contraband pets they find just to be cruel, and prisoners see an opportunity to torment a person through his animals. As a warden I knew in Canada explained: "The trouble was the inmate would keep his pet hidden and then the bonding would get underway. By the time the guard discovered the little monster, be it a mouse, a bird or a cricket, all hell would break loose when the creature was snatched and either released or destroyed."

Those who keep pets also keep it secret as much as possible. Discovery of a pet by a staff member is an instant death sentence for the pet. I strongly suspect the majority of them are very similar to the character of Robert Stroud. To my way of thinking that would just about have to be the case when a man knows that, if discovered, his pet will be brutally murdered, yet he keeps a pet anyway.

The squirrels were loved and welcomed because they were soft, gentle and friendly, which was a direct opposite of the atmosphere in prison. We were always happy to have them around in our cells. And may the gods have mercy on anyone who would harm them, because we wouldn't have. In fact, in '92 there was a guy on lower A who got angry at one of the squirrels – I don't know why – and he threw a full roll of toilet paper at the squirrel. It hit the squirrel, knocking it off the steps. Two inmates instantly jumped him, dragged him into his cell, and beat him – though not too badly, as the guards came running and broke it up. The inmate was locked up for his own protection.

There was a man on this wing once who raised a fledgling bird fallen from its nest. They were great pals. The bird rode everywhere on his shoulder or head, came when he called, and came and went through a window on which the man had loosened the screw. One day, one of the guards stepped on the trusting bird, then picked it up and threw it in the trash can right in front of the man. The man went insane – not, he said, because the guard murdered the bird, but because he threw it in the trash can and wouldn't let the man bury it. We have learned to expect to be murdered by the authorities. The last I heard of the man, he was being transferred to the psychiatric unit, heavily drugged.

Mice are great survivors in prison. They are bought in pet stores and smuggled inside prison, where they multiply and are sold as contraband pets. A con in Missouri told me about the mouse he kept in his cell:

I caught a very young baby mouse. I built him a nice cage out of cardboard and stuff. I'd give him pot by putting him in a plastic bag and blowing smoke into it. He'd become very active and acrobatic then. He liked to play hide-and-seek, but, as soon as night fell, he'd jump out and go prowling. I bathed him regularly in my sink. When I first got him, he once almost drowned. I was trying to get all the dirt residue off him, when he went limp and just floated there like a drowned human. I wanted to give him mouth to mouth, but he came to, and, strange as it then seemed to me, after that moment he stopped biting me. I was sad when I had to leave him. The inmates there would probably kill him. One wanted to eat him. So I just let him go on his own. He had other mouse pals, probably relatives that lived inside an ancient heater across from my cell that would often attempt to come in my cell to hang with him. They would look at me with their beady black eyes as if asking for permission, but they were full of grime. They looked comical. I called my mouse Chocolatito, which means "small chocolate" or "a bit of chocolate" in Spanish.

Some cons become enraptured by the small rodents and breed multitudes of them. Frank Horgen started with the contraband of a single male and female that another con gave him and before he realized it he had a colony of one hundred and thirty. He got them high on hash and weed. They liked it so much they'd climb around his body sniffing and looking in his pockets for the marijuana. The mice brought him peace, he says, and allowed him to forget where he was. Another con talks about his mouse:

> A few years ago I had a pet mouse. I called her T.C. for Terribly Cute. At first I didn't want one, as I associated them with the same league as the dirty, filthy rats infesting this place. But, when a friend of mine put her on my leg and I watched her run and hide under my sweat top, she stole my heart.
>
> Taking her back to my cell I made a temporary home for her using a little box that packages our rolling papers and set about mouse-proofing the cell so she wouldn't wander off. Anything on the floor that I didn't want her to get into was moved or sealed off. Her home eventually became a section of a multidrawer container for nuts, bolts and nails. I made her a wheel out of Q-tips, cardboard and ramps, plus little ramps for her to get up on the desk and bed.

Over time we had a little ritual. At night when the lights went out I'd set up the ramp so she could get up on the bed, which she did immediately. I'd watch her come up at the end of the bed, scoot across the blanket up to my chin, reach up, and grab a Rice Krispie from between my lips. At night, when she wanted to have her ears scratched, she'd crawl up to my ear and nuzzle me until I woke up.

When I would have her in my hand scratching her ears I used to marvel at how tiny she was, especially her paws and the nails at the end of her toes. Ever so small and fragile, yet strong, for the tiny nails would hold her weight even when she was climbing vertically. Just when you thought she'd never be able to get into this or that, surprise, she did.

During lockdowns she kept me company, helping me write my letters while we listened to the music on the stereo. She could even dance. I'd be content to just watch her race on the wheel, going nowhere. Reflecting back on this time I feel she understood when I was feeling down and depressed, because that was when she would be content to lie down between my T-shirt and sweat top, just in the fold at the edge when you're sitting down. It was almost as if she was saying, "I'm here for you. You're not alone," which, until I left, I wasn't.

When I found out I was cleared to move over to c-7 I was happy to go, but saddened by the thought that if I went I couldn't take her with me because anyone caught with mice would be sent back. I cried the night I left c-7 because I missed her and our little ritual.

My friend who gave her to me took her in and, as he had a male, it wasn't too long before she was pregnant. Occasionally I would come back to visit her, but each time my happiness at seeing her was tinged with sadness when I left. Sometimes, when I think about her I wonder if she understood my leaving and why I couldn't take her with me.

One of the first things I am going to do upon my release is to go to a pet store and buy a little female mouse. I'll call her T.C.

Another letter:

> When I was at Laval maximum (St. Vincent de Paul) there was a
> fellow with pet rats. He was about six feet tall but weighed only
> one hundred and fifty pounds. He had shoulder-length light-
> brown hair with a pronounced, receding hairline. He looked
> rather cadaverous and was covered with tattoos. He had them on
> his calves, legs, arms, chest, back, neck, forehead, cheeks, nose,
> eyelids, lips, ears, etc. This is not a guy who will get out and look
> for a job in the local mall as a greeter.
>
> Anyway, Daniel adopted a large Norwegian rat that crawled
> out of his toilet. They became the best of friends. The rat went
> everywhere Daniel did, perched on him like a parrot. It eventu-
> ally had a litter and Daniel raised them also.
>
> At mealtime the tiers and ranges would be opened one at a
> time to pick up a tray of food which was shoved at you through a
> slot in a wall. You would then carry it back to your cell.
>
> Daniel, usually wearing shorts and no shirt, would line up for
> his tray with half a dozen rats clinging to him. The rats would
> scamper down his arms onto the tray to start supper as he
> returned to his cell. What a sight, a mobile meal composed of
> tattoos, tray and rats.

Before I slept in a cell in Kingston Penitentiary I met a prisoner there who I would learn had a phobia about rats. Rats were a dark episode in his journey through life. He was born to a prostitute, used by her and abused sexually. "My mother was a drug addict and a prostitute, and she found out that I could be used to make money for her. Most of this took place at night, so, of course, darkness caused pain and fear in me. Add to this being locked up in closets and cupboards and I think you may be able to see how darkness became such a source of pain and fear for me. It was later when I came to understand and learn that I could control my feelings in the darkness." He used drugs and drank and lashed out at those he associated with his mother, women who were prostitutes and drug addicts. After three attacks, both physical and sexual, he was declared a dangerous offender.

When I met him inside Kingston Penitentiary I was intrigued by his love of nature even inside a stone tomb like that prison. The rat operated as a kind of psychic avenger in his life, a Greek fury that didn't listen to compassion or reason. Here's a saga of rats and other wildlife written by a man in prison, stitched together from several letters:

The first time I had a run-in with a rat was in Toronto when I was in Grade 4. That would make me nine years old at the time. One weekend a few of my friends were playing in a neighbour's yard. The three of us tried to catch a rat. We managed to corner it and it had no place to run – or so I thought. The little fellow saw what he thought was an opening, but it was the bottom of my pants. The rat ran full speed up my pants. Instantaneously I started what was to become known as dancing the Jerk. I was hopping around shaking my leg and holding my pants, trying to get the little critter out. I thought he might take a bite out of something he shouldn't. He finally came out and scurried away. I haven't thought about that for years, but I think it did have a bearing on future events.

Years later I was in Florida. I had run away at seventeen and worked my way down to Florida with truck drivers. I would load and unload trucks heading south. Each time a driver had gone as far south as he was going, he would get on the cb radio and find me another ride and more work. It was a rather good trip in all. I made some money and saw a lot of the United States in the process. It took me three weeks to make the trip, but it was some trip.

In Florida, I soon ran out of money and was living on the beaches, in beach shacks. I could get work every day I wanted, cleaning yards, watching property and so on. Since I was not an American citizen, I could not work per se, but had to find cash jobs. Almost every night there were parties on the beach. Beer was cheap and food was plenty, so things were not that bad.

One day I guess I had a little too much to drink at one of these parties and wandered off down the beach and fell asleep in the tall beach grass. Much later – I am not sure of the time – I was wakened up by a strange feeling. At first, I was not sure what it was, but I soon became aware. I had no feelings or sense of what was happening. Then I opened my eyes and saw, not more than an inch from my eyes, a giant black rat. Then I saw that my whole body was covered in rats, about twenty ocean-type rats eating away at my clothes and running all over me. Terror engulfed me. I soon became aware that the rats had eaten through my clothes. I had gloves on, and they had eaten the fingers out of the gloves. All I could do was yell and run, shaking and pulling the creatures off me. Talk about moving quickly. I was out of there. It took me a good five or six hours to calm down. Each time after that when- ever I saw a rat I was paralyzed with fear and relived the night on the beach. I still cringe to this day when I see rats. So a lot of time at the prison was spent in a deep-rooted fear which had nothing to do with the prison itself.

A few years after I was in a jail in Thunder Bay and I went back to school, a science teacher noticed I wouldn't go near the cages with the rats and froze when I saw others handling and playing with the little critters. He took his time with me and talked to me and for the first time I told the story about the ocean rats and the rat in Toronto. In time he was able to get me to play with one of the lab rats. The rat would run around the table and up my arm and sit on my shoulder. She was a white female with red eyes. After months of this I reached the point where I was playing with all the lab rats. This process helped me greatly, but not totally. Whenever I saw a rat, wild and loose, my skin would still crawl, and I would be guarded.

In prison, in Kingston Penitentiary, there are rats. I was on the very top floor, the fourth, and I only saw one or two on the lower floors, but not on top. One day they started exterminating in the basement and the lower floors and, of course, the rats went to the top floors. I started to see them on the third floor. When I saw them, I would have great trouble falling asleep and, when I did sleep, it was troubled by nightmares of the past.

Since then, I have come to understand the little fellows a little more. If one is around, I just let it be and it lets me be. I came to understand that the first rat in Toronto acted out of fear and the ones in Florida, well, that was just their nature. I was in their place. I was an intruder.

When I was a child animals seemed to know it was safe to be around me and some even went out of their way to protect me. I was drawn to the woods at a very early age, at twelve and thirteen. I would go out into the bush and soon I found rivers, creeks and wild life. I would be the great white hunter tracking down the animals. I had a little air gun which I used to hunt the birds and animals.

Then I ran across some hunters who had a number of kills in front of them – deer, bear and other animals. I saw their lifeless bodies in front of me and started crying. The animals, much like myself and my birth mother, were hunted and overpowered by a force greater than themselves. I spent many hours in the same woods, but this time it was different. I had a common bond with the creatures. I would sit for hours by a little fire and eat my lunch. In time, the little creatures started to come closer, the squirrels and the chipmunks. The birds would come nearer to eat the scraps I would bring. I went to the grain mill one day and bought some mixed seed and set up a little feeding area where I spent most of my time. I would sit as still as possible and watch the animals. After four months, I had my own little zoo. The animals knew I would do them no harm. I wouldn't take children or other people there. It was my place.

I would sit for hours watching them and feeding them. In time it was like I was just one of them. They were giving me a natural peace I did not have in my life. As a child I had a hard childhood. I was assaulted in every way known to man. As such, I think the animals knew that there was something wrong and, in their own way, took to me, for they sensed something such as pain.

There was an old couple who lived in Jackson's Point who had an old St. Bernard. This old fellow had no teeth. One day the couple called me to their front porch and asked if I would like to take their dog for a walk. I said okay. No leash was needed. The old fellow just followed me no matter where I went.

I took him down to the lake for a swim. Well, at least, that was the idea I had. He had a drink, looked at me like I was nuts, and just sat there until I got up to leave. As I was leaving there was a couple of local bullies heading our way. I hoped to just walk by, but they had other ideas. They started to get aggressive and the dog got rather aggressive toward them, without actually biting, which would have been hard since he had no teeth. But they did not know that. Now, what was rather special about all of that was that this was the first time that the two of us, the dog and me, were together. We never knew each other and yet he protected me and knew something was wrong.

Then I had my own dog. Well, not really my own dog, just one in the area that seemed to have no owner. He would follow me around. Of course, I could not have a dog of my own at home, so he would meet me outside the door each morning and walk me home each night. We spent a lot of time in the bush around Jackson's Point. I would chase the animals around in the woods like most dogs would just for fun. In time, I would just sit around and let everyone be.

I worked in the United States with an uncle who owned midways. We travelled all over the east coast of the States. He had many animal acts with his show. Unlike most people, Uncle Bob did not have dogs, but rather cats to guard and protect his trailer and money. Yes, cats – a tiger, a leopard and a lion, who all lived together chained to the motorhome when we were not around.

Then there were the elephants. I spent some time with the beast and her little one. The two of them would tag me when I cooked outside, one keeping me busy while the other one stole fruit and vegetables.

One night I had too much to drink and when I made it back to the fairgrounds the baby elephant was up and trying to get to me for some attention. So I got into the pen with them and the mother was not sure what was going on and got a little aggressive with me. Elephants should be wrestlers for the move she pulled on me. The mother took her trunk and put it around my neck and, at the same time she slammed me to the ground, lifted her leg to hit me with her knee on the way down. I was able to get away, but I saw stars for a few hours. The next day it was as if nothing had happened. I went near the beast and her child with no problems. Who knows, maybe the alcohol in my system changed my odour or something.

The only time this sort of thing [abuse from the mother] was not happening was in the woods or out in nature. That was my escape and only escape. My only friends were animals. I talked to no one nor trusted anyone. Very early in life I discovered many animals would come to me and trusted me. Birds, deer, raccoons, chipmunks, squirrels, just about all. Even fish would play with me. This went on for years, until I was about fifteen or so.

At this time my aunt and uncle took me out of that situation. But it was too late. I was really screwed up by that time.

15   Mirth in misery

It's the second law of thermodynamics: Sooner or later everything turns to shit.

WOODY ALLEN

The longer the road, the more necessary it is to have some laughs along the way. That's true of prison as well as the ordinary preoccupations of our lives. I don't mean to imply that prison is funny, though. Only that humour can be found even in the midst of misery. It's an idea I found in Dante when he exited from the lowest rung of hell and found everything upside down. That's humour. Anybody who thinks there aren't any laughs in hell hasn't been there. I think of what happens when the writer Kurt Vonnegut, a later Cervantes, makes me laugh when I don't want to. A prison humorist would say the same thing but more ruthlessly. As a con told me from his cell in Detroit, "Shit rolls downhill – and we live in the valley." Some prisoners have learned to survive in the valley by turning shit into laughter. I knew a con who wrote satire in prison through an underground newsletter he called *The Bullshitter*. The newsletter mocked the administration heartlessly. It earned him an official reprimand in his offender's file. He was probably the funniest felon in the Canadian prison system – and one of the most reviled. He used humour in a situation where he had no power. When I read the pranks in the letters I receive from prison I laugh and then I wonder why I laugh. The brutality of humour in the penitentiary reminds me of *Don Quixote*. Cervantes, who may have learned about laughter from his time in a cell, referred to his book as "a child born in prison." Jailhouse humour has a bitter edge to it, but it also has a logic. I've tried to capture this by grouping it into simple penal formulas to illustrate the nether end of human nature. May you laugh when you don't want to.

STATE OF WASHINGTON
DEPARTMENT OF CORRECTIONS

OFFENDER COMPLAINT

CHECK ONE: ☒ INITIAL GRIEVANCE, ☐ EMERGENCY GRIEVANCE, ☐ APPEAL TO NEXT LEVEL

RESIDENTIAL FACILITIES: Send all completed copies of this form to the Grievance Coordinator. Explain what happened, when, where, and who was involved or which policy/procedure is being grieved. Be as brief as possible but include the necessary facts. A formal grievance begins on the date the typed grievance forms are signed by the coordinator. Contact a staff member to report an emergency situation or to initiate an emergency grievance. Please attempt to resolve all complaints through appropriate staff before initiating a grievance.

NAME: LAST	FIRST	MIDDLE	DOC NUMBER	LOG I.D. NUMBER
NELSON	MICHAEL	ROGER	908546	

PROGRAM ASSIGNMENT	WORK HOURS	FACILITY/OFFICE	UNIT/CELL
MILLWRIGHT I	8-3³⁰ M-Sa	CBCC	CE07

COMMUNITY SUPERVISION: Send all completed copies of this form directly to: Grievance Program Specialist, Offender Grievance Program, Department of Corrections, P.O. Box 41129, Olympia, WA 98504-1129

MAILING ADDRESS: STREET OR P.O. BOX	CITY, STATE	ZIP CODE	TELEPHONE NUMBER

I WANT TO GRIEVE: REMOVAL OF THE RULE BOOKS FROM THE DUTY OFFICES: IF I AM CHARGED WITH AN INFRACTION, I NO LONGER HAVE THE OPPORTUNITY TO CONSULT THE RULE BOOKS SO THAT I MAY ADEQUATELY DEFEND MY POSITION. CURRENTLY, IF I FILE AN APPEAL, I CANNOT CONSULT THE RULES. I HAVE 24 HOURS TO FILE THE APPEAL. I ALSO CANNOT GET TO THE LAW LIBRARY IN THAT TIME.
I HAVE WRITTEN A KITE TO C.U.S. BOE, 1½ WEEKS AGO, ASKING WHAT ALLOWANCE TO APPEAL WILL BE MADE, IF WE FIRST NEED TO GET TO THE LAW LIBRARY TO CONSULT THE RULES. I'VE RECEIVED NO RESPONSE.

SUGGESTED REMEDY: I REQUEST UP TO DATE WAC'S, FIELD INSTRUCTIONS, AND P.O.R.'S BE MAINTAINED IN EACH UNIT, UNTIL THEN, I ASK THAT WE BE GIVEN EXTENSIONS TO APPEAL UNTIL 24 HOURS AFTER OUR FIRST LAW LIBRARY VISIT. DUE PROCESS REQUIRES THESE REMEDIES.

MANDATORY SIGNATURE: Michael R Nelson DATE: 9/30/00

GRIEVANCE COORDINATOR'S RESPONSE

LOCATION CODE	DATE RECEIVED	LOG I.D. NUMBER
CBCC1130	10/2/00	0020841

Your complaint is being returned because:
☐ It is not a grievable issue.
☐ You requested to withdraw the complaint.
☒ You failed to respond to callout sheet on 10/3/00.
☐ The formal grievance/appeal paperwork is being prepared.

☐ The complaint was resolved informally.
☐ Additional information and/or rewriting is needed. (See below.) Return within five (5) days or by:
Due Date:

EXPLANATION: _____

	INITIAL COMPLAINT OBTS INFORMATION					DATE OF RESPONSE	COORDINATOR'S SIGNATURE
TYPE	CATEGORY	AREA	SPEC	REMEDY	RESOLUTION		
01	02	803	005	08	07 / 07	10/2/00	Akyens

DOC 05-165 (3/99) OCO

DOC 550 100

⊗ **Use humour to relieve the tedium.**

In prison, those who can't laugh are condemned to be a joke. A con in Texas says his nickname in the joint is "Trouble" because of his pranks:

I'd write up a letter as though a woman had wrote it. Then fix up the letter as though it were being mailed to a guy down the run. When the officer comes to pass out the mail and he gives me my mail, I tell him, "Oh, hold on officer. This one isn't mine." And I hand him the one I have fixed up. The officer thinks he made a mistake and takes the letter down to the guy. The guy will get the letter thinking he got a letter from some rich beautiful woman who wants to marry him. When he starts telling people about the letter, we all start laughing. Then we tell him over the run what we did, which leads him to being quite embarrassed for falling for it. All he had to do was look and notice it had no official postmark.

After work we go straight to the shower before heading back to the cellblock. Well, one day while we are at work I notice this guy's soap dish sitting next to his other shower stuff at the desk. His soap was brand new, still in the paper wrapper. So I took it while he was not looking. I went back to my desk, which has lots of office supplies. I carefully opened the soap wrapper and I used clear tape to tape up the soap. I taped it up completely. You could not see the tape since it was clear. I then put the soap back in the wrapper and sealed it up and placed it back in his dish. He never knew it was gone. Now, when we shower about thirty of us are herded in and we have about five minutes to shower before the water is turned off. So, at the end of the night, I tell our bosses who watch us shower to keep an eye on Ponce. So they are, "Like why?" I say, just watch him, and I tell them what I did. So me and Ponce and a few guys are all showering at the same post. I was trying to keep from laughing as Ponce unwraps his soap and begins trying to lather up. He scrubs and scrubs and puts more water on, but no soap is lathering up. He would look at the soap and put more water on and keep trying. No suds! We all start laughing and he says, "My soap isn't working!" Then he takes a closer look and realizes what happened. He starts frantically trying to untape it all the while saying, "One of you go down! I'm going to get one of you!" The whole shower is laughing at Ponce, bosses and all. So, just

as he starts to lather up, the water turns off. No shower for
Ponce. Full of soap, he had to get out and wipe off the soap with
a towel.

José Cruz in Leavenworth likes humour. It is a language that we use
to communicate with each other. I doubt if we could communicate as
well as we do if we were serious all the time. He is one of the great
pranksters of the joint.

There's a simple prank which we do here, which I did to my
neighbour this morning. He's got the habit of asking me what
they give me for breakfast every damn morning, I guess to make
sure they ain't forgetting anything. So today I said, "Orange juice,
toast, coffee, eggs and bread." So he said, "Fuck, man, I knew
they forgot something" and starts hollering and cursing for the
officer. The officer comes over pissed. "Yeah, what's your
problem?" "My problem," says my friend, trying to be sophisti-
cated, "is that in the process of doing your duty for this country,
you forgot to give me juice." "What juice?" the officer yells,
cutting him off. "You ain't special. No one got juice" and storms
away. I don't think that dude will ask me tomorrow what we got.
It's already nighttime and he still hasn't spoken to me.

One time a Spanish guy who spoke no English came to our
gallery. He was dying to smoke a cigarette, so he asked another
Spanish guy in Spanish. The guy answers, "I don't got none, but
call our black brother on the first gallery under us. He's got
smokes. He'll give you some." "What's his name?" says the
Spanish guy. "Take-it-out," says the dude seriously, which
means "show your cock." So the Spanish guy starts yelling out of
his bars, "Oh, Take-it-out, Oh, Take-it-out, I need a cigarette."
We was all dying on that one.

Another time Cruz conceived a joke for a man who farted too much:

The guy I had next to me would fart all day long. I'm talking about unbelievable trumpets that would rattle my bed. He would tell me and the nurse, or anyone else who would listen, that his stomach was exploding, and he was serious. He was a real hypochondriac. He thought he had every disease in the book – AIDS, herpes, syphilis, shingles, the bubonic plague. But each time he'd take a test it was found negative. Then he started seeing things on his dick. So I told him he might have genital warts. So he went to the doctor and showed her his penis. She couldn't find nothing and told him so. "Look closer," he says. She looks closer. "I still don't see nothing," she says. So he comes back upset because he knows he's got it. So I mentioned "microscopic warts." Now he's going around talking about how he's got "invisible warts." He's a cool guy, too. He's the only one I know who took an AIDS test and came back mad because he didn't have it.

Thomas Bodnar in Folsom cites some pranks:

Pranks in prison are a way of life. As far as I know, no one has ever retaliated violently, only by doing a prank back. We once turned a staffer's desk around and put his stuff on the desk forward. He at first thought we took his desk drawer knobs, then realized the damn desk was backwards! The confusion before he figured it out was priceless. We once sent a note to the doctor about some dude saying he could not stop masturbating and needs help. We almost got him into deep trouble. He was called to see the psych. Someone once put in a request in my name to have a tooth pulled. Imagine the look on his face when I came back with a tooth pulled. He just about crapped his pants. I was silently suffering a toothache and needed one pulled. A neat coincidence.

We once made memos in Tehachapi max saying in January all hair must be cut off. So people cut their hair off. My cellie was a clerk, so he had access to the official memo sheets. There was no retaliation. Their fault for being gullible. We did another one

saying all cells must be neat, beds made every morning or disciplinary action will be taken. People filed grievances against it. It
was funny. Everyone bought that one. Allowing people to believe
stupid shit is one of the most frequent pranks. For example,
there's a rumour that San Quentin is closing down, salt air eating
the prison. I hear people convince themselves the place is
closing. But I just fuel the rumour. So, anytime someone
misguides himself I just agree with his disillusion and send him
on his merry way.

Roger Caron, who spent time in Kingston Penitentiary, writes about
an incident where the chief keeper of the joint realized that the cons
were making homebrew in a large old fire extinguisher. The officer
thought he'd play a joke on the cons. He let them make booze, but with
a chaser. He slipped a strong laxative into the mixture. The inevitable
happened and he had a big laugh. This kind of prank is endemic in
prison. It combines the oral with the urinal, in what I like to call the
orinal. Here's some more wit from Kingston Pen:

An ex-homosexual that hangs around with a group known as the
Hillbilly Crew in Kingston Penitentiary says that it is the context
of a relationship which makes the difference between a joke or
an insult. The ability to accept pokes in sensitive areas is a sign
of a bond of friendship, he says. This is our way of showing
acceptance and caring. It lets others know that we are always
there to back one another up in the event of an external problem
and that we are a group that will also stick together.

When I first met the main "hillbilly" I was working in the
kitchen and I was sitting at the back table. He walked up to me
and said that this was his table and that I was more than welcome
to have the seat I was sitting in. He told me there were a few
conditions. The last one was no fags. I sat there for a moment in
shock not knowing if I should decline the offer of the chair and
avoid a conflict, or if I should reveal myself and allow him to
make a choice of his own. I chose to be honest and he told me

that he already knew. It was a way of finding out whether or not he wanted to do his time with me. Now we are the best of friends and there is nothing that we will not do for each other.

We also play on the paranoia of those that we hang with. One day the Kid was at one of his programs and we thought that we would have a little fun with him. After he returned home, he found a note in his cell that said we knew where he was and we knew what he had done. No signature, no traceable handwriting. The Kid freaked. He searched his cell high and low. Watching him get upset over nothing at all was funny in itself and so was the time when we finally did get around to actually telling him that it was us. Yet, if someone who I was not close with tried to do something like that to me, I would have no choice but to end the insult for what it was. In the States, when you are doing time, reaching for a cigarette in another man's shirt pocket either says friend or foe. If you are tight with the guy, then it is okay. If you are not, then it is a punk off and the two of you have a problem.

I am the type of person who can enjoy a practical joke if it has some thought and intelligence involved. One day I returned from a visit and found that my cell had been tee-peed with fifteen rolls of toilet paper and I was not impressed. Basically just an overblown classic. The future victims wasted no time in letting me know that it was them and I set about to pay them back in a manner that I felt was a tribute to my intellect. I took one of my old radios, rewired it, added a light bulb, and hung it inside a toilet bowl in a cell. I arranged the electrical cord so that when a person sat down, the wires would touch and provide power. At this time the cells were fairly dark and this guy had a habit of living in darkness. In he walks after a hard day at work and no sooner does he get home than he needs to relieve his bowels. Down come his pants to his ankles and he lowers himself on the throne. A bright light went on between his legs and a loud voice started to yell, "Hemorrhoid alert! Hemorrhoid alert!" He flew off the can, landed on the ground curled up in a ball, and screamed. I laughed and knew I had won and that he would not try to return the favour.

Our jokes have a tendency to be a little more perverse than what you may hear on the outside. What is the difference between a terrorist and a woman on PMS? You can negotiate with a terrorist. Did you hear about Robbie Knevil's new stunt? He's going to drive through Newfoundland dressed as an altar boy. What do you call the balls on a queer? Mud flaps.

⊗   **Use humour to test mettle.**

Prison humour is part initiation rite, part intelligence test. It's a battle of wits. A typical prank is to booby-trap a cellmate's locker by tying everything to the door with strings. When the cellmate opens the door, all his things come crashing down on him. Another prank, which I got from a con in Soledad prison, is to put clear plastic wrap over a mirror in a cell so that your nearsighted cellmate thinks his eyesight is deteriorating. Since prison is a place of bureaucracy and paperwork par excellence, cons invent fake forms to sign people up for fishing trips or Easter egg hunts. "You'd be surprised how many signatures you get," says a con. Another prank is to tell a new con to push the button by the wall speaker to the guard post and ask for the elevator door to be opened. The con does that and hears the guards laughing at him. Carl Horne from prison in Texas explains a prank once used repeatedly for new cons:

> Several years ago the commissary sold small immersion water heaters [an electric coil plugged into a socket] for instant coffee and food, which we called "stingers." A common prank was to send the "newboot" to test the water to see if it's getting hot. We'd tell him to go stick his finger in the water and see if it was getting hot. What he didn't know, though he quickly learned, was that the water had an electric current running through it. It would knock him on his ass while the entire dayroom busted out laughing. Thinking back on it, I'm surprised no one ever got hurt by

this. Imagine getting a wet rag and sticking it into an electric socket. They were definitely shocked at how hot the water was.

A con in prison in Illinois likes the mail pranks typical of some prisoners. For instance, prisoners will put a straight con on the mailing list for a gay publication.

The extent of my pranks has been to send in another man's name to one of these nocturnal enuresis or bedwetting foundations and watch his face when he keeps getting these letters in the mail that advertise on the envelope for bedwetters.

And . . .

Yes, there are the usual pranks, like putting five gallons of pure hot sauce in the officer's vat of chili to commemorate Cinco de Mayo (a celebration of Mexican independence on the fifth of May). Or the inmate who would gross out newbies by standing outside the chow hall and biting a live rat's head off, and then commence to eat the rest of it. (This was back in the early eighties. He hasn't done that for a while.)

Another prisoner explains simple pranks:

You fill up a garbage bag of water and you place it under the mattress of the top bunk and when it's time for bed, it's time for a shower. The weight busts the bag. Another prank is you place the name and number of an inmate and tell the nurse he needs an enema. Since the medical kite is in his name and all, and the nurse comes around with that glove. An inmate will drop his pants and take it, only to find out days later that it ain't routine.

Here's an example of using humour to initiate cons, as Ty Midgette of Attica prison explains in a story about a jail where blacks and Latinos got along well.

Tito, who was the head of the Latinos, comes to me and says, "Yo, Ty, I got this new Latino who just came in. Everybody says he's tough. I want to see how tough he is." So, Tito goes on, "I want you and your boys to pretend like y'all have a beef with him." I say okay. I get four of my boys and wait in the back. I see Tito talking to this new Latino. Tito is saying in Spanish, "Hey, do you know those black guys? Did you have any trouble or beef with them?" This guy is looking toward the back at us. I tell my boys look mean, look tough. So the guy starts walking toward the back where we were. He asks, "Wassup, mon?" I ask him questions about the other jails he's been in. He says, "Yes, I've been in that jail." I yell, "That's the motherfucker, get him," and start moving toward the guy. This guy took off like a bat out of hell for the front door. We all burst out laughing. Tito comes toward me saying, "He's pussy. The guy is at the door. The door won't open." He turns around and sees everybody laughing. He comes back, starts smiling like what's going on here. Tito explains to him that we do this to all newcomers. So we all shake hands and had a good laugh.

A variation of the rite-of-passage prank:

The most famous jailhouse prank is called "a blanket party." When a fellow prisoner reaches his release date, a blanket party takes place with the departing inmate being the guest of dishon-our. A blanket is thrown over the inmate and a good ole-fash-ioned spanking (or whipping) occurs. In the more extreme cases, the inmate experiences difficulty walking because of hits to his legs. So he hobbles out of the institution. The ritual is supposed to remind the inmate of the prison experience. I believe it is the party-givers way of venting stress. Without a doubt no one will know when I reach my release date.

To defeat boredom and create entertainment, cons and guards push language to absurd limits. They engage in ironic conversation. They exchange primal wit. "Some guys humour themselves when they take a shit and yell they're feeding the warden as they flush the toilet."

⊗   **Anything sexual is funny.**

People expend a lot of energy trying to hide their sexual inclinations, with hilarious consequences. Sex is a constant source of amusement.

Most youngsters can't stand to be sex played. We just had this happen a few days ago. A young man, twenty-one years of age, had his towel and boxers taken from the shower and he didn't want to come out of that shower for nothing. He was holding a washcloth over his private parts (his dick) so no one would see it. Us old-timers don't care. We will walk down the run naked with nothing to worry about. A youngster is scared to death.

Another prank happened a few weeks ago at visitation. I walked up to a friend of mine and acted as if I were gay in front of his girlfriend. I asked him who he was cheating on me with. It gave us a big laugh. Sex play is the biggest prank that goes on around here.

One guy was telling me how he knew of a homosexual prisoner who was led on to believe that a guy wanted to have sex with him. Then the guy rubbed Ben Gay on the poor guy's sphincter. Ouch. I was told that the homo danced and screamed and rubbed and all that. The thing is, the more you move and sweat, the more it burns. It was kind of cruel, but what the heck. That shows the guy not to give his ass to just any Tom, Dick or Harry.

Another prank I heard of was also in solitary confinement. One of the guys told his neighbour, "Hey, that nurse is a real freak. She loves to eat." That means to watch guys naked or masturbating. He went on to explain how he does it every morning by telling her his illnesses, whipping out his member and jerking off and how she would stand there watching, enjoying, and wait till he finishes. Well, of course, the neighbour decided to try it. The next morning the nurse came by on her sick call run. But when he pulled out his boner with a smile, she was not happy. She began to scream, "Put that away. Put that away," as if he had a weapon in his hand. The guy exposing himself was baffled. He was whispering, "Shhh. What are you doing?"

Four inmates held down one inmate and wrapped him in a chain. They then lifted him with a power hoist until he was dangling in the air. One inmate pulled the hanging inmate's pants down, boxers and all, and held his legs while the others, using automotive grease, greased the inmate's butt cheeks. He freed himself when they were attempting to insert the hose. Usually the pranks I see consist of grease in the pants or the shoes. Did the individual retaliate? Yes, in his own way. He waited until one of the guys was under a truck and dropped a wrench on his head through the engine compartment.

Here's one from a prison dorm in Kentucky:

There was this fag, some young white kid, had this so-called date with a fairly large black inmate. Well, it was late at night, so the kid got out of his bunk and made his way to the black guy's bed. You could hear them talking softly. He was telling him to go ahead and suck his prick. Well, the young fag wasn't really all together in the head anyway. About fifteen minutes into the sex the young kid said, "Testing, testing. Is this thing on? Hello! Hello! Can anyone hear me? Houston, we have a problem." Of course, pretty much the entire dorm burst out laughing, which brought in the guards yelling at everyone to shut up and go to sleep.

⊗   **Dire circumstances call for dire jokes.**

To probe deeper into the deep-shit principle, consider those in the penitentiary system who take bodily wit to the extreme.

In these prisons in New York we have professional shit-slingers. They call it "busting the cup." You'll find guys bragging, "Man, I bust my cup," and they're serious too. I don't do it. Never did. But you got experts who can make it reach thirty feet with spray action from squeeze shampoo bottles. It's usually done in the solitary confinement areas where inmates can't reach each other. At times there's an argument and one guy would get so offended that he'd bust his cup. Sometimes the victim will take it as a loss. But other times it goes on to a full-scale shit war. For instance, me and you got a beef. Well, if I go to the shower, I'll pass by your cell and whack you, or vice versa. Where can you run? Now they got it like that in South Port Correctional Facility, which is an entire prison for solitary confinement. Everyone that goes to the shower must use a rolling fibreglass shield that blocks his whole body so that he won't get shit down when passing all the other cells. Remember, these are barred cells, which makes shit-flinging easy.

Officers and snotty nurses get it the most. They get it soooo much that the state of New York is now giving new court charges and additional jail time if you hit any staff with feces. The reason why they get shit down is because officers and nurses love disrespecting prisoners that cannot get to them. So they get shitted on. And then there are some inmates that just do it for fun. Just recently two officers here got shitted on and these cells have a sliding iron door with a food slot in the middle of it. The inmate said, "C.O. [corrections officer], let me talk to you," and the officer opened up the slot and caught it as he put his face on view, all over the face and in the mouth. The next day the same guy caught another victim. Now all the officers knew not to open his slot. But the law library guy fell for the oldest trick in the book. The guy in the adjoining cell said, "Hey, my neighbour got some books for you." I heard a momentary pause as the officer considered his situation. He knew the kid was a shitter, but he had to pick up the books – or so he thought. He must have rationalized, "Nah, the kid won't shit me down. He already shit the guy he did not like and I ain't done nothing to him." And when he opened up the slot, pow, he was caught. All we heard the officer say was, "Oh, he got me." No shit, Sherlock.

Even the officers play that crazy game. One group of officers got tired of this one slinger and started filling up a bucket with shit. Then all the officers took turns busting their cup. Crazy. I bet the guy felt real shitty then.

This jail stuff is like a whole other world, a diverse culture, a subculture. The police here become just as evil and spiteful as the prisoners. But, as in regular good and bad, you can tell the difference. Slimeballs, freaks, perverts and whatnot, they give themselves away by their actions. The perverts we call "hot pockets" because they walk around with holes in their pockets and every time they see a female officer or civilian, their hands go into their pockets and they start jerking off. No joke. I saw one guy get pat-frisked by a female officer. He had purposefully got himself hard, and when she touched his side pocket, she said, "What's that?" "What's what?" the guy responded, hands still on the wall. "This," she said, digging into his pocket and grabbing his brown dick. And, when she realized what it was, she screamed, "Oh, my god, you dirty fuck." Now that's funny.

⊗   **Use humour to discipline and correct.**

From a prisoner in San Diego:

I worked as a diesel mechanic in an automotive refurbishing prison enterprise. One person had a bad habit of "sex playing" people by making off-colour jokes and comments, grabbing butts and crotches, throwing cold water on people while they were urinating in the stalls, etc. One day, everyone on his crew in the woodworking shop had enough. They acquired a mechanic's creeper (used to scoot under cars and trucks) from our shop and rolls of tape from the paint preparation shop. His crew grabbed him and promptly taped his ankles together. Then the guys relieved him of his shirt and taped his hands together behind his back. Then they carried him to the creeper and laid him down, unfastened his pants, and yanked his trousers to his shins, fully exposing him. With a running start, they rolled him onto the open paved area. The creeper rolled downhill toward an observation tower for about sixty metres before it stopped. He just had to lay there – out in the open and fully exposed – by himself until the tower officer called to make someone go out and untape him. He never "sex played" anyone again.

A prisoner in a supermax prison in California used a prank to awaken remorse:

There were four cells on my tier. We had individual heat sensor switches in our cells to operate our lights. For some reason from cell one I could also control cell four's light. They move a guy in there who just committed a double murder. I tell him, "Look buddy, that cell is haunted. A guy hung himself in there two months ago and his ghost has been in there ever since." So, later the next day I start playing with his light. I tell him it must be the ghost. We are all locked down and cannot see into each other's cell. The guy is kinda weirding out, but he is not going for the ghost story hook, line and sinker, yet. I say, "Let's have a séance." I speak to the "evil spirits," ask them to do us no harm, and say that they can answer our questions by turning the light off for yes and turning it on for no. We ask the ghosts many questions and they answer them all. The guy is down there trembling when I answer yes to the question, "Are you the spirit of the guy Joe murdered?" Then he was more fearful yet when I answered yes to "Have you come back to seek revenge on Joe?" The guy is now swearing that his cell is possessed. I write a note to the night duty guard and ask him to play along by flushing Joe's toilet from behind the wall. I ask the spirit, "If you've come back to kill Joe for killing you, give us a real strong sign by flushing his toilet." Everybody is quiet and listening. After about ten seconds we hear Joe's toilet flush. That's it. He's on the door screaming for the guards to get him outta there – and make it quick. The guy does not quit screaming and kicking at the door until they come and move him away from the ghosts.

⊗ Watch out for the joker, life.

Life has a wicked sense of humour. Here's a note on that from old-style con Timothy Crockett in a federal joint in Atlanta, Georgia:

> I was taking college courses at Central Correctional Institution in Columbia, South Carolina (an extremely violent and old prison now closed except for a museum). There was a convict – can't remember his name, but his nickname was Bam Bam – who graduated with a B.A. while I was there. This guy had raped and murdered a young lady in Columbia while driving a prison work-release van. He was sentenced to the electric chair. While he was on Death Row, a famous prison preacher converted ol' Bam Bam and somehow assisted him legally and got Bam Bam's death sentence overturned. Well, a few years later, while we were doing time together, ol' Bam Bam was sitting on the stainless steel shit jacket in his cell repairing his TV. ZAPP! Killed the shit out of Bam Bam. He avoided ol' Sparky just to electrocute his stupid ass on a toilet. Fuckin' ironic to the limit.

⊗ And lastly, a couple of summary pranks.

The humour of prison is infinite, the ingenuity of penitentiary pranksters without limit. Let me end this brief survey with two final examples, which the humorist Freud would enjoy for the way they reveal the nature of prison. The first prank is a joke played out in various forms in various prisons. Time will not tarnish it. It will always be worth a laugh.

In the classic prison joke, the prankster applies a layer of honey to the seat of a toilet, and then waits for someone to get his ass stuck like a fly on flypaper. "What the fuck!" It's gotcha time in the joint, a moment of liberation for humanity. And finally, from the supermax prison in Fort Madison, Iowa, comes the release of pent-up quixotic humour:

> There was one inmate, a good friend of mine we call Chopper, who was psychotic. He was all right when he had his medication, but when they started messing with it, look out. One incident occurred when he missed his meds the night before. A new doctor just taking over here wanted to see how he reacted without the drugs. The next morning at breakfast Chopper was outside standing underneath the guard's gun and observation tower, with a pile of rocks at his feet which he commenced to throw at the tower. Sort of a Don Quixote windmill type of thing. But he was really funny trying to take on the evil guard tower with nothing but pebbles for ammunition. They subdued him in force and gave him his medication, then let him back out of lock-up the next day.

16 Prisoner of the airwaves

Humility is only doubt.

WILLIAM BLAKE, "The Everlasting Gospel"

Robert W. Rowbotham smokes outside the Collins Bay prison.
Photo by Shawn Thompson

Monday was my night out with the felons. I was a volunteer escort for federal prisoners who were "cascading down" – dropping to lower-security prisons as they got closer to release to the street. My boss at work said it wasn't the sensible thing to do. My wife sided with the boss, describing how I was going to be beaten and whipped to a miserable pulp by prison thugs. I did it anyway.

Oddly enough, it gave me a sense of liberty. I don't mean the contrast between the incarcerated and me. I mean it was liberating to be among people who had broken with convention or, at least, who weren't sure what convention was. I signed the convicts out from the Frontenac minimum-security prison in Kingston, just behind the seagull-grey walls of the tougher, medium-security Collins Bay prison. My small car heaved and sagged like an overweighted baby carriage as the enormous felons climbed in. With that kind of load, I had to be careful to avoid the potholes of the prison road, which I suspected were a simple deterrent left there by the administration. A guard in a truck with a rifle patrolled the short stretch of road between the Frontenac prison and the Collins Bay prison.

I had strict instructions to drive the felons straight to the television studio where they were producing a program about prison life for the local community cable channel. Then, straight back to prison with no stops along the way. I obeyed the instructions somewhat. I took the prisoners to the drive-through window of a McDonald's restaurant so they could gorge on hamburgers and fries before we got back to the joint. They had to eat everything by the time we pulled into the prison parking lot and could not exhale the aroma of fried foods once inside. I suppose it didn't help the springs of the car to feed the cons.

I was given an official Corrections Canada volunteer escort card, number 44100-000043, with a photo that made me look like somebody who spent too much time in a library. I was warned that cons would try to persuade me to take them to see their wives or girlfriends, and that they would make all sorts of passionate pleas, which I was to ignore. The best word to use with cons was "no," I was told, not "maybe." Ex-con jailhouse lawyer Howard Massicotte, who became an aide to a criminal lawyer, gave me the same advice. Don't dally with a con. If you're not sure about saying "yes" to a con, say "no." The next piece of advice I got from the prison official was what to do when I got conned, as inevitably happens. "Laugh at it," the official said, "and say, 'Oh, man, that was slick.'"

The convict crew for the program included a talented Native painter who had almost killed his wife in a cocaine frenzy, a computer analyst with a ponytail and a conviction for murder, a drug dealer who had supplied cocaine to the female stars who had been my idols growing up, and Robert W. Rowbotham, the king of

Canada's cannabis offenders. Years ago, Rowbotham had been nick-named La Fleur, or Rosie, which suited his flamboyant manner and his flowery shirts. Barbara Amiel called him Johnny Reeferseed in the late 1970s.

When Rosie joined the television program, he was coming to the end of serving a nineteen-year sentence for a series of cannabis offences. He was a con with no violent history and no involvement with hard drugs. During his years in prison he was able to win the trust of both the cons and the administration. The official who briefed me for my job as a prisoner escort told me that Rosie was the only con he knew, in all his years with the prison service, who could be trusted absolutely. The official didn't know that in exchange for hash Rosie had acquired lobster dinners in the Collins Bay prison for himself and others or that he'd found ways to have sex a dozen times while incarcerated. He had sex several times in the Roman Catholic chapel in Collins Bay and once under a table during a social event in Millhaven. The sex and the lobster dinners boosted Rosie's morale in the joint. His main passion at the time I knew him was getting food while he was running a television program. I admired his ability to enjoy life whatever the circumstances. I wanted to know how he did it. How can somebody endure prison for almost two decades and still emerge as a human being? It was a puzzle. I needed to investigate.

I discovered that Rosie and I were contemporaries who'd led divergent lives. Robert W. Rowbotham was born a year before me, in 1950, on Halloween. I went to university to study English literature while Rosie went to Rochdale College in Toronto to sell marijuana and LSD and to listen to Allen Ginsberg read his poems naked. While I studied in the library, Rosie travelled the world. He used ex–Vietnam War pilots to fly marijuana in from Mexico, survived dysentery and the complications of the Bangladesh-Pakistan war, and ran eight tonnes of hashish out of Beirut through a United States naval blockade. I've never even had dysentery, let alone adventures like that.

Then my Ph.D. thesis stalled and Rosie was caught smuggling hash through the airport in Toronto. That was a difficult year for both of us. I accepted a job working for a minuscule newspaper in potato country north of Toronto, in the exact spot where Rosie once had a farm, and Rosie went to prison. Eventually, Rosie and I landed in Kingston, the prison capital of Canada, and home of Queen's University, where I had once studied literature and gone deeper into the wilds of the library.

At that time Rosie was in his chrysalis phase as a journalist, hosting the show *Prison Life TV*. I volunteered to be the prisoner escort for Rosie and his crew. Prison is where Rosie learned journalism and added to his streetwise savvy and his understanding of how society really functions. He was a frank and innocent soul. He'd discuss with prison officials why it was forbidden to have sex with a prostitute while out on a pass. Any other offender would just do it. But that was part of his ability to focus on the essence of life and to talk openly to people. Everybody liked Rosie. With his wide girth, halo of curly white hair, and laugh that peaked in a high-pitched *hee-hee*, he had a funny, charming streak that made him a kind of prison Falstaff. He'd play with an idea until out came the high *hee-hee* and you understood the absurdity of the situation. How could you not yield to a laugh like that?

Rosie liked jokes. One time he called from prison and left a message on my voice mail that he was holding the officer in charge of us volunteer escorts as hostage for pizza. Another time, I was about to talk with the American writer Norman Mailer about prisons. Rosie wanted me to tell Mailer that he and Woody Allen had led the march on Washington that Mailer turned into the book *The Armies of the Night*. Rosie wanted me to ask Mailer why he hadn't received proper recognition in the book.

The transformation of Rosie into a broadcast journalist was a phenomenon that I discussed with Norman Mailer. Mailer had an interest in prisoners, and in 1962 he had written a haiku poem: "Rip the prisons open / Put the convicts on television." And that's just what Rosie's program did. Cons and officials, from long-time offenders to criminologists, discussed prison issues on television. Mailer knew Rosie, having spoken in his defence at his trial in Canada in 1977. "There was a word you apply to him that you can't really attach to too many people," said Mailer, in the low, husky voice that has become an accent unto itself, "and that word is 'unquenchable.' You can't stop Rosie." Mailer thought back to the trial and how Rosie's unquenchable

personality affected his chances in court. "He just had a kind of roguish humour about the whole thing and I think it drove them up the
wall. You know, you're not supposed to be roguish when you're in
court and in the dock. . . . [The judge] couldn't stand Rosie. It was
obvious. He couldn't pretend to be impartial. He was virtually snorting
with annoyance every time Rosie would open his mouth." Rosie, said
Mailer, was "a political prisoner," and continued, "One of the ways you
can tell how just or unjust a society is, is by the measure of its prisons.
A society that has evil prisons is an evil society. A society that has
relatively decent prisons is a relatively decent society."

Most of my memories of *Prison Life TV* are now a blur – scenes of
Rosie getting lobster take-out at the studio, of studio disasters with
cons who had scant training to operate television equipment, of Rosie
sweating as if he had the flu because of his girth and the hot studio
lights. I remember the night someone brought a toddler to the studio.
With the cameras rolling, Rosie sat the child in his lap and sang "Row,
Row, Row Your Boat" while he clapped the child's hands. Another
time, a woman came to the studio to operate a camera, wearing skin-
tight pants in full, supple, mind-bending, elastic view of felons whose
hormones had been locked up in prison for years.

The first night I was there, the cons decorated the studio set in a
Hawaiian motif. In part, it was homage to La Fleur, who continued to
wear his flowery shirts in prison. A warden once told me he remembered being stopped in the prison halls for long conversations with a
large human butterfly in tropical shirts. So here was a program about
Canadian prisons with a Hawaiian theme. In the midst of a discussion
of how female offenders feel threatened inside a male prison with
male sex offenders, the camera would pan to a Hawaiian cactus or a
picture of a Hawaiian woman, as if to make an obscure point.

One mild day in February I visited Rosie in prison to discuss the
television program, and recorded the visit in my journal:

> He has a manoeuvre, birdlike or childlike, of thrusting his
> head downward and his chin upward, in a kind of sassy arrogant
> insouciance.

I don't know why I called it arrogance. It was the largeness of the personality of someone who had played big around the globe and then had learned to protect himself in prison, without being corrupted by the environment.

The insouciance of the man was seen as contempt in court. Having the American Norman Mailer speak as a character witness further jolted the Canadian justice system. Imagine the irritation of the judge having to listen to a lecture on marijuana from Norman Mailer. Mailer told the judge that Rosie the cannabis entrepreneur was a swashbuckling hero like Captain Blood.

While writing this book, I talked to Rosie on the phone and mentioned this perception of arrogance. After all, he'd once told me that his biography would have to be six hundred pages long. Rosie paused and thought about the perception of arrogance. He explained it by talking about the scope of his life before prison and his strong resistance to his present humbling and degrading circumstances. Because of Mailer's Captain Blood comment, I got a swashbuckler's cape and a big feathered hat from a costume store and photographed Rosie doing a sweeping courtier's bow in front of the prison walls. Eventually, I came to believe that Rosie had a roguish taste for the pleasures of life – for marijuana, sex, seafood – that rooted him in humanity but at the same time put him at odds with society's conventions.

Rosie set a humorous tone at the prison television show. I made an entry one night in my journal after driving the crew back to prison:

> Going home Rosie complained that someone had stolen his roast
> beef sandwich at the studio and we made a joke of it. I said that
> all the footage the cbc had of him showed him eating. I also said
> that it was a rough world outside the walls, a sandwich-eat-sand-
> wich world. Rosie went on and on half in jest about how you
> never took another man's can of pop in prison and how untrust-
> worthy people on the outside were.

I had gone inside Collins Bay prison with Rosie and his felon film crew.

Drove to Kingston through rain that was freezing on the windshield. Spent the whole day in Collins Bay prison, starting at nine a.m., with Rosie shooting video of convicts for his show and the CBC shooting him. At the end, the CBC reporter enraged Rosie by asking him the expected question about his arrogant assertion years ago in court that he could never be reformed. That got him very angry and defensive. He said that he was just being honest and that, if he had lied and said he would change, nobody would remember.

Rosie was my prison guide and guarantor to the cons. Prison is the kind of society where trust can be passed from person to person only in an individual's presence. It needs personal verification. And so with Rosie I had the rare opportunity to talk to cons simply as men in their typical prison environment. During one excursion with Rosie into the Collins Bay prison I talked to a lifer, a bank robber and an East Indian who chaired the inmates' Bible study group and who was caught smuggling drugs into Canada. There was a man I remember only as big and bald with wild tattoos in green on both forearms. A nervous man with glasses, who was serving a double life sentence for two first-degree murders, said he read books on philosophy. He had written a novel in Millhaven prison, he said, but it had been confiscated. I also spent ninety minutes talking to the free-thinking warden.

At one point he said he didn't understand the way that a criminal can be converted religiously in prison and think that everything can be changed. He also talked about people like himself being moral and law-abiding all their lives.

From another night of *Prison Life TV*, during a snowstorm, I found this entry in my journal:

Rosie was in fine form. A woman brought him dinner at the studio of lobster and clams. He talked on the phone to a woman who was in jail in Toronto. He said she had a body like a *Pent-*

house playmate, about one hundred and fifteen pounds. She dressed in long furs, which he didn't like, but was sometimes naked under the fur. He said that he had sex with her just before going to jail.

That I could picture. Rosie had a way of making you see things.

She is on the criminal fringe and has two kids. She's tough, he says. A man took her money and so she tied him up with duct tape. I asked how such a small woman could overpower a man. He said with a gun. He joked with her on the phone asking if she'd like to tie him up with duct tape.

Then there was the guest on the prison program who called himself a "psychiatric survivor."

Rosie's guest was a man with a balding pate and flowing white wisps of hair at the edges. He says that psychiatry is a fraud, creating pseudo-medical diseases with Latinate names. He says these diseases don't exist and can't be proved empirically.

That's the kind of information you don't get in the newspaper. After nights like that, I'd take the cons back to prison and, on the road home, would see signs of a wider world. My eyes had been opened. The veil of conventionality had been torn away:

Coming home I saw the small form of a coyote cross the road quickly in front of the car. I also saw a shooting star above the trees to the east.

Time passed. On October 6, 1997, Robert W. Rowbotham was released from prison on day parole. I picked him up early that morning at the prison, no longer his official escort, in the car with the springs he had offended. We went to a restaurant for the ritual coming-out-of-prison breakfast. It was simple – scrambled eggs, hash brown potatoes and a cup of coffee. Then it was time for him to catch the train to Toronto, to a liaison with his lady of the duct tape. A new career would bloom with CBC radio in two weeks while he was still living in a halfway house. "This is the dawn of a new era," he said, already practising to be a broadcaster. After nineteen years in prison and a few clandestine lobster meals, La Fleur, or Rosamunda, as I called him, was getting out. He'd had a heart attack in prison, partly due to his Falstaffian girth. He'd been incarcerated with violent and sadistic sociopaths, such as the one who told him how much he "loved" the young con he stabbed to death. He'd been inside Millhaven during a riot when felons broke through his cement-block cell using the iron from their cots as battering rams. He'd been cut with a razor blade. A con tried to drown him in a sink full of water for calling him "a joint man," or an ass-kisser. He'd been reviled and condemned by the justice system as an offender of gargantuan proportions.

I wondered how he could endure nineteen years without being sapped mentally and spiritually, without turning into a vindictive misanthrope. At breakfast the morning of his release from prison he'd said, "If I had an attitude that I was bitter, then I lost. That nineteen years in prison is like a bad debt. I'm going to write it off." I went back to some of the comments Mailer made to me about this man. "There was something so positive and sweet-living about Rosie that the thought of him being in jail for so many years struck me as just like cutting the air away from a fine plant, from something living."

When Rosie was released on parole, I had sent him the clipping of what another journalist had written about the "moxie" of the CBC hiring a man on parole. It was just after the weekend I spent voluntarily locked in a cell in Kingston Penitentiary. Rosie said:

Funny how things pop up over the years. . . . So how was your ordeal in lock-up? Did it make you humble?

Hee-hee.

17   It doesn't have to rhyme

He misunderstood Shakespeare.
              JOHN RIVES, prison poet, in a poem about a prisoner

Drawing for a bookplate inspired by the artwork of William Blake

I heard that a parolee named John Rives had a passion for the poet William Blake and had written two books of poetry about prison. I wanted to meet him. It was the kind of literary encounter I'd dreamed about all my life, after failing twenty years ago to finish a dreary Ph.D. thesis about Blake. I became a journalist instead, covering weird crimes and trials, writing about felons. The distance between the violence of the daily news and a dead poet from the eighteenth century seemed great, but here was a man who had read Blake in prison. He had lived the life of the prison metaphysic, those "mind-forged manacles" of the prison world that Blake had envisioned. I wanted to meet this Rives.

Rives lived in a rented farmhouse with a field and a pond in the rocky countryside outside Kingston. He'd been released on parole after being imprisoned for second-degree murder. "In a drunken rage," he told me, "I shot my grandmother, brother and an innocent bystander with a .44 Magnum carbine rifle. My grandmother was killed, but the other two recovered." He had been a university student studying history, with a welter of black emotions he said he had been suppressing all his life. "It all exploded that night." As it happened, that was not a happy catharsis. Rives was convicted. A decade passed in prison. He was released. He wrote the first letter to me in January, when the snow was blowing, recalling that the last thing he did in his life before going to prison was to shovel snow. The snow would set off a chain of associations.

> After I completed the job, I settled down to liquor, movies and murder. I remember the look of the snow outside my first cell window at Metro West Detention Centre [in Toronto], known as The West in joint parlance. The grounds were eerily lit by powerful halogen lamps of an odd magenta shade. And the snow became a nightmare fluorescent goo swept up against the brick walls of the surrounding courtyard.

At the farm, Rives, thinking in literary terms, balanced memories of prison with nature. He named the three-acre pond out back after the noble talking horses in Jonathan Swift's *Gulliver's Travels*.

Bush wolf tracks are in evidence out by Houyhnhnm Lake.

I liked the wolf tracks by the lake of talking horses. It sounded as though he was finding his real creative self in that spot. Professors have a word for the moment of discovery – the anagnorisis – taken from Greek tragedy.

> Sitting here, listening to Irish music, wondering what this literary experiment of ours is likely to do, if anything, I recall all those years of letter writing in prison. Mostly writing to young women I longed to impress . . .

The seduction of women by fancy words is an old trick called the pastourelle by knights who used it on the shepherdesses of the thirteenth century. The modern version is the prison pastourelle. The women are young criminologists, nurses and prison officials who care for the wounded flock in prison. The offender captivates the woman by his charisma and candour. Rives was aware of the aura he cast as a felon and a poet, but it also bothered him. He was having a small anagnorisis of the heart.

> As I gained some recognition for my writing, all the poems, articles and public appearances came to represent the superficial. Life was a dry fuck. Signing a book was like signing a centrefold, only my public preferred to dream me disembodied, not in the flesh. Ultimately, poetry saved me. I met Daphnee at one of my readings at the University of Ottawa.

I should point out to anyone who has not had the misfortune to study Blake as obsessively as I have that the name Daphne is an important literary reference. It is Greek for the Latin word laurel, or bay leaf, a living part of the natural world, and it figures prominently in the poetry of Ovid, travelling by literary infection to the poems and paintings of Blake. Daphne is the natural woman bringing the vitality of nature into the prison for Rives. Writers hope that a natural woman, through the alchemy of hormones, will inspire them to be poet laureates. The letter continues with the nature motif:

> Last weekend, the bitterest cold took me out on the frozen surface of spring-fed Houyhnhnm Lake. With a cry of "landfall," I finally set foot on each of the two wee islets at the centre. Lilliput and Blefescu I call them. While I was tracing animal tracks out on the lake surface, I heard the unmistakable moan of ice giving way. I beetled it quickly back to the shore.
>
> Later that afternoon, after paying respects to an ancient maple I call Grandfather, I marked some territory in the forest. First time I've pissed outside in fifteen years. Imagine. Imagine. Another thing about the country, the snow here is very white.

The letter continues and Rives's poetic self emerges again. This is what Blake calls the "moment in each day that Satan cannot find." It is the pure moment of the inspired self when the mind drifts by itself, unwatched, untended. It is also the moment when we are open to nature. Rives remembered being a child during the spring break-up of the ice in Sault Ste. Marie:

> At break-up, my friends and I used to venture out onto the ice floes. It was dangerous and exciting. Sometimes a chunk would break free and start to carry one of us downstream. We'd always be quickly caught up again on the shore where we would leap to freedom with no more than a soaker. Upriver, where Lake Superior dumped its load into the stream, winter came as massive sheets upthrust and fractured like the milk teeth of a mountain chain.
>
> I always think about what lies below the ice. Are there fish? Is there enough oxygen or swimming space for them? Ice remains a mystery, a tangible link to the other side of things.

Then back, led by association with ice and snow, into prison, back to the old dry fuck of sensation again. A pattern was emerging.

In January 1982, the magenta obscenity of snow outside my barred window drove me utterly into myself. It was alienating. I was separated from the universal reality of winter. Behind the bars it was cold, one hospital blanket on a dirty cotton mattress cold. The hideous Technicolor snow looked warm by comparison – a weird reversal of perception.

In the joint, fog was a blessing. Fog meant the guards couldn't see the perimeter security. Fog meant no work today and sleeping in. Fog meant half-pay, a sick day zero pay. Fog was a warm blanket and a morning in bed.

Fog is a fine medium for musing. Collins Bay was prone to fogs. It was built in a wide hollow bracketed by two streams. Fog softens the outlines of the prison, confuses with the walls and diminishes their solid strength. The limestone towers of the Bay took on an even more medieval appearance. The razor wire disappeared and you could imagine ancient warriors manning the walls. The fact that fog disrupted normal institutional routine only accentuated the difference.

Fog is a passage to another world. I never feared fog as a child. Some pretty good ones rolled in off the St. Mary's River. You could hear the great lake freighters bellowing in the distance. Fog was a link from prison to the world of imagination. It is still a link from this existence to another, but not back to prison. Fog is still progressive.

Now picture a pale full moon glowing like a fatal eye through a damp and sinuous fog. That moon could penetrate anything, even the angry yard lights surrounding the prison yard. The stars weren't so lucky. Yet even then the Big Dipper and old Orion would bully their way through to our eyes. Starlight is a gift of freedom, easily lost. The city steals it. The prison almost obliterates it. The first time I was out on a day pass late enough for stars to appear out of the blue dusk, I was ecstatic. They were only dim city stars, but they were there. Lots of them.

I'd sent him some descriptions of the moon glimpsed from inside

Kingston Penitentiary in letters I'd received from felons. It reminded him of the moon seen from Collins Bay penitentiary, which has red turreted roofs that make it look like a chateau in the distance.

> I love their Kingston Penitentiary descriptions of the moon. I was fortunate at Collins Bay to have southern exposure. Every night the moon rose over the gothic pinnacles and roofline of Two Block and sent her rays probing into my hole.

The first of his prison poems to be published was one where he used the light of the moon to make puppet shadows against the wall of his cell. Prisoners call their cell their "house."

> I recall one night dragging a friend into my "house" to witness a lunar eclipse. He had never seen one.

Then he returned to the part of him that on parole is outside prison but feels inside. It was somehow triggered by the memory of the child-like wonder of seeing the lunar eclipse in prison.

> I am a prisoner. I am the one the hang-em-high reformers want to flog. I am the erstwhile violent offender out on parole and I cannot escape it.
>   You ask if anyone died while I was in prison. Several hundred. Some dozens had names and faces for me. Fast Eddie had his throat cut after a hockey game in the yard at Millhaven. Bled to death in his goalie pads. Wally strung up at the Psych Centre; so did what's-his-name. There was Greg, Coco, Jimmy, Carl and Christopher, Bruno, Danny, Dennis and all those others. Seven men died violently at Millhaven during the nineteen months I was there. But there were other deaths. No one dies of natural causes in prison. There is nothing natural about death in a cage.

He remembered his days before murder and prison as a young

geologist working in the bush for mining companies, north of Flin Flon, Manitoba, and in northern Saskatchewan.

> My chief accomplishment was to go for six weeks without bathing. Oddly enough, one of the reasons I quit geology was because of the isolation. Yep. Prison was much less isolating for the soul than to be afloat on the tide of nature.

He talked about fishing in his spare time, which triggered a childhood memory, as fishing often does in people.

> When I was five, I had a tumour removed from my left leg. While I was laid up my sisters and I would cut up construction paper fish and then they'd hide under the bed while I fished with a cardboard pole and safety pin. When I'd snag a paper fish, they'd reach out and pin it on. During this time my invisible friend put in his final appearances. His name was Dooney Boogerson and he was a Swedish ghost.

His parents were worried that his imaginary friend was a kind of tumour too and summoned the family physician to investigate. It reminded me that as a child William Blake saw a tree full of angels on Peckham Rye by Dulwich Hill. That worried Blake's parents too. Another letter:

> Hello again. Good to hear from you. . . . Have you ever travelled in the far north? One of the first things you notice after the drone of the float plane engines have receded back into the southern part of your brain is the lack of crickets. Or frogs. When it is silent, particularly at sunset, it is really silent. All the chirrupings and peepings and the like have somehow evaporated into the ether. You wonder if there is any living thing at all out there in the dark. Then the loons begin their song.

A break, a letter about nature, dreamscapes. I'd asked how he dreamed in prison, as I did other prisoners. Our dreams and sensations are the part of us that aren't manipulated by our rational side, which makes them revealing. To find the essence of the individual and what prison does to people, I asked prisoners how they slept, what kind of dreams they had, and what their bodily sensations were.

> My earliest experiences with dreaming in prison tended to revolve around waking to discover reality was indeed worse than the nightmares. No, not nightmares, dreams offered healing through removal from the intolerable guilt, fear, despair and apprehension of my daily existence and through imaging my need for reconciliation with family and those already dead. In dream I could experience the justifiable anger that went unspoken during visits with my family, emotion that required release before true healing could occur. And I could walk with my dead grandmother. It would be okay.
>
> Later prison, as the commonplace, would insinuate its presence into my every dream, even as it imposed its limits on my waking life. When I would dream, I would always be on a pass from the joint. I could be reliving some vague fantasy about grade school and yet, like Cinderella, I had to be back before the time ran out on my pass.
>
> The only exception was when my frustrations and sublimated anxiety and anger overflowed and found expression in the prison-break dream. They were extremely violent affairs. And they were empowering. I would take on all comers – guards, police, the citizenry – and overcome all barriers by brute force alone. I would tear people from limb to limb, without fear, without remorse. I had become the monster in the movie. And I always felt better in the morning. What most would call nightmares, I viewed a great adventure. Occasionally I would dream of tunnels deep within old stone castles, libraries and the like. These usually necked down, down, until I was wedged tightly in the narrow space (which recalled our teenage spelunking days along the limestone fault caves of the Niagara escarpment). But I

could escape this entrapment, often by physically forcing myself up through the floor.

He eventually progressed to our old friend Blake. I enjoyed this because it felt like the resurrection of a dead part of my life. What Rives said was livelier than the academic versions of literature I got from my university colleagues. Rives had read Blake superficially when he was younger. And then, "in the county bucket awaiting trial," unable to go to an exhibition of Blake's artwork in Toronto, he asked the brother he'd wounded in his shooting spree to bring him the exhibit catalogue.

> I was particularly struck by the images of the damned both from single plates and series illustrations [by Blake] for Dante's Inferno. Shocking. All too real for an accused murderer. I could see myself in the rolling eyes, the anguished gape, the awestruck horror in the face of one confronted by the irrefutable loss and perfect shame. I felt sick. Physically sick with despair. All I could see ahead was years of trial, degradation and quite literally deliberate gouging of open wounds by the media for public amusement. Then, at the end, condemnation to a life behind bars. That was William Blake's fine art.

The letter went on with misty speculation, then came back to what Blake called the mundane shell, the material world we create out of our unimaginative selves, with a postscript about washing contact lenses down the drain, a pressure tank on the water system needing repairs, a car exhaust pipe replaced. I asked again and again about Blake.

> "Tyger, tyger burning bright" felt like power in the darkness. Like a secret literature. And most appropriate, in the jail where I first read these words, they turned out all the lights (except for one dull red spot) to keep us from subversive work like writing letters through the night. Those red-cast shadows from the spot were just enough to shit by and provided such a hellish vision.

The night after I was sentenced to life imprisonment, and before the lights went out, I opened up an art book which my brother had sent in to me. He got it at the travelling Blake art exhibit when it was in Toronto. I looked closely at a favourite and troubling picture. Blake titled the engraved portrait Head of a Damned Soul. It was the shaping of the mouth, the silent scream, the numbness of the lips – I raised a hand to my own face. It was the shape of an incomprehensible way of being which was my reality.

As life unfolded, I found much more than solace and escape in imaginative literature. For the symbols of illusion fit my reality, igniting meaning, if not reason. I read its fearful symmetry and put my prison in its place. I dreamed the terrible dreams and then I wrote the hell out of it.

It was in the writing where we actually met. Blake says that on the other side, the blood I taste is only mine and those shadows are cast by little words awaiting my creation.

There were often lapses in our correspondence. The next letter came after a gap of silence caused by the giant ice storm that paralyzed eastern Ontario in 1998, and by the disruption of Rives's divorce from his wife Daphnee, a criminologist. It sounded as though the feelings he was experiencing were a reversion to the painful old "mind-forged manacles" of prison and release. I'd made the descent to the filing cabinet in my basement to read the letters again. I'd forgotten so much. I saw again in the letters what had fascinated me about the mind of this man. He tried to live in a world of poetic thought that he had created for himself. Rives thought and wrote from inside his experience. He did not seek sanctuary in fiction to avoid the difficulties of writing about life. That's the kind of false creativity that he calls "the dry fuck." I wrote to Rives. He answered after the gulf of years by e-mail.

There is failure, loss and I must once again deal with the sense of being unwanted, undesired and alone. However, I like the freedom. My buddy Gerry (the cab driver and ex-con thief) has moved in with me. Mostly I need a girlfriend. And I have turned forty. I kept the farm and Daphnee moved north of the city. My friend Gerry is sharing the place. We live an idyllic bachelor's existence along with my lovely new dog, Cassie, short for Cassiopoeia.

The wet air filled with the sound of . . . the vibrating membranes of
thousands of cicadas.

REDMOND O'HANLON, *Into the Heart of Borneo*

As a writer I'd been searching for years for the perfect question. I'd
started writing to prisoners and wanted a question that was as simple
and straightforward as Freud asking, what do you dream? It had to be
a question that wouldn't threaten the ego. The question had to be
revealing about people in ways they would not realize. I was working
late one night on my correspondence with prisoners. I decided to take
a break and went for a walk in the dark in the small town where I lived
on the St. Lawrence River. My mind was consumed by the letters I was
reading. I stopped thinking about prisoners for a moment. And then I
was overwhelmed by the sweet, brute, ruthless music of crickets
pulsating out of the night. It was as if the resistant old me had been
swept away by a rough cosmic harmony. It was like the shock of
coming out of a crowded building and gazing up at the wide night sky
aclutter with stars. Why didn't I hear the crickets before? I asked
myself. And it occurred to me that I'd found a question that would
appeal to a mind open to contact with the world outside the ego. I sent
out letters and the responses came back from certain types of prisoners, the articulate ones, the thoughtful ones, the humorous ones. I
asked felons in the toughest prisons a question they'd never been
asked before: Do you hear crickets?

José Cruz, or Blaze, liked the question. At first he couldn't hear the
crickets, but then, one night during a hot summer in Leavenworth, he
went into the prison yard about eight-thirty and . . .

I heard them. I heard the crickets. They were out there. Kind of
deep, too. I strolled to a grassy area, laid back, and looked up to
the brilliant blue sky. I guess that was the problem, too many

U. S. Department of Justice
Federal Prison System

United States Penitentiary
Leavenworth, Kansas 66048-1254

Office of the Warden

September 8, 2000

Shawn Thompson, Assistant Professor
University College of the Cariboo
P.O. Box 3010
Kamloops, B.C.
Canada   V2C 5N3

RE: Jose Cruz
Reg. No.: 14065-074

Dear Mr. Thompson:

This is in response to your letter dated August 15, 2000, wherein you request approval to introduce crickets into the United States Penitentiary, Leavenworth as part of a research and experiment for an article. You also, request to photograph Jose Cruz, an inmate confined at the Leavenworth facility.

Unfortunately, I am unable to accommodate your request to introduce crickets into the Leavenworth facility, as well as, your request to photograph inmate Cruz. Your request does not comply with Bureau of Prisons policy governing Research or News Media Contacts.

If you have any questions or concerns, please feel free to contact my office.

Sincerely,

M. E. Ray
Warden

people out drowned the sound. Can't hear them or, as the convicts say, they went "on the lam."

Before he was in Leavenworth, Blaze was in the Riker's Island prison, where it is hard to hear the crickets.

Riker's Island is a little jungle. It's amazing how such a small area could be so noisy – talking, yelling, cursing, keys jangling,

iron doors slamming, footsteps. The dude next door is hollering
to his friend five cells down, with me in between, about the injus-
tices of the world and the devils who run it. An airplane is
passing over us, louder and louder and then slowly fading away.
Man, it's noisy and tense. You had to stay alert. But, if you listen
intently, under the noise, you could hear a cricket chirping away.
They are all one mind in a million little bodies rubbing their
wings like a million violinists.

I could understand why Blaze would be able to hear crickets in the
prison yard. I had the boy from the Bronx figured for a stargazer.

Yeah, I love the stars. I'm an astronomy buff. Really. I know all
about the planets and stars, more than anything else. I certainly
miss the stars. Sure do. Want to hear something weird? As a kid,
I would go up to the roof of my six-storey building at night and
gaze at the stars all night, daydreaming, writing poetry or telling
made-up adventure stories to an enthralled audience of kids. Do
you notice when you drive how it seems at night as if the stars
and moon is following you? Look at it the next time you drive at
night. I felt like I was the chosen one. I often wished aliens would
take me away and show me the wonders of the universe. And,
yes, I used to think the stars and moon used to follow me on
those long nightly drives, like when we took a three-day drive to
Florida. I spoke to the stars all night long. Come to think of it, ma
never mentioned nothing. So what do you think? Was I a crazy
kid? A bored kid? A dreamer kid? Or is it natural for kids to wish
they were abducted by a UFO?

I wrote letters to my other correspondents in prison asking if they
heard crickets too. Kesley Foreman, in prison in Arizona, heard them.
She said that she rescued crickets that came through the cracks in the
walls of the prison and protected them. She did that, she said, because
they had no ill intentions. Another letter came from the Bath prison, at
the eastern end of Lake Ontario, from an offender who, after eighteen

years in prison, could be fitted to neither prison nor the outside world, and didn't care.

> Yes, we certainly have crickets here. I hear them all night long. I moved my bed so that my head, when I lay down, is level with the window ledge and I can look out at the view. It's very nice. I find the sound of them soothing, and it's a good thing because there are sure a lot of them making their sound at night. For the past couple of weeks I've been serenaded to sleep each night by a cricket. It was very loud and I became accustomed to the sound. Since I sleep with my head right next to my window, which has been open since the spring, I assumed the cricket was in the grass outside my window. But one morning early last week I got out of bed at my usual time, four-forty-five a.m., and went to put my feet on the floor and almost landed on a sleeping cricket. I quickly grabbed an empty plastic container with the intention of capturing him and putting him outside. I snuck up on him and scooped him into the container and quickly tried to put on the lid. But he was out of that container faster than a politician to a fund-raiser, and he got out before I got on the lid. He could really jump and I think he thought he was a frog. He got away under my bed amid the boxes and I was not interested enough in getting rid of him to search. So he's still there and still singing.

A con in solitary in a prison in Texas told me he heard the crickets there:

> Crickets are funny. Sometimes when you are laying there at night, the cellblock totally quiet and you are alone with your thoughts, a lonely cricket will begin his chippering. Sometimes you try to find him by looking under the crack in your door. If they see you looking at them, they are quiet, maybe thinking you are a predator. They sometimes give you a break in the silence that gives you company, but, other times, their noise brings an unwelcome intrusion to silence, depending on your mood, I guess.

Letters from Prison

A woman in prison in Las Vegas heard them:

> I listen to the crickets. It really has a calming effect on me. It reminds me of the days when I was sitting on the porch at my old house, when I'd sit and reflect on the day's events. The crickets find their way inside all the time. You'll be cruising along the hallway and find one cruising up the wall or in a corner. One time I had a cricket that lived in a vent that connected my cell and the one next door. It would get quiet during the day, but at night you would hear it singing all the time.

From a con in a prison in Texas I heard the sound of crickets infiltrating a sterile world:

> Sometime in mid-December I heard the crickets again. If you are willing to allow your mind to just drift, the sound of crickets can be rather soothing, as can the sound of wind through leaves or a slowly moving stream.

A Chicano in solitary in Illinois heard them:

> It was a long time before I heard crickets after my incarceration, about five years. It really blew my mind. I felt like a child when I was back in Mexico. My grandmother had the largest house in the centre of town. We had two outhouses, a well and different kinds of trees – pine, pomegranates, lemon, orange, lime, guava, papaya, avocado, mesquite and different kinds of cactuses. She was a medicine woman, so she had all kinds of plants for healing. So I grew up loving the plants and trees and cactuses.
>
> Crickets always sound spooky to me, like creepy, but sort of warm and very endearing. Because of the sort of rattle they remind me of a car purring, and the whistle-type sound is rather pleasant to my ears, like a musical instrument. The sound always keenly draws my attention, as if I'm trying to decipher a message from the crickets, sort of like expecting them to be playing a song

in unison. I always feel like the crickets can tell me something.

My grandma taught me to be wary of the dark, so crickets remind me of hiding in the bushes in our yard at night under the light of stars, sort of fearsome, yet delighted with the different wonder of the night. My grandmother had all kinds of plants and flowers, so the crickets remind me of that.

I had some crickets in my cells at times. I fed them bits of bread and little drops of water and sometimes they stayed a few days. But I've never found one dead, nor do I know how they get in because the window screens are too close together. I remember when I was in Vandalia Correctional Center I heard cicadas that spring. I was there from January to May of 1990. I hadn't heard cicadas since I was a little boy in Mexico. So I sent for a book at the library, which the guard brought me faster than I could remind myself what I'd just sent for – about cicadas. They bury themselves for something like sixteen or seventeen years underground before being born. And that blew my mind because I'd read a book on the folklore of ancient Ninjas. And, after they have completed their decade-long apprenticeship, they are buried deep in the ground in a fetus position under a full moon. They have to materialize up on the ground to become Ninjas.

Patrick Rasmusson mused from his cell at night in Illinois:

I remember crickets well. Dad recorded them on a cassette tape once. He records homemade sounds of all sorts from Mom Nature. Then he plays them back as he picks at his electronic work on his home desk.

Last summer, in the middle of an August night, there was a flock of crickets somewhere outside my cell window. The window was already open. I pulled my chair to the open window, which reminded me of my father and his nature-filled concerts. I miss that music as I miss him. But, tonight, I have a pleasant rainstorm. Now, back to the little fat black crickets that do not ever bother a soul, but are sometimes used as bait for fishing. Isn't that ironic?

To hell with the damn crickets for a moment, professor.

The cricket question was assuming a life of its own, sallying forth like Don Quixote in search of nobler things. I thought of it as an experiment in the workings of the human ear, how people learn to listen to the sound of the universe ticking. The question would reveal earsight. I was asking prisoners the question, but what about scientists? Charles Darwin wasn't ashamed to make notes when he heard crickets, or when he didn't. "No crickets," said Darwin when he was exploring the coast of the Strait of Magellan in 1834 during his voyage around the belly of the world.

No crickets? Crickets live in most places on Earth, no matter how remote. More people on the planet know the sound of crickets than know Beethoven's Ninth Symphony. There have always been crickets, too, across the latitudes of time. They are three million years old, emerging long before the dinosaurs. There are twenty-six hundred species – ground crickets, tree crickets, mole crickets, aquatic crickets, ant crickets, you-name-it-and-it-exists crickets. NASA shot fifteen hundred crickets into space on a shuttle mission. The idea was to study the effects of gravity to help with the colonization of Mars some day. Crickets are everywhere, without inspiring an evil thought, never poisoning or biting, just providing entertainment according to the right invocation of dark and light and heat. Listening to crickets is like listening to the heartbeat of life itself.

And so the cricket question sallied forth around the globe to scientists too. I got responses from a cricket biologist in Japan who raised crickets when he was a child. "They give us nice background music for our life," he said. A cricket scientist from a university in Wisconsin, Bradford G. Rence, mused on cricket incarceration. He said, "Caged crickets will sing all night in their inevitable pursuit of unrequited love. Maybe this is a powerful metaphor for human incarceration." He kept a cricket caged at home as a pet. Others, like Carlos Frankl Sperber at the Universidade Federal de Vicosa in Brazil, said that the natural stimulus of something like crickets might encourage the sanity of prisoners. Werner Loher, the co-editor of the thick cricket book *Cricket Behaviour and Neurobiology*, and a professor at the University of California at Berkeley, was even more daring. "I do believe that cricket sound improves life, and, if convicts could be exposed to cricket songs for short periods every day before they go to bed, that might ease tension and lead to dreams about a life without bars." Loher said that a singing insect appeals to him because he has been "an acoustical animal" since childhood. He learned to play the violin and viola in primary school and has played in string quartets all his life. He thought that crickets would improve life on Mars as well as in prisons.

The chief crickateer on the NASA mission that shot crickets into space was Dr. Eberhard R. Horn of Ulm University in Germany. The scientist told me that crickets would be good for prisoners. "The life of a cricket is short compared to the sometimes long time men have to stay in prison. So, if a prisoner keeps a cricket as a pet, he will have to recognize the perishableness of life. Thus, he has to form a cricket colony. This will give him positive thinking about the future and, in particular, a sense of the continuity of life." That's about as good as it gets, from a crickateer with formidable credentials as a scientist.

The cricket scientists had gone further than I expected with their comments about prison. Maybe it's not such a wild idea that prisoners would benefit from breeding crickets in their cells. I thought Blaze in Leavenworth might like that, and the idea might proliferate. It would be an interesting experiment to see if breeding crickets in a cell would soothe and focus the minds of felons. I wrote to Blaze's warden at Chateau Leavenworth, Mickey Ray, who received my letter a few weeks after becoming warden. Taking the hint from Loher, I suggested to the warden that the felons in his facility be allowed to breed crickets. "Unfortunately," the warden responded, "I am unable to accommodate your request to introduce crickets into the Leavenworth facility."

I wrote back commending the warden for his promptness and his decisiveness, which are important qualities for a warden dealing with riots one day and letters from professors in British Columbia the next.

"Thank you," I said, "for your encouragement to 'feel free' to clarify the issues with you." I continued:

> Strictly speaking, crickets are not new to Leavenworth. You have them already, roaming free and unsupervised, according to the cricket watcher inside the walls. (There are also lots of ants and other bugs crawling around the cells, but they don't produce natural music like crickets.) The message of crickets to us is that Nature doesn't want to be kept out of people's lives. My suggestion is that you allow inmates to have crickets as a kind of simple nature therapy, much simpler, for example, than the messy pigeons kept in Leavenworth years ago by Robert Stroud, the Birdman of Alcatraz. The warden of Leavenworth at the time of Stroud, the early days of the twentieth century, was a Civil War veteran and "one of the hardest of the old-time wardens," according to Stroud. The next warden in 1913 came in with new ideas, allowing a convict newspaper, tango dancers and a brass band that played during prison meals. Those were the days in Leavenworth! I bet you don't still have the tango dancers.

I also asked the warden if he would waive the rules to let me do an interview with Blaze:

> I realize there may be problems getting access to Cruz, judging by the time he spends in the Dog House, or the hole. Maybe he would be spending less time in the hole if he were raising a family of crickets. How about this for a slogan: raise crickets, not hell!

I also asked for a personal interview with the warden, promising "no trick questions about crickets," and tried to end the letter on a sympathetic note:

> I've interviewed wardens in the past and enjoyed their point of view, although, in a sense, they are suffering from a type of

incarceration too, because of their work. Once again, thank you for your consideration and I hope this doesn't make you feel like you have a dwarf on your back.

Mickey Ray wrote back again, bless him, but he had reached his bureaucratic limit. Maybe some time in the future we'll continue our correspondence. Meanwhile, the cons kept me informed from that listening post on the edge of the known universe, the prison front. From a prison in Huntsville, Texas, came a letter from a prison crickateer with the time to think and observe that a forty-five-year sentence can give a man.

> The crickets are back in force. They don't usually come inside until the weather turns cold, but this year they started coming in about mid-June. Even the other men are beginning to notice them. One of the men assigned to work on my wing as a porter asked me in an accusing tone, "Where did all these crickets come from?" He looked at me as if he thought I gathered them up and brought them in. It might really get thick in here if the weather ever does turn cold again.
>
> Along with the crickets has come an invasion of ants, who obviously came to eat the stepped-on crickets. And we have something new this year – grasshoppers. Usually we don't have too many grasshoppers in this area, but they're pretty thick now. I saw in the paper an article that said they have reached plague proportions in the Dallas area.

Between letters from the cons, I was never sure if the cricket experiment would work or flounder on the shoals of half-answered questions. There were delays in the letters from prison. Felons are easily distracted, and one never knows what's happening to them behind the walls. They can lose interest in a topic. They can get beaten up, transferred, stabbed, thrown in the hole, sick, despondent or just fucked up. All this creates stress and anxiety for a writer like myself who depends on prisoners for his inspiration, like a little pig suckling the big institutional teat of the penitentiary. Add to that stress the influence of the paranoia that came in the letters, and it's nerve-racking as hell. So I was in suspense waiting for the mail. Then a letter arrived from the Texas felon in that tiny, inky, cricket-sized script of his with deep chirrups of information.

> Here's a curious coincidence, although I wonder if it was coincidence that on the twentieth and twenty-first of September we were invaded by a swarm of crickets. I did notice with some curiosity that they were totally silent. The crickets, hundreds of them, came inside, probably in response to our first cold spell of the season. Though the place appears to be impenetrable, it obviously isn't. For several hours it was impossible to take a step without stepping on at least one of them. It almost looked like a carpet of black crawling from the walls across the floor. I flushed at least a dozen dead bodies down the toilet during the hours of the invasion. Then they vanished as suddenly as they appeared. As to why they were silent, I could not begin to guess, especially since the invasion took place in the early night when crickets are usually quite vocal.
>
> You asked how the guards and other inmates dealt with the cricket invasion. Like the butterflies, I don't think they even noticed. The only mention I heard of it was the following morning when the porter came in to sweep and mop and asked, "Where did all these dead crickets come from?" There are occasionally crickets in here through most of spring, summer and fall, but this is the first time I have ever seen an invasion of this magnitude.

That letter was like hearing nature write its signature on the tablet of a lost soul in prison. And all from a deeply troubled man in a Texas penitentiary, and from Blaze in Leavenworth, and from the others. Yes, there are things to be heard outside yourself, if you pause and listen.

In the end, the question of crickets exhausted itself like a season in the year and there were other issues to explore. Blaze, it could be predicted, would be in and out of the hole in Leavenworth, writing letters with an aching wrist, trying to keep the paper dry from sweat. In the prison yard he would pause and listen outside himself, like Darwin, who could hear when the crickets stopped in a world that's sometimes deaf to their music. The conversation will resume. There will be more questions to throw out like seeds. The letters will bloom.

I have never lost a sense of distance and a need for solitude.

ALBERT EINSTEIN

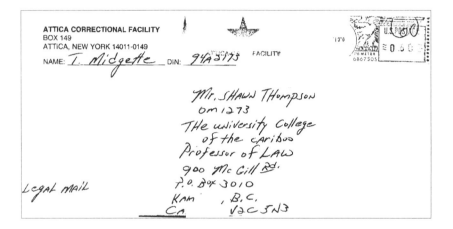

ATTICA CORRECTIONAL FACILITY
BOX 149
ATTICA, NEW YORK 14011-0149
NAME: *T. Midgette* DIN: *94A5173* FACILITY

Mr. SHAWN THompson
om 1273
THe university College
of the cariboo
Professor of LAW
900 Mc Gill Rd.
P.O. Box 3010
Kam , B.C.
Ca V2C 5N3

Legal mail

Don't think for a moment that being in prison is some kind of grand mystical experience. It's not, no more than a bout of the flu or a toothache, and prison lasts a hell of a lot longer. Nor is solitude the romantic notion we have come to believe. Or at least that is what I believed until I spent a summer by myself in the Spice Islands. I almost went berserk in a small Indonesian airport near Pungkalan Bun when I learned the airplane was broken and wouldn't be fixed until the next day. I jumped onto another airplane that was leaving in half an hour for Java because it was going somewhere else. Solitude in small doses is wonderful. But I don't know how human beings endure years of it. And yet, in prison, solitude and night can ease the burden of the place.

Most of the letters I receive from cons are written at night when the men and women are locked in their cells. I asked them about solitude in prison and solitude in their experience of the world before they went to prison. I wanted to know how being solitary shapes us as human beings. Here's a convict who is the night janitor in the prison in Beaumont, Texas, to begin a meditation on the solitary night self:

> I report to work at ten p.m. I enjoy the job mainly because of the peace and quiet. Most of the prisoners are asleep and most of the guards are laid back. I hear and see all types of things, some of which make me mad, but, in this place, minding your own business is the law of the land. I see men having sex with other men. I hear people fighting in the cells. I hear people snoring. I see Muslims making Salat (prayer). I see and smell people using drugs, or just sitting quietly enjoying the silence. Night differs from day because the noise level in the day rises to the point that you can't even hear yourself think and you must isolate yourself from everyone and everything. I try to stay in my cell all day if I can, only leaving to eat or attend some function. When I do leave, I always put my earplugs in. I go outside at night to clean the rec yard and when I'm finished, I just sit down and gaze at the stars and think how big this world is and how I'm confined in such a small part of the universe. When I look at the stars, it gives me a sense of freedom. My body is incarcerated, but my mind isn't. Looking at the vastness of space also makes me realize how I should be gazing at the stars with my son in the free world.

From Kingston Penitentiary:

> After ten-thirty lock-up a great silence falls upon the prison, so we can all hear sounds that we can't during the day. For instance, the wind. It is nine-forty-five a.m. Saturday morning as I write this letter to you. My window is open about one inch to let in fresh air. I can hear the wind. I can even feel it push against the window, feel it rush into the cell. Why? Because at present most everyone is still sleeping and those who are awake are being quiet. There's an unwritten prison law: on weekends and holidays we're quiet until noon so that others may sleep in. However, during the week it's noisy. The guards are always using the

intercom system to call someone. So much noise, so much activity, even if one wanted to, it would be very hard to hear the wind. So nighttime, after darkness and silence, that's the only time we can really pay attention to nature.

Time progresses differently at night in prison. It goes way too fast. Sometimes it just seems I no sooner lay down and go to sleep than I have to get up right away. Some say it goes too slow. However, I am sure these people don't like being alone because they have to think about things they'd rather forget.

I prefer the night and darkness. Staying in the darkness in my cell is a good way to shut out the rest of the world. In a way, it's like pulling a tent around yourself and zipping it up so that no one else can get in. Perfect for privacy.

In many cases, many times, this is a welcome time, as it gives each prisoner a chance to be alone, be away from the rest of the prison, even escape prison for a few hours, sleeping, watching TV, reading, daydreaming. It is also very welcome as it is the only time we can really relax, let our guard down, release stress and tension, because in prison there is just so very much tension it continues to multiply every day and the only way to escape it is when we are alone at night in the darkness.

Listen to a prisoner in Detroit savour a rare taste of night:

We are not allowed on the yard after dark. When the sun sets and the lights come on, the yard closes. But, on certain occasions, there is a chance to walk from one building to another after dark. It is an eerie déjà vu experience, to say the least. Like a lost sensation. I remember my first trip outside after dark in quite some time. It
was January 5, 1998, and I was in handcuffs being taken to the segregation unit. My last step out into the night by the light of the moon had been May 6, 1996 – nearly two years – so it was a real treat. I slowed right down and tried to savour every step, like you'd try to remember a sexual encounter with a pretty girl so

you could relive the experience again and again in her absence. But the hook was trying to rush me into my concrete cubicle so he could be done. I'm sure he was totally unaware of the fact I was getting off on something as common as a walk after dark.

Night is a time to find the solitude that eludes one during the day. I wondered while writing this book why solitude can either bring vitality to a life or poison it. What is the right amount of solitude? Do I need more solitude than you, or less? Beginning with the Lone Star State, some thoughts:

Solitude is something which is in short supply here in Texas. On many units here a single cell is rarely seen and the only time solitude is obtained for me is when I go out to the yard at night. I attempt to get as far away from people as possible. I sit down and enjoy the space I'm able to gain.

The nights here are filled with the hum of machinery. To help keep the cellblocks from getting unbearably hot or cold there is a system of blowers. They are going constantly. Along with that there is also the hum of human conversation going without stop some times.

I am comfortable in either the city or country, yet feel the need to get away from people every now and then. I have memories of forests and rivers while growing up. They seemed so alive compared to the city. The cities seem so dead even with all the people. The night to me was a time of mystery, when more things seemed to come to life. The night to me was more of a friend and teacher. At times it seemed like a fleeting kiss, much more alive and willing to give comfort than the daylight, and much more seductive. Prison has brought a taint to the night for me, a bitter sweetness. I used to be able to go and sit among a grove of trees and be at peace, not here.

Some inmates like solitary time while others hate it. In a solitary cell a darkness comes over the cell and the person. It's a darkness that has a weight to it, sometimes a heavy weight. There's almost no room to move, so you lay on the bed. You can feel yourself melt into the mattress and all your strength leaving your body. At first, it's pleasant and relaxing. After a number of years in prison, it gives you a chance to get rid of built-up tension. But then days and weeks pass. You are stuck in a cage with nothing to do. Many people no longer get off the bed after two or three weeks. Laziness has set in, an I-don't-care attitude. One person smokes twice as much, another eats twice as much, another doesn't eat at all. The silence and the darkness grow. The weight gets heavier. For some, this is a time to spend sleeping, twenty-four hours a day, just to avoid having to face the situation. For others, it's a time to reflect. For others, it's a terrifying time; from their past come the faces and voices of people they've loved and lost as well as people they've hurt.

A person in solitary is like a snail that crawls back into its shell, except that we are forced into the shell and it's locked and we don't get out unless somebody else says okay.

This is true for all people in solitary to some degree. And each will deal with it in their own way – crying, committing suicide, yelling, destroying the sink, toilet and bed, and still others will simply lay back, read a book day after day as if nothing happened.

I enjoy solitude, because it is part of me as I am of it. We're inseparable because I grew up with solitude. When you become part of something that you enjoy, you don't want it to go. It is almost like being with a woman that you truly love and cherish. I have been with solitude since I was four or five. Being in prison you have all the solitude that you want. Yes, there are other people around, but solitude is in the mind, as well as the heart. Darkness, that is funny, 'cause no matter how much light you have, you're still in darkness. Darkness and solitude connect with each other.

Yes, I had grown up with solitude. The solitude is different in prison for me. There are too many people to really get any solitude.

Darkness, that is when I enjoy the day the most. It's because I really cannot stand the sun. It hurts the eyes. To me, the light is a type of love that you will only know if you didn't have anyone that would listen to your problems, but the darkness is always there with you. You can talk to it and, if you listen real carefully, you can hear it talk back.

I am thinking about solitary pursuits as I type revisions to this book. It is raining outside. I have not gone anywhere tonight, although I stop typing from time to time to see how far I can listen through the depth of the rain. Not far. The rain has thickened. It protects me from distractions like the layers of a forest. I wonder why it is that I want solitude when I'm with people, and company when I'm alone. Am I the only one with that ambivalence? I don't think so. I have been reading the prison letters of the German pastor Dietrich Bonhoeffer. Maybe it was this imprisoned man who inspired my interest in prisoners. When I was a child the pastor of my church talked from the pulpit about the wisdom of this man locked in prison. Not long ago I read a letter that Bonhoeffer wrote to his fiancée from prison where he said that in spite of his need for people he needed solitude too. In the last letter his fiancée received from him before he was executed by the Nazis in 1945 he wrote, "It is as though in solitude the soul develops senses which we hardly know in everyday life." Once that sounded deep to me. Now, tonight, I'm more skeptical. And certainly the solitude of a troubled man or woman who has committed a crime is different from that of a man like Bonhoeffer.

As I work alone on this book I think of how, years ago, I started hunting for the quality of solitude that strengthens and invigorates the mind. I searched for it on rivers, in the mountains and valleys of British Columbia. I pursued it to the dry, sandy stretches of Morocco, to the jungle rivers of Borneo, looking for the perfection of solitude, as though it were the cusp of a wave, the smoothness of a stone in a river,

253

the shy embrace of shade from a tree on a hot day. A hermit I found living on an island in the St. Lawrence River told me, "Like anything else, it starts out as an adventure, and becomes a habit, and then it becomes a way of life. I like solitude. I like reading. I only gotta answer to the dog."

In a clinic near the jungle in Indonesia I found a vet from Spain who had devoted two years of her life solely to orangutans. It was a fitting choice for a solitary woman to isolate herself with a beast once thought to be a human being gone wild. Orangutans are not social primates like chimpanzees and gorillas. The male orangutan lives by himself like a hermit in the forest. On the spectrum of socialization I wonder where human beings fall among the three great apes – gorillas, chimpanzees, orangutans. Is there an evolutionary or hereditary spin to solitude? Is our solitude made for us in ways we don't know?

Trying to understand the experience of solitude through prisoners makes sense, I hope. The modern idea of the penitentiary started in the late 1700s as an experiment in reforming offenders through the power of silence and isolation, like that experienced by monks in a monastery. That seemed to make sense then. Now, prisons are so crowded they feel as dismal as the cities outside the walls. Solitude in prison is used as both a punishment and a refuge. Some felons say that the last place on Earth to find the comforts of solitude is in a penitentiary. Others say that they live for the moment when they can be locked in a cell at night. In the Auburn prison in New York State, Ty Midgette is sent to "the box" for resisting transfer to Attica, "the bottom of the barrel."

> We have just the bare necessities here in the box. The heat in here is oppressive, no air ventilation whatsoever. So, I'm sitting here in underwear and undershirt writing you. Excuse my writing, because this is not really a pen. I'm in a cell, not a room, not a room-like cell. No door, just bars that open electronically. On the bars is a big plate of fibreglass so you can't stick your hand out. The officers are escorting a handcuffed prisoner who

just cut his wrists. Some will resort to such behaviour just to get out of here. This is my second time in the box. The first time I did sixty days for having Masonic order lessons. So, I always try to use this isolation time to re-evaluate my future. It's quite peaceful, if you know how to utilize your time. Sometimes it gets very noisy. It's a chain reaction. All it takes is one or two people to start it. Right now there is one prisoner having a loud conversation with himself. Some people do different things to maintain their sanity. Ninety days is really not that bad compared to two or three years in here.

A man writes from a cell during lockdown:

My cell is my house, my space, my cave, my abode. Many of my peers distinguish between these, while waiting to return to outside society, to combat feelings of institutionalization. I'm resigned to the permanency of my confinement and merely strive to live as best I can in here.

I have a corner cell on the third tier. The window cranks open approximately forty-five degrees to allow airflow through the metal bars. I've done more stretches in solitary than I can count. I actually prefer certain aspects of solitary. It is the only climate-controlled housing in the Texas system. I've been through isolation in psychiatric facilities, jails and prison. I am either psychotic or self-absorbed enough to disregard the social deprivation and focus on my writing. I have some dear friends outside who keep me from becoming too desensitized. I keep my window open virtually all the time, so weather and nature remain close by. I closed my window two nights this winter when the temperature was just unbearably frigid. I feed insects rather than kill them. I get the sun during the afternoon recreation period and once in a while catch the moon.

Another voice from the hole:

Ah! There's nothing like clean white walls and a fresh paint job. You get kind of sick staring at the same old generic graffiti day in and day out. I have no view of anything beyond my tier. And, to be honest, I haven't seen anything worth looking at in so long, I don't even bother trying anymore. For those of us that have to spend any real time in the hole, most get on a medical subscription for depression or to help themselves sleep. Others, such as myself, embrace the challenge of isolation "all natural." Not to imply that it's an easy thing to do. And then there are those who decide it's just not worth enduring. They usually hang themselves. One just did that last month. The hardest thing a man has to face in the hole is himself. There's no distractions. Nothing to take your attention off yourself and your haunting thoughts, whatever they may be. And you know what they say: "Some people just can't live with themselves." There's always something to keep you awake in here. Someone yelling, banging on a door, and even those quiet times when yourself wants to slap you with some reality. So sleep for myself comes from exhaustion.

I asked the prisoners where solitude began for them before they came to prison. Are people who like solitude able to adjust to prison better than others?

I am very comfortable with solitude. From the time I was old enough to be cognitive of the actions of other people (about age two) I have always found that I am my own best friend. Having learned to love and enjoy myself, though I feel a need for companionship, as does virtually everyone else, I do not suffer when the need is not being met, as most people do. Also, in the free world, when you clash or have problems with someone, you can simply walk away. In here, you can't do that. The minute you turn your back to the other man he's going to put a shank in it. In here the staff work deliberately to reduce us all to the level of wild animals, their own level, the result being that the law of the jungle prevails.

Being a solitary entity I have far less trouble of that nature
than most prisoners. I hate violence, even when I am forced to it
for survival. I don't like to hurt people.

I enjoy solitude. Being totally alone in the wilderness is a spiritual experience. When I was a boy my family rented a cabin from
the same Natives who lived on the White Lake reserve in Northern Ontario. The cabin was located on Little Cider Creek, hidden
in the pine trees. It looked like the trees pierced the sky to let the
spirits come down.

I remember the rain hitting the roof. We would leave the door
open to watch the drops hit the trees outside. The bush seemed
silent, as if all the life there was taking shelter from the rain. It
was almost the silence of death.

My father was a very abusive man who had been abused
himself as a child. The bush was special because I could escape
the abuse of my father. I walked out of the bush once when we
were flown in and we had run out of food. The bush waits for
you. It waits until we are aware of what is happening.

As a child I enjoyed nature. I remember when my parents would
go out drunk (just about every night) I would run to the woods
and, on this hill was a big pine tree, and I used to climb it and I
would go all the way to the top and just look at the beautiful
sight. We lived in a valley in New York State of two hundred
people. The only thing in that town was a welding shop. Everything was miles away. I was at peace when I was in this tree. I
would hold on real tight and close my eyes and feel the wind
blow against my face and as a child I swore up and down the
trees talked to me.

I am still a country boy and when I get out I am going to buy
some land and build me a cabin or a big stone house. I want at
least one hundred acres across with a stream on it and some hills
and a waterfall running off one of the hills.

But peace in prison is fleeting. From Stephen Pang I heard about the peace that comes with a lockdown:

> Things have been pretty calm around here recently and we all anticipated a lockdown, but no such luck. I say no such luck because I wouldn't have minded being able to sleep in for a few days. Some guys, such as moi, relish lockdowns – the privacy, the quiet, being able to sleep in. Guys who have served time in max enjoy lockdowns, while young guys who are relatively new to the system hate them. The young guys are the only cons I've ever met that have that TV mentality – gotta have fresh air, can't be locked up, all that crap. I have personally never felt that way. I think the reason max guys aren't bothered is that we're used to extreme levels of stress in max joints, and when we're locked down it provides us an opportunity to do our time without that stress.

Pang and I discussed desert landscapes, which have an affinity with the prison landscape. Pang saw the desert as a test and challenge, as prison was for him. He spent twenty days by himself in the desert to see if he could live off the land with the survival skills he had learned from the American military. I'd been to the small tip of the Sonora Desert that protrudes from the United States into south central British Columbia. The place is called Osooyos. Where I live in the small city of Kamloops, a four-hour drive from Osooyos, it's so hot and dry in the summer that there are rattlesnakes and tiny cacti on the slopes at the edge of town. Pang wrote:

> This desert thing really intrigues me. Keep me posted on that. I've always liked deserts, anyway – silent, no reference points, a hostile wasteland, yet life adapts, improvises and finds ways to flourish.

I wrote back, unable to restrain my exuberance:

You like the idea of the desert? Yeah, it's an intriguing idea and I'm grappling with how to write about it. The desert has an impact on you, but it's difficult to get into words, and next to impossible to photograph. It's a similar difficulty to writing about prison, another hostile wasteland, another barrenness with signs of life. The first thing that comes to me is that it's wrong to go into the desert during the daytime. The desert comes alive at night. It's dead in the daytime. So daytime is the night of the desert and night is the day. Last weekend I talked with a welder who lives near the desert in Osooyos and has been intrigued by it for years. He told me about hearing the coyotes at night calling to each other from different hills. And one time, in September or October, he found a depression in the ground filled with crickets singing their hearts out before they die. Insects such as the cricket are symbols of the ability to survive in a harsh landscape, which is partly why I'm gathering stories about crickets in prison. The honey that the bees make from fireweed in the desert is also a symbol of this. So I think if I am going to understand the desert I should go hunting for crickets at night, under the cool stars, in all the glory of nightbloom.

Pang responded:

Yes, go into the desert at night to see the life, but go into the day to appreciate its power, its Ka. The desert draws its power from its daytime desolation, the heat, the aridness. That is what challenges you. The lack of reference points, the solitude, the total alienness of it. To be accepted by the desert, you must survive its power. Well, that's it, dudely. Tomorrow I finally get a single cell. Yee-haw! Be cool. Pangster.

I pursued the question of the desert as an extension of solitude and the mind. He answered:

Got yer latest yesterday. Have I ever been to the desert? Yep – California, Nevada, New Mexico, Utah. Solitude, dude. The only privacy left on the planet, uno? I found New Mexico's the emptiest, just thousands of square miles of nada except the old A-bomb test sites and jackrabbits. Each desert seems to have different coloured sunsets, too, probably due to how inversion layers compress the smog from the nearest cities.

The desert has always either killed men, driven them mad, or freed them. See, cultures have recognized their power for centuries. Hebrews, Australians and American aboriginals, all undertook "spirit walks" of one sort or another in the desert. It is total isolation – silence, no landmarks, no meaningful horizon. Its barren hostility forces you to examine life, yourself and death. It is a land where one mistake means death. Spent a week, alone, in the barrenness.

Postcards from Borneo

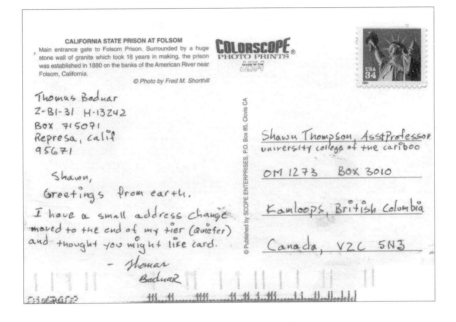

CALIFORNIA STATE PRISON AT FOLSOM
Main entrance gate to Folsom Prison. Surrounded by a huge
stone wall of granite which took 18 years in making, the prison
was established in 1880 on the banks of the American River near
Folsom, California.
© Photo by Fred M. Shorthill

COLORSCOPE
PHOTO PRINTS ®
MADE IN THE USA

Thomas Bodnar
Z-B1-31 H-13242
Box 715071
Represa, Calif
95671

Shawn,
Greetings from earth.
I have a small address change
moved to the end of my tier (quieter)
and thought you might like card.
   - Thomas
        Bodnar

Shawn Thompson, Asst Professor
University College of the Cariboo

OM 1273   BOX 3010

Kamloops, British Columbia

Canada, V2C 5N3

I spent the summer before I finished this book travelling to the great eastern extremity of Borneo, fermenting in the heat like ripe jackfruit, staring at the dense foliage to see if I could see through it and beyond, meditating on the joys of my fellow primates in the dwindling rainforest, writing postcards to my advisors in the joint. I'd heard that Borneo was a wild place and wanted to see it for myself. In 1984, Redmond O'Hanlon published a book titled *Into the Heart of Borneo* that even my lawyer in Toronto had read and raved about. There were descriptions of the jungle where "the river grew louder in the darkness. Something hooted. Something screamed in earnest further off." There were poisonous butterflies and descendants of the old headhunters. I wanted to feel that river and hear that screaming. I was also wondering about the wildness of the human heart. There is the intensity that we need to be alive as human beings and the intensity that leads us to destroy ourselves and others. Are they the same quality or different? How should they be tapped? I sent postcards from Borneo to Blaze in Leavenworth, Ty in Attica, Paco in prison in Illinois.

I was glad to put some distance between prison and myself. I was coming to realize that writing a book wrestled from correspondence with prisoners was interfering with the freedom of writing letters to them. There was too much purpose in the work. Revising the chapter on Huck in prison was good therapy for me. It made me realize that I'd become too abstract and analytical, which is what I wrote the book to avoid. I wanted to be caught in the flow of the letters again as though it was a river I was navigating with the liberty I once had.

In Borneo I stayed in a town on the edge of the jungle, in the best hotel, where it took me three weeks to learn I was also staying in the best whorehouse in town. But then the bartender also mixed margaritas that tasted like a mixture of tequila and orangutan piss. Nothing is ideal, is it? Not love. Not margaritas. While I watched the parade of nipa palms from a boat on the river, a team of editors toiled in the weary city to make sense of the jumble of a manuscript I'd sent them. I returned and made the revisions they wanted with absolute stoicism, because writing, like crime, isn't committed in isolation. It needs help.

At the moment I departed for Borneo, the Pangster was also departing from prison on parole. He was taking with him Snowball, the prison feline suspected of causing the death of a fellow cat. "He's eight, which, in cat years, gives him fifty-six years in, so it's time he got paroled." I learned months later that Snowball was on the lam as soon as he got out of prison and hasn't been seen since. I could have used Pang in the jungle to keep me safe, but, with his criminal résumé, he can't cross borders easily. His only advice to me was to buy a gun in Borneo with a calibre that would penetrate the foliage. "Personally," he wrote, "I think you're nuts to go to Borneo. If I were you, I'd buy a gun as soon as I got there. Maybe a .45 auto (heavy calibre and slower rounds are better for jungle conditions since they punch through the foliage rather than being deflected by it). Take a tube of strong antibiotic cream, a big tube. In hot, humid conditions, any cut will fester rapidly. Medics in 'Nam learned that very quickly." He finished by saying, "Remember, in Borneo you're exotic food." A person couldn't go wrong with advice from the Pangster. The last letter I got from him in the joint was signed The Edge Master.

More advice, this time on combatting malaria, came from Jackie Reynolds in Estelle High Security prison in Huntsville, Texas. Reynolds is studying pharmacy in prison through a correspondence course, and he quoted from a number of obscure texts. To ward off malaria he suggested cinchona bark (*Cinchonae cortex*) instead of the Lariam prescribed by my traditional doctor. Lariam comes with a warning that it can cause "abnormal dreams, convulsions and distur-bances of mood," although I don't know how you can tell the differ-ence in the insanity of the heat of the jungle. I went with traditional medicine and, between that and mosquito spray with a high concen-tration of DEET, I fared okay. As for the other cons, most of them did not sally forth that hot, dry summer from the seclusion of their concrete sanctuaries. "I'm not going anywhere," a number of them said, "so keep in touch."

My summer in Indonesia was my year of turning dangerously fifty. It is the time in a man's life when the hormones wane and the obses-sions take hold. I took comfort watching the senile president of Indonesia being evicted from his palace like someone who didn't pay the rent. I delayed as long as possible returning to my cage in the university.

When I got back from Borneo, a pile of prison letters was waiting, like the first snow of the season. From the wildness of Attica prison, Ty Midgette wrote:

> I'm wondering did you get back yet. I hope you're safe and sound, and your hide is in one piece. I also want to thank you for the postcards. Too bad I couldn't go. I was a little worried about you. I swear, if I were in the free world and you were my friend, you would drive me to grey hairs. I find myself thinking of you at times, wondering if your crazy ass is all right.

Letters from Prison

I wrote back to say that my ass was fine and that Attica is wilder than Borneo.

Mike Schoen in a prison in Yuma, Arizona, wondered what happened to me. He wrote:

> Well, not much going on around this camp. We had a small riot while you were gone.

There were two letters waiting from Blaze in Leavenworth:

> What's up, brotha? Got your card dated August 15 from Jakarta that you're on your way home. I received all your cards.

Blaze said he'd just watched a documentary on television about Julia Roberts and orangutans in exactly the place where I was. I'd stayed in the same hotel room as the movie star in Pungkalan Bun, a town on the edge of the jungle. I was telling anyone who'd listen that I'd slept in Julia Roberts's bed and had the room key to prove it. Small world, isn't it? Too small maybe.

One night in Borneo I slept on the deck of a boat I'd rented, with the stars of the jungle splashed over my head. I was wrapped in the gauze of mosquito netting and had doused myself with so much insect spray that I was melting the paint on the boat. But I heard the crickets singing, out of the jungle into the sky, just as Blaze heard the crickets singing in the yard in Leavenworth. Maybe we were all linked by one long chain of cricket harmony strung around the globe. At least, I'd like to think that, in my last wild, solitary thought of this prison meditation. I'll end with words of bright clarity in that letter waiting from Blaze:

> By the way, we also have a guy here by the name of Cricket, small skinny kid with an odd twitch.

Acknowledgements

This book takes its strength and character from conversations, by mail or in person, with people willing to open their hearts and minds. I want to thank these people for the generosity of their conversations with me: José (Blaze) Cruz, Stephen R. Pang, Kesley Dawn Foreman, John Rives, Thomas Bodnar, Robert Moyes, Victor Masci, Ty Midgette, Doug Strain, Doug Lagossy, Ray Medina, Harvey Wendt, Charles Huckelbury, Charles (Chuck) Armstrong, Dave Desorcy, Jackie Reynolds, Michael Ivie, Steven W. Zehr, Alexander Bernal, Mark Fisher, Stan Hedger, Carl Horne, Richard Peebles, Harvey K. Fair, Patrick B. Rasmusson, Craig Scott, Nancy Martz, Dale Adesamya, Vernon Maulsby, Anthony Hamilton, Forrest J. Killian III, Shelton Thomas, Ignacio Pesqueira, David Hinman, Kathryn Oliver, Ronald F. Rose, Yuri Khomaash Luckette, Allen Graves, Gregory Dadisi Rivers, David Weidert, Timothy Crockett, Don Williams, Larry Joseph Grass Jr., Paul Wolfe, Yraida L. Guanipa, Rafael Vasquez, Herbert Diaz, Ted W. Palmer, Oscar Andrew Hanson III, Michel (Mike) Schoen, Christopher S. Sohnly, Edward Huggler, Leonard Freeman, Daniel Rees, Jesse Butters, Jeffrey Lee Heath, Michael Lee Hood, Richard Abood Lyon, Robert J. Carlson, George King, Eric Furzland, Carlos Martinez, David Gaspar, Jimmy Jarrell, J.T. Orcastias Jr., Michael Roger Nelson, Tghambe T. Blake, Christopher Dye, Serafin Flores, Michael Kerak, Clint Corbeil, Jerome A. Scope, Joseph Richardson, Dennis Alexander Pashko, Nebuchadnezzar N. Wrisper, Dale Darling, Frank Horgen, Fred Hyatt, Andrew de Groot, Jerry Broude, Rita Clarkson, Lionel L. Rogers, Robert M. Williams, Ozie B. Collins Jr., Anthony Pestello, Edwin D. Wolff III, Allen Washington, Michael Runnels, Ronald Keal, Ellen Young, Paula Bettencourt, Tracy Armstrong, Joan Blackwell, Gail Stoddart, Shari Boyd, Allan Kinsella,

Gerald Trudeau, Dave Biggins, Mike Rolls, Larry McCullough, and Roger Caron.

In the process of writing the book, I had generous help from a number of people outside prison walls who gave information or advice or helped me gain access to prisons. I want to thank David St. Onge (curator of the Kingston Penitentiary Museum), Andrew Graham, William Gladu, Bill Chitty, James Blackler, Maureen Blackler, Ron Fairley, Paul Urmson, Dennis Finlay, Barb Hill, Carol Sparling, Chris Stafford, Jim Stevenson, Bernie Aucoin, Lynn Baker, Mickey Ray, Peter Tilt, Fionna Jordan, Wayne Scissons, Frank Heaney, Tommy Atkins, Chip O'Connor, Josh Zambrowski, Bob Bater, Howard Massicotte, Guy Paul Morin, Frank Polson, Tom Mann, Harvey Valiquette, Brian Rogers, and Vicki White.

Several others were instrumental in guiding and shaping the book (and the author) into something better. Some of the first discussions about the nature of the book were with Robert W. (Rosie) Rowbotham. He lent his enthusiasm for the project, his insight into prisoners and the prison system, and his help to make contacts for the book. Pamela Erlichman improved the manuscript with her copy edit. And, finally, Karen Hanson at HarperCollins made the book a reality by believing it should be published. She championed the book and guided it through editing and production with intelligence and enthusiasm.